Rohinton Mistry's

Such a Long Journey

A Critical Study

Celebrating Indian Literature

Rohinton Mistry's

Such a Long Journey

A Critical Study

Santwana Haldar

abc

asia book club

an international publishing house

Published by
Asia Book Club
C 3/1, Janakpuri
New Delhi 110 058
Ph. 9818755529
www.asiabookclub.com
ISBN: 81-7851-25-1

Printed at Chaman Offset Press, New Delhi 110 002

Contents

Rohinton Mistry's *Such a Long Journey*:
A Comprehensive Analysis
by
Santwana Haldar

Critical Perspectives

Rohinton Mistry: Life and Works

Rohinton Mistry is an important figure in contemporary Commonwealth literature and he occupies a significant position among the writers of Indian Diaspora. A glowing star in the galaxy that contains luminaries such as V.S. Naipaul, Salman Rushdie, Amitav Ghosh, Shashi Tharoor, Vikram Seth and Bharati Mukherjee, to mention a few, Rohinton Mistry has drawn the attention of the world as an absorbing writer of human experiences. Having been born in a Parsi community, a minority community in India, and having recorded the complex tradition of Parsi history and culture in his writings, Rohinton is also famous as a Parsi writer and is grouped along with Bapsi Sidhwa, Dina Mehta, Firdaus Kanga, Keki Daruwalla and Boman Desai. His scholarly insight into the Zoroastrian faith as well as his objective detachment and capacity for self-analysis enabled him to be regarded as an authentic Parsi writer of his time. An India-born novelist settled in Canada, Rohinton Mistry has remarkable capacity for capturing the crowded, throbbing life of India.

Rohinton was born on 3 July 1952 in the metropolitan city of Bombay. He availed the opportunity of studying in Theresa Primary School and St. Xavier's School, the two famous institutions in the city. He graduated from St. Xavier's College in Bombay, completing his degree in science (Mathematics) in 1974. He emigrated to Canada in 1975 and studied English and philosophy as a part-time student at the University of Toronto. In 1982 he received a second Bachelor's degree. It was in 1975 that he married Freny Elavia, who was also Bombay-bred and a student of St. Xavier's and who had gone to Canada in 1974. It is interesting to note that Rohinton Mistry was not much of a writer in his early days. Nor did he visualize a writer's career for his future. Rather, he was interested in making a career in music and even gave performances in Bombay to fulfil his ambition. Having arrived in Toronto he tried to make name in the musical world. His own compositions of folk songs were recorded in Canada in 1975; a disc *Ronnie Mistry* was released by Polydor. There was however little progress in music, particularly after his joining as a bank employee. During 1975 to 1985 he acted as a clerk and accountant in the Canadian Imperial Bank of Commerce. Rohinton and Freny lived in a Toronto suburb Brampton for twenty years. Rohinton is known as a reticent man, an admirer of quiet existence, even after he became an international figure.

Having passed some years in search for a proper medium for expressing his genius, Rohinton Mistry came to the channel that suited him most. In the year 1983 he wrote his first short story "One Sunday" which won him the Hart House prize. For another story, "Lend Me Your Light," he received the same award. In 1985 he received the prestigious Contributor's award of Canadian Fiction for his "Auspicious Occasion." Thanks to these prizes, the publishers got interested in publishing a collection of his short stories. And the result was the publication of *Tales from Firozsha Baag* in 1987 by Penguin Canada. The stories collected in this book were set in Parsi Housing Estate in Bombay where he had not lived during his stay in Bombay but of which he was well aware through his friends. His father was in the field of advertising and he was brought up in an average middle class Parsi family. That he never forgot the titbits of Parsi life in India after his settlement in Canada is manifest in his stories; the dreams and desires, the sufferings of broken dreams, attempts to adjust oneself in unwanted situations, the anxieties shared by the minorities in the rise of fanaticism and a concern for corruption are examined and expressed in his writings that demanded immediate attention all over the world. Being a Parsi himself, Rohinton Mistry had an easy access to the glorious years of Parsi existence in India during the British Raj when the Parsis enjoyed freedom, patronage and dignity. The misrule and corruption in postcolonial India affected the Parsis no less than it affected any common Indian, unprotected by the all-powerful political leaders. Rohinton Mistry experienced all these during the early Seventies and he also had the opportunity to get detached from these actual experiences, for he started writing about all these after eight long years when he had settled in Canada. The distance of time and space helped him to offer an objective rendering of the situations that could defy all sorts of cheap emotions.

The collection of Rohinton Mistry's stories was brought out later in Britain and USA under a modified title, *Swimming Lessons and Other Stories from Firozsha Baag.* The book was short-listed for Canadian Governor General's Award. Firozsha Baag is a fictional Parsi enclave in metropolitan Bombay. The stories differ from one another, but they are interwoven by the common setting that evokes a Parsi world—the customs, traditions, food habits and erotic details of a community that likes to remain confined. Some characters such as Kersi and Rustomji make their appearances in more than one story. Kersi figures in "One Sunday," "Swimming Lessons" etc. while Rustomji figures in "Auspicious Occasion," "Squatter" and "The Paying Guests." There are other characters like Najamai (seen in "Condolence Visit" and "One Sunday") and Jehangir (seen in "The Collectors" and "Exercisers") that appear with different roles in different stories. As a result, the readers have the experience of remaining in the same world where situations change but the mood remains the same. The ironic rendering of Parsi customs is a characteristic feature of the stories. The most holy occasion of the Parsis, 'behram roje,' is displayed as an unholy occasion in "Auspicious Occasion." The patriarchal set-up in the Parsi families is also rudely exposed in "Of White Hairs" and "Cricket." The secret eroticism of a puritan culture is evoked in "The Ghost of Firozsha Baag" through Jaakaylee's belief that she is seduced by a ghost. With sharp eye and gentle wit Mistry displays the inhibited desires of Parsi women. In "Gathering," the gathering of the Parsis in a closed world of their own is placed side by side with the gathering of the Parsi immigrants with their cross-cultural experiences. "Lend Me Your Light" and "Swimming Lessons" relate the experiences of the Parsi immigrants, of the prevalent racism and cross-culturalism in Canada. These stories are appreciated for a successful evocation of a sense of loss and nostalgia in the immigrant's experiences and of alienation.

Rohinton Mistry's first novel, *Such a Long Journey* (1991) won Governor General's Award for fiction in English in Canada in 1991 and the Commonwealth Prize in 1992. It was also shortlisted for the Booker Prize in 1991. Through the fluctuating fortunes of the protagonist, Gustad Noble, the writer projects the socio-political turmoil in the Sixties and the early Seventies in India. The setting "Khodadad Building" is an imaginary Parsi enclave in Bombay like the Firozsha Baag in his short stories. Though imaginary, it is based on real experiences of life. The backdrop of the Indo-Pakistani war also helps the socio-cultural scenario appear real. The protagonist's remembrances of his childhood days—of the time when his father was a rich man and again when he was declared insolvent—expose the rich past of the Parsis in India. And his present experiences are closely linked to the contemporary political crisis. The crisis in Gustad's life is rendered as a part of the corrupt dynastic rule that hardly bothered about the well-being of the common people. Gustad's crisis was somehow over, but his friend Major Bilimoria, who had been working for the RAW, got trapped and had to face death. Gustad's personal life is also projected as a part of the Parsi community in India. The inhabitants of the Khodadad Building are representatives of a cross-section of middle class Parsis who express the anxieties of a minority class in multiracial India as well as the age-old superstitions and customs that have cornered them and have also alienated them from the main stream. The novel is also rich in symbols. The title "Such a Long Journey," taken from Eliot's poem "Journey of the Magi," links Gustad's journey of life to the spiritual quest of the wise men from the east who witnessed new born Jesus. Though the novel is written, apparently, in a simple narrative style, the writer has also adopted postcolonial methodology.

Rohinton Mistry's second novel *A Fine Balance* (1995) has a wider range of characters and a larger fictional territory (the novel contains more than 700 pages). Critics tend to compare the novel to Vikram Seth's *A Suitable Boy* and Shashi Tharoor's *The Great Indian Novel.* While *Such a Long Journey* is confined to the Parsi community and to Bombay, *A Fine Balance* projects the Indian life—its people, climate, cities, ethnicities, classes and castes as found in cities as well as villages. The novel starts with Dina Dalal, a Parsi woman, and her story in Bombay but soon enlarges its scope through the inclusion of the characters such as Maneck Kohlah, Ishvar, and Omprakash who came in contact with Dina in some way. The writer's attention is still on the pessimistic and sordid state of affairs as it was in his first novel. The real situation of the Indian political system beneath the high-sounding democracy and federalism is laid bare. The wretched condition of the poor and the middle class people, tortured under the brutal forces of corrupt rule, offers a criticism of the postcolonial government and reveals the writer's sympathy for the subaltern. The criminalization of politics during the Emergency (1975-77)—the autocratic rule of Indira Gandhi and the end of the Nehruvian era—is Rohinton Mistry's chief area of interest and the novel offers a faithful record of the shameful episode in Indian history. *A Fine Balance* ironically renders how the marginalized and the powerless are forced to maintain a precarious 'fine balance' between life and the death-in-life existence while passing through the impossible ordeals of life. Take, for instance, the incident of Nawaz, a tailor, who was arrested by the police presumably for smuggling gold from the gulf. In reality, poor Nawaz asked the influential customer for his payment. An observation of the stall owner may be quoted to show how Rohinton Mistry took up the method of direct criticism. "With the emergency, everything is upside-down. Black can be made white, day turned into night. With the right influence and a little cash, sending people to jail is very easy. There is even a new law called MISA to simplify the whole procedure." (299) Feminism is another aspect of the novel. Dina's attempts to live on her own income through a tailoring shop were rudely challenged in the male-dominated society. Ultimately, she was compelled to live with his brother Nusswan, a condition that she never liked. The writer comments: "Independence came at a high price: a debt with a payment schedule of hurt and regret. But the other option under Nusswan's thumb was inconceivable." (473) Dina has to maintain fine balance in some way, as Nawaz has to do in some other way. Thus, the details of the narrative raise some important issues concerned with gender, caste and power oppression.

Rohinton Mistry's third novel *Family Matters* (2002) goes back to Bombay for its setting and for its characters it goes back exclusively to the Parsi community. The city has been renamed Mumbai, though its old cosmopolitan look prevails. The change in the political scenario is marked in the reference to the acquisition of power by the BJP and Shiv Sena, but the focus in *Family Matters* is more personal than political. A nine-year-old boy Jehangir is projected as a witness of family quarrels. The novel shows how the boy tries to understand the quarrels and puzzles of the family and how he desperately wants to bring peace and harmony. Much to his disappointment Jehangir finds that the grown-up people always fail to bring peace among them. The novel uses the flashback method successfully. During the family get-together politics intrudes into close family circle as do other events like the Indo-Pak cricket matches. The topic of contemporary problem among Parsis about inter-communal marriages also comes up. Rohinton Mistry creates a close domestic and identifiable situation. Despite the criticism of Canadian politics, Bombay is clearly celebrated in *Family Matters.* Despite grave disturbances and fatal blows of violence, Bombay continues to provide shelters to all. The narrative moves in a complicated manner, recording the ups and downs in Noriman's family including the emotional turmoil and maladjustment in the background of pressing, external events.

The characteristics of Rohinton Mistry's writings may be stated as follows. The diasporic space that he occupies as a writer helps him to write from a distance and his postmodern imagination is provided with a scope to flourish. To quote Vijay Misra, "the idea of India exists in the minds of the Diaspora through forms of spatial displacement in which the site is transformed into a word. This form of transference/transformation of space means that India gets internalized and projected on to other geographical space without so much as a hint of dissonance. Where epic textuality requires a fixed point of reference, a past that cannot be duplicated but only extensively rememorated, what we get in the Diaspora is a whole series of displacements that lead to the construction of new spaces as metaphors of India" (Trivedi and Mukherjee, 1996). In Mistry's novels, there are little traces of Canada; he is rather obsessed with the colonial and postcolonial experiences in India. He often intermingles history with the personal lives of the characters and this practice is characteristic of an immigrant writer. (Salman Rushdie's *Midnight's Children* may be referred to as an example). Like V.S. Naipaul, Rohinton Mistry also writes critically about India, particularly about India's political scenario and the picture of rampant corruption. Though written from outside, it is an insider's view and hence the writer's concern for India cannot be overlooked.

A noted post-Independence Parsi writer in English, Rohinton Mistry shares both ethnocentric and minority discourse features which characterize Parsi literature. Being a small minority group in India, the Parsis are constantly being threatened by the possibility of being devoured by the dominant Hindu culture in India. Their sense of insecurity and urge for removing identity crisis are artistically presented by Rohinton Mistry. Besides these two major issues there are other disturbing features such as declining population, late marriages, low birth rate and gender discrimination. All these issues are carefully dealt with in his novels. The sensitive characters are often tortured by an awareness of a slow, steady and almost imperceptible extinction of the community and yet, they try hard to support the central government of India with the hope that the secular nature of the Indian constitution would safeguard their interest. The Parsis had left Iran after the Arab conquest in the eighth century and a group arrived at Sanjan in Gujarat. They sought refuge from King Jadhav Rana and stayed there obeying some conditions laid down by the king. Since then the Parsis in India lived a secluded life, but in the course of time contributed to nation building. During the British period they felt rather comfortable and some prominent Parsis were bestowed national honour. In the postcolonial days they lost the importance at the national level and even suffered disgrace during Internal Emergency. The Nagarwala incident, that involved a Parsi, jolted the self-image of the community. In fact, *Such a Long Journey* is based on that incident. Major Bilimoria, who was used by the prime minister for taking out sixty lakh rupees from the nationalized bank, and was arrested and killed in the hospital, is the fictionalized version of Mr. Nagarwala who was trapped by Indira Gandhi. Laying bare the corrupt practice at the highest level, Rohinton Mistry expressed his strong reaction at the disgrace of Mr. Nagarwala whose disgrace was a direct insult to the Parsis who had retained a strong ethical tradition. In this way, Rohinton Mistry's fictional works reflect Ethnic Atrophy Syndromes. Besides being faithful records of the Parsi life-style, customs and rituals, these are also the domestic, social and political commentary concerning the Parsis. It is often observed that the Parsi community is the real protagonist in his works

Rohinton Mistry writes with a honest perspective. His sense of detail never bores the readers, but makes them more inquisitive. The writer's ready wit and his capacity for cracking private jokes make his fiction popular. He uses imagination to connect the private lives with the outer reality, the social and political world outside the individuals' private existence. In *Such a Long Journey,* Gustad's private life is interfered with outside events. If Major Bilimoria had not sent Gustad ten lakh rupees and Gustad had not decided to oblige his old friend, Gustad could remain free from trouble. Major Bilimoria's trouble, again, was closely linked to Bangladesh War. In *A Fine Balance*, too, the personal lives of Dina, Om, Ishwar and Maneck are intervened with the external agencies and political changes. Though the private world of the individuals in *Family Matters* is more pronounced than the outer world, public events obtrude and influence the private life again and again. The Bombay riots, for example, remain a threat to the individuals. Ultimately, the focus is on the fate of human existence in a world devastated by violence and conflicts.

Rohinton Mistry is also noted for his treatment of the subalterns. His protagonists are necessarily ordinary people, devoid of power and money. Hence, they are subjected to various sorts of pressure. Besides the major characters, there are shopkeepers, vagabonds, ayahs, rogues and such other figures in each of his works and these people often belong to the lowest position in the social hierarchy. The old woman Ms. Kutpitia, known for witchcraft, and the mentally retarded Tehmul, noted for their subaltern existence, are the two important characters in *Such a Long Journey*. A good number of characters belonging to the working class may be sorted out in *A Fine Balance*. These characters belong to the subaltern in its different forms, that of gender, class, caste, economy etc. In *Family Matters* too, the poor and the weak, the politically and socially exploited persons, are exposed with much care. Rohinton Mistry's deep-rooted concern for the poor and the downtrodden is expressed in his presentation of the marginalized and the underdog.

Lastly, Rohinton Mistry is known as a writer of urban life. In fact, he has no first hand knowledge of the village and he has not tried to trespass his limit. Born and brought up in Bombay, Rohinton Mistry had the opportunity to observe and analyze the compulsions, tensions and contradictions of urban life. And he fictionalizes the life in Bombay as experienced by him during his stay in India.

An Introduction to *Such a Long Journey*

Such a Long Journey (1991) is the first novel written by Rohinton Mistry, a writer of Indian Diaspora, who settled in Canada. Though the novel was published sixteen years after Rohinton Mistry had settled in Toronto, it has no trace of Canada. Rather, it reveals the author's deep concern for the Parsis in India in particular, and for the development of postcolonial India in general. This feeling may not be explained with the word 'nostalgia' which is loosely associated with romantic feelings. Rohinton Mistry's feeling for India is not just longing for the past, but a mixed feeling of unpleasant jolt when the Parsi community felt hurt at the Nagarwala incident and of restoring the honour of the Parsi community through a realistic portrayal of the said incident.

It may not be an exaggeration to observe that the Nagarwala incident was the basis of the novel. During the regime of Indira Gandhi in India, one Parsi gentleman Mr. Nagarwala was accused of imitating Indira Gandhi's voice while talking over the phone to the chief cashier of a nationalized bank from where he took sixty lakh rupees presumably for the fighters in Bangladesh. Mr. Nagarwala was pronounced guilty by the court and the entire Parsi community felt shocked and disgraced. Rohinton Mistry's pride for his community, which had been maintaining a high moral standard and which had secured a prestigious position in the past, got hurt and he decided to take revenge on Indira Gandhi through his fiction. No one has any doubt that Major Bilimoria in the novel, the Parsi gentleman working for the RAW, is none but Mr. Nagarwala. Bilimoria is accused in the way Mr. Nagarwala was accused, and Mistry gives Bilimoria a scope to justify himself when he arranges a meeting between Gustad and Bilimoria in jail. Bilimoria has not lived long after this confession. Though the entire world thinks him guilty, he feels relaxed that his friend Gustad has learnt the truth. Some extracts from his confession may be quoted to show how Mistry took revenge on Indira Gandhi for exploiting patriots and humanists like Bilimoria. Bilimoria says to Gustad,

> She [Indira Gandhi] said, I arranged for money . . . because Mukti Bahini must be helped. . . . Having second thoughts she said, I have enemies everywhere. If they find out about this money, they will use the information against me . . . our country will suffer if government destabilized. Very dangerous border situation. . . . She said, only problem is my telephone call to chief cashier . . . he might talk . . . but he did not see me speaking . . . we can always say someone imitated my voice. . . . Very clever woman, Gustad. She said, if my enemies try to make trouble, all you have to say is . . . you imitated my voice. I laughed . . . who would believe this? But she said, under the proper conditions, people will believe anything. She promised . . . nothing would happen to me. Like a fool I agreed . . . trusted her. Then she said, maybe . . . we should make our plan watertight . . . you can write a few lines just now. A confession. That you imitated my voice . . . because you wanted to continue helping Mukti Bahini. . . . What can I say, Gustad? Even to this . . . I agreed . . . . I wrote my confession . . . like an idiot. My respect for her . . . grown so much over the months. Such a strong woman. Trusted her completely (277).

Bilimoria uttered those fragments of sentences with much effort. He was very ill and after he was injected, he could hardly utter any word. Gustad still had his doubt as he could not understand how a worldly wise man like Jimmy could be so foolish. Bilimoria continued after a pause. He said that after physical verification he could learn that the Mukti Bahini had received no money. Then he had verified through his personal channel where the money could go. And it came out then, that the money disbursed by him had been intercepted by P.M.'s office and rerouted to a private account. Bilimoria also observed that the money might be used "to finance her son's car factory" or for election. Then Bilimoria disclosed his own sin. He had been so upset at the revelation of the P.M.'s real nature that he wanted to get everything exposed. But it was impossible to reveal the fact. Then, in a frenzied mood, he decided to put aside ten lakh rupees which could be distributed among his friends who were really needy. He thought that no one would bother about missing ten lakh rupees after getting fifty lakh rupees. But he was wrong. He had been arrested for that ten lakh rupees, though the charge against him was that he had taken the entire sixty lakh rupees. Bilimoria concluded,

> Everything is in their control . . . courts in their pockets . . . it is beyond the common man's imagination, the things being done by those in power. (280)

Indira Gandhi's role is further criticized through the reporter's comment on the acceptability of the P.M.'s phone call to the cashier of a nationalized bank. The reporter wrote,

> While the alleged facts of this case are certainly unique, what strikes this reporter as even more unusual are the circumstances surrounding this highly imaginative crime. For example, assuming that Mr. Bilimoria has the talent of voice impersonation, is it routine for our national banks to hand over vast sums of money if the Prime Minister telephones? How high up does one have to be in the government or the Congress Party to be able to make such a call? And was the Chief Cashier so familiar with Mrs. Gandhi's voice that he accepted the instructions without any verification whatsoever? If yes, does that mean that Mrs. Gandhi has done this sort of thing frequently? These questions cry out for answers, and till the answers are heard, clearly and completely, the public's already eroded confidence in our leaders cannot be restored. (195-96)

This direct attack on Indira Gandhi makes it clear that Mistry exposed the nature of corruption she was involved in and thus tried to make up the disgrace brought to the Parsi community.

It will however be a mistake to think that Rohinton Mistry's only concern was to restore the lost glory of the Parsis through an exposure of Indira Gandhi's criminal role in the fraud case. He was equally concerned for the poor Indian people, irrespective of religion and creed, who were suppressed under corruption at high places and the autocratic rule during the Emergency. Through Bilimoria's anguish, Rohinton Mistry's concern for the poor and the oppressed is expressed:

> Whole day and night I sat in my flat. Doing nothing . . . just thinking. What hope for the country? With such crooked leaders? . . . I sat thinking of all the people I had come across in my life . . . men in the army, good men. And my Ghulam Mohammed. Khodadad Building . . . the families living there. You and Dilnavaz, the children, the ambitions you have for them. And those bastards, those ministers and politicians, those ugly buffaloes and pigs . . . getting fatter and fatter, sucking our blood. . . .' Jimmy trembled, choking with vehemence. (279)

Through the accusations of old Cavasji directed at God, the wretched condition of the poor and the marginalized is hinted at:

> Monsoon is coming, so you be careful! Year after year, your floods are washing away poor people's huts! Enough now! Where is your fairness? Have you got any brains or not? Flood the Tatas this year! Flood the Birlas, flood the Mafatlals! (127)

Mistry however is not sentimental about the poor and the marginalized. His attention is also drawn towards the heartless attitude of the common man. When Gustad was seriously injured at the accident and a water-seller was asked to give a glass of water, the man demanded the price. When the taxi-driver told him, "You have no shame? You cannot see the man has had a serious accident, he is in pain, fainting?" the water-seller stuck to his point that he should get the price. The crowd that assembled began to argue on the topic.

> "I am a poor man," said the water-seller, "I have children to feed." He had a large purple mark on one side of his face, and a high-pitched voice with an irritating whine.
>
> The crowd took sides in the argument. Some said the heartless scoundrel should be driven away with a kick, while others saw his point. Determined not to be done out of his only sale all day, he spoke up again. "The man has had an accident. So? He will pay the ambulance and the doctor and the hospital, to get mended. Why

> should I be the only one left out? What is my sin that I don't get my twenty naye paise?" (59)

At last Gustad's son Sohrab, who accompanied him, paid the water-seller and the crowd dispersed. Such objective renderings revealing the variety of man's nature abound in the novel and the writer's urge to focus on different types of characters is explicit.

Rohinton Mistry's capacity for story-telling is another aspect of the novel that attracts the readers. He is able to create suspense so that the readers never lose interest in the flow of action. Though the protagonist is a common Parsi gentleman with modest aims in life and the surrounding is also about Parsi customs and way of life, non-Parsis are not less attracted towards the narrative. Mistry developed the skill of powerful narration even in his first novel. Thanks to this skill, the loopholes in the plot are neglected. Mistry has depended too much on coincidences: the same character comes back to the same place incidentally. For instance, the driver who helped Gustad at the time of accident and carried him first to Khodadad Building, and then to the Bonesetter, was the same man, Ghulam Mohammed, who handed over the money to Gustad. Gustad had not known earlier that his close friend Bilimoria was so much attached to Ghulam. It is also not probable that a mere bank clerk Dinshawji deposited large amount of money every day, and also withdrew the same amount in the same way, without attracting others' attention. A sort of willing suspension of disbelief on the readers' part explains why the readers do not very much bother about this type of incidents. They are so much engrossed with Gustad's anxiety that they start sharing it and wish that Gustad should remain safe.

The novel deals with a good number of characters most of whom are the residents of Khodadad Building, a Parsi enclave. All these characters are of varied nature and are rendered as types. With the use of some bold strokes Mistry sketches these characters which are lifelike and deserve to be remembered. Ms. Kutpitia with her superstitions and black magic, the idiot

Tehmul with his child's brain and an adult's body, Mr. Rabadi with his fascination for dog and old Cavasji with his unending complaints against God are remarkable creations. All these characters may be Parsis, but basically they are human beings having the peculiarities and shortfalls which may be found in people all over the world. Peerbhoy Paanwalla is another type who attracts the customers with his erotic stories, and yet changes the nature of his stories replacing them with patriotic ones in accordance with the changing mood of circumstances. The physician Dr. Paymaster is noted for keeping up his smiling face while examining his patients. He appears rather comic when he is compelled to keep the old signboard bearing the name of another physician with whose name the patients had been acquainted. Mistry has an eye to observe the little ironies of life such as this. Dinshawji is another character who is remarkable not only as a fine portrait but also for his contribution to the plot. His jokes that attracted his colleagues are in contrast with his sad demise. Bilimoria's character is sketched from Gustad's remembrances of his friendship with him and from his confession. Gustad's doubt about his confession is actually the doubt of the readers who raise questions about the acceptability of the Major's views. Gustad's satisfaction in regard to Bilimoria's statement is also shared by the readers.

Broadly speaking, *Such a Long Journey* is written in traditional method of novel-writing. The modernist method of experiments did not attract Mistry, as he has faith in his power of presenting facts from the point of view of a social realist. Though he uses memory in the construction of his plot, here is no flashback method and the development is chronological rather than spatial. Almost in the method of classical writers he seeks to project life in its fullness, bringing together a variety of beliefs and ideas—scientific attitude and superstitions, radicalism and secularism, broad nationalism and narrow party-politics—which are skilfully woven to the textual fabric. The central character Gustad Noble is designed as a common man having the grandeur of a classical tragic hero. A god-fearing man of modest aspirations, Gustad hoped that his eldest son Sohrab would join I.I.T. and would bring material prosperity to the family. He was rudely shocked when Sohrab refused to enrol himself as an I.I.T. student and chose arts stream instead. Though he loved his children very much, Gustad did not hesitate to declare that he would have no connection with Sohrab. This strong mentality became more prominent when he accepted Bilimoria's proposal to deposit ten lakh rupees, though he knew that there was fear of being caught and losing his job. His patriotic feeling as well as his gratitude to his friend who had helped him so much got the better of his fear. And when he learnt that Bilimoria was a fraud, he was tortured by internal suffering. He went to Delhi despite the difficulties, only to learn the truth from the Major. His anxiety and fear while depositing the large amount and again, while withdrawing it, may be compared to the sufferings of a tragic hero who takes up a hard work not for any gain but for performing the work. Gustad's ethical stand adds grandeur to the story. In strong contrast with Gustad is Ms. Kutpitia who has hardly any ethical standpoint when she proposes to do good to somebody at the cost of bringing misfortune to other. Gustad's wife Dilnavaz accepted Kutpitia's black magic that assured her of a good fortune at the cost of Tehmul's misery. At the end of the novel when Tehmul dies and Sohrab returns home, Mistry has no intention however to show how black magic wins. Rather, he projects the different attitudes to life. Any person having scientific view of life knows that these are mere coincidences, but a superstitious person will explain Sohrab's return as a result of black magic that demanded Tehmul's life. All these happenings fill the reader's mind with awe and compel him/her to think over the mysteries of life and death.

Such a Long Journey is not only a realistic novel revealing strong views about corrupt politicians—they are not imaginary figures, but respected chiefs of the country—but also a symbolic one that projects life on the earth in terms of journey. On one level, the 'journey' in the title suggests the 'journey' of the Parsis who had left Iran in the eighth century and settled in India.

They had to adjust themselves to the new surroundings: they adopted Gujarati language, their women began to put on saris and their men surrendered their weapons. They were also ordered to venerate the cow and strictly forbidden to proselytize. With these conditions the Parsis remained alienated in India, but gradually they became a part of India's multi-racial society. They were gratified to play an important role at the national level during the colonial rule. They also received a setback in postcolonial India when they lost the importance that they had enjoyed earlier. Long ago they had lost their literature and art, and the journey taught them how to adapt to a new home. And now that they have to face disgrace such as the Nagarwala incident, they are required to accept it as a passing phase. They have to be prepared for their journey ahead, for it is not the end of their journey; they have to continue somehow. The metaphor of 'journey' may be applied to the life of Gustad, the protagonist of the novel. Just as 'journey' in Eliot's "Journey of the Magi" is not physical journey but man's spiritual quest, so also 'journey' for Gustad, who is bound to the wheel of destiny, is the continuous struggle for gaining the values of life.

On another level, 'journey' is the metaphor of life and the pavement artist, a significant character in the novel, clarifies it through his activity and his reflection on life. The pavement artist has no home of his own. Nor has his art permanence. Gustad asked him to paint the compound wall of the Khodadad building and he did it. He painted pictures of gods, goddesses and saints of different religions and the wall that caused stink, turned to be a holy place. The painter was also happy that the religious-minded people offered money with which he could purchase oil paint. He even replaced his earlier paintings with oil paintings with the intention of making them permanent. But the municipality's decision to remove the wall came as a sudden blow. It was a coincidence that a 'morcha' that was on its way to the municipality to protest against its corruption, faced the labourers of the municipality engaged in breaking the wall and attacked them. The idiot Tehmul was killed when stones were flung, and the pavement artist had to leave the place. When Gustad asked him where he was going, the painter said, "Where does not matter, sir. In a world where roadside latrines become temples and shrines become dust and ruin, does it matter where?" (338) The pavement artist became ready for going, but he did not take the box of oil-paints. He said that he had his box of crayon and that would do. The implication is that nothing is permanent in life which is also a journey.

A Critical Analysis of the Text

Chapter1

The first chapter of *Such a Long Journey* introduces the readers to the inner world of a Parsi family—a minority community in multi-ethnic, multi-regional India—and highlights the Parsi life-style including their dress, food-habit, details of prayer and other tit-bits of daily life. The protagonist, middle-aged Gustad Noble, is sketched as a self-made man who had to shoulder hardship and humiliation to stand on his own feet after his father had been declared a bankrupt. As the novel starts, Gustad is exposed as a holy Zoroastrian performing religious rites. Facing the eastern sky, illuminated by the first glow of dawn, Gustad offered his 'orisons' to Ahura Mazda; as usual he was listening to the chirping of the sparrows while reciting his *kusti* prayer. He was sure that the sparrows were always first to awake, and the cawing of crows came later.

The surrounding of the Khodadad Building that accommodated some Parsi families including Gustad Noble's, is also exposed side by side. The milk man, called 'bhaiya' in the locality, started pouring milk from his tall aluminium can into the vessels of the housewives with the help of his little measure having a long, hooked handle. In spite of the women's disgust and grumbling, the tranquil hour and early light preserved the peace. Through the milkman's amusing hair-do, his Hindu identity is marked: he had a thin, short tail of hair growing from the centre of his otherwise perfectly shaven head. The camera is again focused on Gustad's physic—his prayer cap that hung on his wide wrinkled forehead was settled on his grey-white hair—and the tall broad-shouldered man with his black, groomed moustache comes up. It is noted that Gustad's sound health was the envy and admiration of his friends and relatives, though he had crossed fifty and had suffered a serious accident that made him limp. Guided by superstition, his wife Dilnavaz would say 'touch wood' to herself on such comments by others, lest there be any harm to his body. The mutual love of the couple is expressed through such insignificant descriptions. The old resident of the building, Miss Kutpitia is introduced through her regular scolding and threatening to the milkman for selling adulterated milk. Though she did not purchase milk from him, she took it up as her duty to keep the milkman in line through periodic berating. The milkman, however, ignored her with the remark: "As if I make the milk. Cow does that." She was also ignored by the women who had been waiting with their pans, for they were anxious to purchase the "sickly, watered-down white fluid" and return to their chores. Miss Kutpitia's isolation from others as well as the pathetic condition she was in—she had acquired over the years, the reputation of being mean, cranky and abusive—is further expressed through the description of how she was heckled by the children: "To children, Miss Kutpitia was the ubiquitous witch of their fairy stories come to life. They would flee past her door, screaming, 'Run from the *daaken*!' as much from fear as to provoke her to mutter and curse, and shake her fist." (2)

Gustad's wife Dilnavaz was one of those women who would regularly purchase that 'white fluid,' as the Nobles could not collect much coveted milk ration card from the government office even after a long waiting. She remembered the days when ration cards were only for the poor and the servants, and that time the Nobles could afford to buy the fine creamy product of Parsi Dairy Farm. She wished that Miss Kutpitia would stop screaming at the milkman who, as a result, might resent them more. Her inner sense of insecurity and fear is expressed through her thought: "God knows what he might do to the milk—as it was, these people in slum shacks and *jhopadpattis* in and around Bombay looked at you sometimes as if they wanted to throw you out of your home and move in with their own families." (4) The minority complex brewing up in the mind of a Parsi housewife throws light on the theme of the novel. Dilnavaz's tender and sympathetic nature becomes clear from her attitude towards Miss Kutpitia's idiosyncrasies. "She [Dilnavaz] found nothing repugnant or irritating about them—something amusing, sometimes tiresome, yes. But never offensive. After all, for the most part Miss Kutpitia only wanted to offer help and advice on matters unexplainable by the laws of nature. She claimed to know about curses and spells: both to cast and remove; about magic: black and white; about omens and auguries; about dreams and interpretation." (4) Dilnavaz never encouraged her, but gave her a patient hearing; for, at her age, a patient ear is more important than anything else.

The narration goes back to the prayer scene, again. Gustad recited the appropriate sections and unknotted the *kusti* from around his waist. The detail of the ritual is given: "When he had unwound all nine feet of its slim, sacred, hand-woven length, he cracked it, whip-like: once, twice, thrice. And thus was Ahriman, the evil one, driven away—with that expert flip of the wrist, possessed only by those who performed their *kusti* regularly." (4) The writer makes it clear that Gustad's prayer was not a mechanical performance, but a spontaneous urge that comes from within. "One day, while exploring the selves in his father's bookstore, he found the story of England's beloved dragonslayer. From then on whenever he said his prayers, Gustad was a Parsi Saint George, cleaving dragons with his trusty *kusti* wherever he found them." (5) The inner world of the Parsi life style and of Gustad's psyche is juxtaposed with the outer world of politics and the role of government as is revealed through references to radio and newspaper. Gustad's prayer is not disturbed by the news broadcast of "government controlled All-India radio." The newspaper headlines about Pakistan and the photo caption of soldiers using Bengali babies for bayonet practice project the setting: it is the time of Bangladesh war in 1971. Mistry consciously juxtaposes the outer incidents with the personal matters of his characters.

The past of the Noble family is exposed through Gustad's remembrances. As he sat on the chair while waiting for *The Times of India,* he caressed the arms of the chair "thinking of the decades since his grandfather had lovingly crafted it in his furniture workshop." (6) The signboard of the shop contained the words: *Noble & Sons, Makers of Fine Furniture.* Gustad's nostalgic feelings are described in first person enabling the readers to grasp the nature of the torture inflicted on young Gustad:

> A glass-fronted cabinet with gleaming cherry-coloured wood . . . a profoundly dignified black desk: all of it like the furniture in my childhood home.
>
> Some of it now here, in my house. Saved from the clutches of bankruptcy—the word cold as a chisel. The sound cruel and sharp and relentless as the cleats on the bailiff's shoes. The cleats had sounded their malicious clatter on the stone tiles. Bastard bailiff seized whatever he could get his filthy hands on. My poor father lost everything. Except the few pieces I rescued. (6)

Gustad also remembered how his good friend Malcolm Saldanha helped him to rescue a few pieces from the clutches of the bailiff. He felt sorry that he had not kept touch with Saldanha. One friend brought the memory of another through association. Gustad remembered Major Bilimoria with disgust and sought to keep his mind free from the thought of his activities that threatened to disrupt the piece of his mind. He gathered comfort from the old furniture, the pieces that "stood like parentheses around his entire life, the sentinels of his sanity." (6) The incident of Major Bilimoria is not disclosed and the readers are kept in suspense.

The narration comes back to the present with the I.I.T.'s entrance exam results published in the newspaper. Gustad had been anxiously waiting for the result; the roll number of his elder son Sohrab on the list of successful candidates filled his mind with immense joy and pride. He stroked sleeping Dilnavaz impatiently to give her the good news, but his wife did not express her emotion in the way he did. She went to fill the water drums, and a long tail of air bubbles reminded her of the bubbles that used to gush in her younger son's little fish tank. She recalled how Darius, their younger son, would fondly preserve the tiny coloured fishes. But the tank was empty, as were the birdcages. They lay covered in dust and cobwebs, along with Sohrab's butterfly display case. Dilnavaz's presence of mind is also displayed when she told her husband not to awaken Sohrab for giving him the news of his being selected. Gustad obeyed his wife and looked upon his son with his eyes filled with joyful pride. He also observed Darius and their only daughter, little Roshan. Since his father's business had been treacherously ruined, Gustad could hardly have a peaceful morning. He had always wished that his sons' and daughter's lives would be filled with peace and tranquillity. He hummed the wartime song he had adapted to sing the children to sleep when they were little:

> Bless them all, bless them all,
> Bless my Sohrab and Darius and all,
> Bless my Sohrab and Darius
> And Roshan and . . . (9)

The wartime song along with the blackout paper taped over the glasspanes of the windows and the ventilators reminded Gustad of the war with China. The year 1962—the year of India's war with China—was also a dreadful year for the Nobles. Gustad recalled,

> How much happened that year, . . . Roshan's birth and then my terrible accident. What luck. In bed for twelve weeks, with the broken hip between Madhiwalla Bonesetter's sandbags. And riots in the city—curfews and lathi charges and burning buses everywhere. What a dreadful year 1962 had been. And such a humiliating defeat, everywhere people talking of nothing but the way the Chinese had advanced, as though the Indian army consisted of tin soldiers. (9)

Funds were raised to support the Indian army and much of the donated goods were reported to have turned up for sale in specific areas (Chor Bazaar and Nul Bazaar) exposing thereby the corrupt nature of the people. The Chinese war broke the heart of the prime minister, Jawaharlal Nehru who, disappointed by the behaviour of his son-in-law Feroze Gandhi for exposing scandals in the government, became obsessed with the ideas of how to ensure that his daughter Indira would become Prime Minister after him. During the war the people were asked to paste blackout papers on their ventilators; even after the war was long over, Gustad left his blackout paper undisturbed with his plea that it helped the children to sleep better. Dilnavaz taunted him, but he stuck to his point, being almost monomaniac like Jawaharlal. Blackout was declared again during the war with Pakistan three years later, and the blackout paper was needed much to Gustad's triumphant attitude. Gustad read out the morning paper describing the sensational news of war on the eastern front to his wife who was busy in collecting water. They remembered on this occasion Major Jimmy Bilimoria, their friend and neighbour, who left Khodadad Building abruptly a year ago without a word to his neighbours, and leaving them surprised. Thus the narrative is woven out of a juxtaposition of historical and familial incidents which run side by side. The first chapter introduces the setting and the important characters through Gustad's recollections as he observes his early morning prayer. The chapter ends with his recollection of the day of his accident nine years ago: the diesel smell of a lorry reminded him of the day of the accident when he lay, with his shattered hip, in the path of oncoming cars spreading diesel smell.

Chapter 2

The second chapter describes Gustad's attempt to celebrate Roshan's birthday and Sohrab's success in the I.I.T. entrance by purchasing a live chicken from Crawford Market. Gustad's nostalgic remembrance of his father's weekly expeditions to Crawford Market, his bargaining with the shopkeepers and triumphant return with live chickens reveal the difference between Gustad and his father: the father was then the owner of a big bookstore in the marketplace, and the loss of the store compelled the son to manage somehow from private tuitions. Gustad's father was always accompanied by at least one servant, arriving and leaving the market with taxi; and Gustad was alone, with his meagre wallet and worn basket lined with newspaper to soak up meat juices lest that could start dripping in the bus. Gustad's apprehension that he might cause embarrassment or, worse still, angry protests from vegetarian passengers, and his reluctance therefore to purchase chicken from Crawford Market, reveal his nature clearly:

> Throughout the trip he felt anxious and guilty—felt that in his basket was something deadlier than a bomb. For was he not carrying the potential source of Hindu-Muslim riots? Riots which often started due to offences of the flesh, usually of porcine or bovine origins?

The second chapter weaves the present incident of purchasing chicken with the remembrance of how Gustad's Christian friend Malcolm had advised him to eat beef and guided him through the Crawford Market giving him first-hand knowledge of how to choose the best beef. Gustad remembered his friend's humorous comments:

> "Lucky for us," Malcolm always said, "that we are minorities in a nation of Hindus. Let them eat pulses and grams and beans, spiced with their stinky asafoetida—what they call 'hing.' Let them fart their lives away. The modernized Hindus eat mutton. Or chicken, if they want to be more fashionable. But we will get our protein from their sacred cow." At other times he would say, mimicking their economics professor, "Law of supply and demand, always remember. That's the key. Keeps down the price of beef. And it is healthier because it is holier." (23)

The differences in food habit, closely linked to different religious practices, offer an inner picture of India where people belonging to different religious sects have settled. Gustad's tolerance of others' religion while maintaining his faith in his own becomes explicit. On the way to Crawford Market, his friend Malcolm would regularly attend the Mass in the church, and Gustad also followed him, dipping his finger in the holy water and crossing himself. When he came to the church for the first time, Gustad was quite intrigued by the church and its rituals, so different from what went on the fire-temple. But he had been conditioned from childhood to resist the call of other faiths. He was taught that all religions were equal, and yet, one must remain true to one's own, because religions were not like garment styles that could be changed at whim. Hence he clung to the sense of peaceful mystery and individual serenity that prevailed in the fire temple. Following the flashback method of narration, Rohinton Mistry focuses in one paragraph on Gustad's confusion in selecting the best chicken, and on the next paragraph takes the readers to Gustad's past days when Malcolm, while guiding his friend through the market, would continue to relate how the early Christians had settled in India. Malcolm would proudly proclaim that Apostle Thomas had landed on the Malabar Coast nineteen hundred years ago. Gustad would thereon retort that their prophet Zarathustra had lived more that fifteen hundred years before Jesus was born, and a thousand years before Lord Buddha was born. He also declared that Judaism, Christianity and Islam were much influenced by Zoroastrianism. On the following Sunday, as per Gustad's recollections, Malcolm described how Christianity was spread in India, thanks to Saint Thomas's process of mesmerizing the mass through the display of how a handful of sea-water, flung in the air, remained suspended there, reflecting the sunlight and sparkling most wondrously. All this was delivered by Malcolm in the market, while sharing his knowledge of how to choose the best beef. Years later, when Gustad started shopping on his own, he was always willing to share Malcolm's wisdom with friends and neighbours. But gradually stopped coming to Crawford Market as he felt embarrassed when the Hindu 'sadhus' started nationwide protest against cow slaughter. "It was easier to remain the silent, unknown apostle of beef." (26)

The second section of the second chapter focuses on the commotion in Gustad's family created by the live chicken bought by Gustad from Crawford Market. The daughter Roshan was first frightened as she had never seen a live chicken earlier. But as she found the bird pecking busily at the grain offered by her and clucking contentedly, she was fascinated by its movements and began to imagine it as her pet. Darius and Sohrab also came to inspect the bird and all were making fun. But Dilnavaz grumbled as the bird made the mess and there was no servant to clean that. In order to appease her, Gustad proposed that he would clean the mess with Sohrab's help and Sohrab also agreed. As Sohrab calmed the chicken, holding down its wings, Gustad was very pleased and commented that he would do wonderfully at I.I.T. Sohrab was annoyed at this and asked his father, clenching his teeth, "How does a chicken have anything to do with engineering?" (27) The hilarious mood was gone and Gustad was taken aback at this reaction of his son. The son's enraged remark, "Ever since the exam results came, you are driving me crazy with your talk of I.I.T.," hints at the gulf between the father and the son. The parents had been discussing the matter endlessly, making plans and provisions of how Sohrab would live in the hostel and would come back at the weekends, and when he would go to America after completing his engineering degree, but they had no idea that their son could not tolerate all that silly talk. Dilnavaz tried to appease him by telling that it was just an expression of his father's joy; she also reminded him of his father's life-long suffering as he had to support his father from childhood. Sohrab left the kitchen without any comment, and Gustad also left with the remark that the bird should be left undisturbed. It is found that all the members in the family were attracted to the chicken. Even Dilnavaz, who first disliked the idea of keeping a live chicken in the kitchen, gave some rice to the bird at midnight when she heard it making sound and thought that it must be hungry.

The third section of the second chapter describes in detail how the chicken was let loose when the butcher was going to dress it and how it was caught by Lame Tehmul, a resident of the housing complex. The character and activities of Lame Tehmul, called so because of his hip-fracture for which he was condemned to years on crutches and sticks and could never walk properly but limp, throw light not only on his character, but on other residents in the complex as well. Tehmul's parents were long dead and his older brother, a travelling salesman, looked after his needs. His schooling was terminated as he could not follow the courses and even in his mid-thirties he behaved as a child and liked to be among children. Mistry writes, "Things that travelled through the air enchanted him—things that soared, swooped or dived, things flying and fluttering in freedom. Whether it be bird or butterfly, a paper dart or a falling leaf, he never tired of trying to possess it. Aware of his fascination, sometimes the children would toss a ball or twig or pebble his way, but always slightly out of reach. Always, he would gamely persevere to catch it and fall over himself. Or they would throw a football away from him, then stand back and watch him stumble after it. Just when he thought he was catching up, his uncoordinated feet would kick the ball further, and his frustrating chase began over again." (31) Though he got along well with the children, the grown-ups could hardly tolerate his annoying habits such as following people and scratching his own body with a circular movement. When he would follow people from the compound gate to the building entrance, they waved their hands till he understood that he was unwanted, "though utterly bewildered as to why this should be so." The ladies, in particular, could not tolerate the sight of scratching and always avoided him. It was also difficult to understand his abbreviated vocabulary that always emerged at breakneck speed. He had a special liking for Gustad who always treated him in a more humane way. That day, after catching hold of the flying chicken, Tehmul entered Gustad's flat grinning, and left after sometime, waving goodbye to all. Gustad was harping on the question of how the string could be untied from the chicken's leg and at that time the screeching of the chicken in the kitchen made it clear that the bird was killed. Roshan burst into sobs and all four looked at Gustad accusingly. The chapter ends with the description of two crows peering through the wire at the mass of feathers and flesh on the stone parapet beside the tap.

Chapter 3

The third chapter of the novel projects the birthday dinner in Gustad's flat. Gustad invited his friend Dinshawji and his wife and Dilnavaz invited Miss Kutpitia. Hours before the dinner party, Miss Kutpitia excused herself from the invitation on the ground that a lizard fell on her breakfast table and to make the matters worse, its tail broke off when she wrenched her leather sappat from her foot and threw at it. The news provoked uproarious laughter and Gustad could not control him easily. Among the other two guests, Mrs. Dinshawji did not turn up and Mr. Dinshawji was the only guest. The presence of only one guest did not lessen the fun of the party; Gustad and Dinshawji started with Golden Eagle and remembered the sweet old days they had passed together in bank. Politics made an obvious way in their reminiscences of the days before the banks were nationalized. The anxiety of the Parsi community in regard to the growing insecurity of the ethno-religious minority group in a vast country like India also comes up. Dinshawji recalled that the Parsis had been the kings of banking; but the whole atmosphere got spoiled after Indira Gandhi nationalized the banks. Gustad retorted that nationalization had worked nowhere in the world. Dinshawji explained the process of nationalization of banks as 'vote-getting tactics.' Expressing his disgust at the shrewd woman's tactics, he also recalled how Indira, after she was made the president of the Congress Party by her father, began encouraging the demands of a separate Maharashtra and thus let loose communal violence. "How much bloodshed, how much rioting she caused. And today we have that bloody Shiv Sena, wanting to make the rest of us into second-class citizens. Don't forget, she started it all by supporting the racist buggers." (39) The two friends then remembered the horrifying days of riots when the big processions at Flora Fountain could not be seen any more. Dinshawji said, "Everyday fighting and some 'morcha' or other. . . . In the bank we thought our innings were over when those 'goondas' broke the windows, even the thick glass of the main entrance. There goes our bonus, I thought. They were shouting 'Parsi crow-eaters, we'll show you who is the boss.'" Dinshawji also described how one elderly employee Ratansa, nicknamed Goover-Ni-Gaan, covered his head with his white hanky and began doing his 'kusti,' like a 'dustoorji' in the fire temple, and how they were saved by the two Pathan gatemen. His hatred towards the Hindu majority is exposed in his comment which he must not have uttered in public:

> Yes, but because of the Pathans and their guns, all those Sakarams and Dattarams and Tukarams only stood outside, screaming like fishwives. If they came close, one of the Pathans stamped his foot and at once they went in reverse gear 'Bhum'! That's all, and the Maratha brigade ran like cockroaches. . . . Lucky for us that just as the bloody cockroaches were getting braver, the police came. (40)

The conversation reveals that the Parsis as the minority community have to cope with the hegemonic forces so that they may get their own space secure.

When the two friends were thus chatting, the three children came to greet Dinshawji who first wished a happy birthday to Roshan and then turned to congratulate Sohrab for his success in the I.I.T. entrance exam. The jolly mood was disturbed as Sohrab glared at his father asking if he had already told the world about it. Gustad asked him to behave properly, but Sohrab teased him with the remark that Gustad was so much boasting about I.I.T., as if he were going there himself. He also told that he was not interested in I.I.T. Gustad asked him to stop any idiotic-lunatic talk. Dinshawji tried a diversion tactfully, giving attention to Darius's capacity for doing fifty push-ups and fifty squats. Gustad had the occasion to recall his grandfather who had taught him 'kusti' and had also inspired him with the stories of the wrestlers and strongmen. Gustad's grandmother, also an ardent wrestling fan, attended the matches with them. She could anticipate falls, escapes, take-downs and reversals better than

Gustad or Grandpa, and very often outdid them in predicting the winner. Inspired by his grandparents, Gustad had always been devoted to body-building and he suggested that one hundred push-ups and squats every morning would increase one's biceps by one inch. As Dinshawji praised Darius's muscles and requested him to show them, Darius rolled up his sleeves to make poses and was secretly happy for his capacity to draw others' attention. He had earlier developed hobbies of keeping fishes and birds as pets, but was not successful. And at last, he turned his attention to himself, and his physique became his hobby. On Roshan's repeated request to sing the donkey song, Gustad started singing and was appreciated by all, including Dilnavaz who came out from the kitchen to listen and announced that the dinner was on the table.

The second section of the third chapter gives details of the dinner. Dinshawji was much pleased, but he appeared to be lacking in manners. When he said that the aroma of the chicken curry could even make a corpse at the Tower of Silence sit up with an appetite, Dilnavaz eyed him distastefully. She felt that one should have the minimum sense of decency that would forbid him to utter such things at the dinner table on a birthday. She was further hurt to notice a similar indecency in her husband who commented that the chicken that tried to escape in the morning was now patiently waiting to be devoured by them. When the two friends started discussing on the utility of buying live chicken, Dilnavaz interrupted him and said that Gustad could very well explain the thing to him later. Her sentiments echoed silently from other three faces, and Gustad apologized. Yet, the children pushed their food back and forth on the plate. Realizing his mistake Gustad wanted to change the mood by saying that the happy birthday song was not yet sung. Despite Dilnavaz's mild protest that the food would get cold and tasteless, the song was sung and it was followed by wishing good luck through tasting wine. Dinshawji began reciting to Roshan a song wishing her good health and wealth. And suddenly the flat was plunged into darkness and everybody was touched with fear and silence. Gustad went to check what was wrong and found that the entire neighbourhood was dark and so he gave up the idea of checking the fuse. Dinshawji was in a good mood and liked to recite other songs, and Gustad called him Poet Laureate. Dinshawji's reaction shows how Dinshawji as individual and the Parsis as a community wanted to be recognized as Indian:

> Laureate-baureate nothing, I am a son of Mother India. Call me Kavi Kamal, the Indian Tennyson! (47)

As he started a song on ghosts, prowling like a spectre around the table, everyone cheered and clapped except Dilnavaz who was now frantic about the food getting cold. Flushed with success and inspiration, Dinshawji uttered, "Though dark is the night, please take no fright, we shall eat by candlelight. Or kerosene light." The jolly mood was once again disrupted as Gustad began to wish for Sohrab and expected his brilliant career at I.I.T., much to his annoyance. Not anticipating Sohrab's reaction, Dinshawji also cried out, "For he's a jolly good fellow! For he's a jolly good fellow!" Everyone joined in and the voice was so loud that Sohrab's protest was drowned. The voices ceased abruptly, in mid-melody, just after Sohrab's shout 'stop it' was audible. He sat staring angrily at his plate. "The candles cast nervous shadows that shivered or yawned wildly when the flames were disturbed by breathing." (48) Dilnavaz again reminded that the food was getting cold. Unable to gauge Sohrab's mind, Gustad asked what was wrong with him. The boy said, "I'm sick and tired of I.I.T., I.I.T., I.I.T. all the time. I'm not interested in it, I'm not a jolly good fellow about it, and I'm not going there." It was indeed a great shock for Gustad that all his hopes in regard to his son's bright career were going to be nipped in the bud. He sighed and felt that the rum taken by Sohrab had left him crazy. Sohrab repeated his view once again and Gustad became more confused than angry at his son's behaviour and proposed that they might discuss the matter next day. Sohrab was not ready for any discussion and declared that I.I.T. did not interest him, that he was going to change to the arts programme so that he would remain with his friends in his college. Gustad could control himself no longer and fired up, commenting on the word 'friend.' He reminded his son of his own great friend Major Jimmy Bilimoria, also called Major Uncle, who had left the building without telling anything about his whereabouts. Dinshawji squirmed uncomfortably at this type of discourse. And finally, they started eating though the gloom could not be dispelled. Silence governed the meal for most of the time and no one was found jolly.

Chapter 4

The fourth chapter of the novel starts with the departure of Dinshawji, the only guest of the evening. Locking the door for the night after his friend's departure, Gustad started accusing Sohrab who was alleged to have spoilt the party. Sohrab immediately retorted that it was Gustad himself who was responsible for making the mess as he bought the live chicken home and made everybody feel sick at the table. Gustad was not in a mind to digest whatever was said by his son. And as a result a quarrel broke up during the birthday party of Roshan. Sohrab said that his father had scolded him for his own stupidity. He also said that his father could not face the truth. Thereon the father was hurt and reminded the son that he had to work hard in his youth to earn his own college fees. He had to study late at night with an oil-lamp, keeping the wick very low. Sohrab said that he had been told the story hundred times. This was a great insult that Gustad could hardly digest. He ordered Roshan to bring him the thick, brown leather belt with which he intended to give Sohrab a good lesson. Roshan stood still, her eyes wide with fear. Dilnavaz recalled the old days when the children were small and were being beaten by their father and would remain afraid of him. But now the fear was gone and the boy would not retreat. Sohrab declared that the father might bring the belt, and he was not scared of him or of anything. Panting with rage, Gustad brought the belt himself and wanted to hear from Sohrab what he had to say. The son said that he had already said everything, and if the father had not heard that, he was ready to repeat. "Gustad swung, and the leather whistled as it cut through the air. Dilnavaz ran between the two, the way she used to when the boys were little. The cowhide lashed her calves and she screamed. Two red weals started to emerge." (51) Roshan started sobbing and screaming, and appealed to his father to stop all that. The belt continued to swing, though nobody was hurt. The misplaced blow had taken much of Gustad's energy and he shouted that Sohrab was cowardly hiding himself behind his mother. Before either Sohrab or Dilnavaz could respond, Miss Kutpitia's shrill cry was heard. She said, "Enough is enough! This is sleeping time, not fighting time! Save the rest for morning!" Gustad was furious. Rushing to the window he replied that he also paid rent for his lodging and so if one had to say something, she must come to his door. Dilnavaz supported her, much to Gustad's annoyance who waited defiantly by the window in case a retort from Miss Kutpitia was forthcoming. Dilnavaz took the opportunity to hustle Sohrab and the other two out of the room and into bed. Left alone, Gustad's anger started to ebb. He threw the belt in a corner, and then blew out the candles on the dining table. He could not tolerate light, and so adjusted the wick of the kerosene lamp. Dilnavaz returned after sometime and asked Gustad to go to Sohrab who was reported to be weeping. Gustad did not agree. He said that Sohrab should come to him. He also said that as Sohrab forgot how to respect, he was dead to him. Dilnavaz protested and said that Sohrab was already nineteen and it was not the way to treat a boy of nineteen. Gustad defended himself by saying that he did nothing except being proud of him. The bewilderment behind his anger was touching, and she wanted to comfort him. Gustad recalled how he had patiently suffered all his life-looking for a bright future for his son, and this was the result of all his suffering. He also recalled how he had saved Sohrab's life at the cost of his fractured hip. Dilnavaz touched his shoulder once again and then went to complete the work in kitchen.

The second section of the chapter describes Gustad's activities that night. Feeling reckless, he mixed together whatever was left in the wine bottles and soda water. He then drank half of the glass and opened the cabinet door of his grandfather's black desk. The smell of the old books, rescued from his father's bankrupt bookstore, took him to the past world. "The rich, timeless fragrance rose from the precious pages, soothing his uneasy, confused spirit. He shut the book, tenderly stroking its spine with the back of his fingers, and replaced it on the shelf" (53). The upper shelf was full of books which he had planned to keep in a bookcase to be made by him and Sohrab, and now the boy was nothing to him. The bottom shelf was full of files, folders and old magazines. In that shelf he had kept a letter secretly which he now took to the lamplight for further reading. The envelope was typewritten. The return address was a post office box number in New Delhi, and the sender's name was absent. Inside the envelope there was a sheet of paper, of excellent quality, thick and fibred. It was a letter of his long lost friend Jimmy who was referred to by Gustad when Sohrab had expressed his desire to get admitted in the arts stream and to remain with his friends in the college. Jimmy's letter was mysterious. He had not explained why he had abruptly left Bombay without telling anything even to Gustad, his best friend. He even did not write where he was staying now and for what purpose. He only wrote, "I am still not at liberty to tell you details except it is a matter of national security. You know I was doing work for the government after leaving the army." (54) In the letter, Jimmy requested Gustad to receive a parcel on his behalf, as he acknowledged Gustad to be the most reliable. He also begged his forgiveness. Quite naturally, Gustad kept the letter in secret, lest the matter be known to all. Rereading the letter, Gustad had the occasion to reflect not only on his friendship with Jimmy but also on the troubles of his own life.

> Gustad lowered the wick of the kerosene lamp and leaned back in the armchair. The light, very soft now, made the room dreamlike in the glow. O Dada Ormuzd, what kind of joke is this? In me when I

> was young, You put the desire to study, get ahead, be a success. Then you took away my father's money, left me rotting in the bank. And for my son? You let me arrange everything, put it within reach, but You take away his appetite for I.I.T. What are You telling me? Have I become too deaf to hear You? (55)

Gustad's concern for his son is a part of the concern from which the minority suffers. He was anxious because of the rise of the fascist Shiv Sena politics and demand for Marathi language. It was like the condition of the black people in America. There was hardly any future for the minorities. And he was unable to make Sohrab understand all this. How could one refuse the chance of getting admitted to an institution like I.I.T. where one's future could be secured? It was not clear to him to what kind of life Sohrab was looking forward. At the beginning of his life he had some hopes in the midst of sufferings, and at this stage there was nothing but sorrow.

Gustad also remembered the day his hip had been fractured. It was a rainy day and he had got on the wrong bus with ten-year-old Sohrab while heading for lunch. Gustad had taken a special half-day's leave to celebrate Sohrab's first day at St. Xavier's High School. The conductor of the bus was rude and refused to pull the bell when it was clear at the time of purchasing the ticket that they had boarded on a wrong one. Gustad was asked to pay for the next stop where the bell would be pulled. And if they were to get down, they were to take the risk when the bus ran slow because of traffic jam. Embarrassed by the exchange of talk between the conductor and Gustad, Sohrab was ready to get down as the bus was at a standstill in the middle lane. The bus jerked forward at the very moment that Sohrab stepped off. He lost his balance and fell. Gustad leapt from the moving bus and realized within a fraction of a moment that he could either land on his feet or save his son. He kicked Sohrab out of the path of an oncoming taxi and his left hip took the burnt of the fall. The taxi-driver slammed on his brakes inches from Gustad and he was saved. The taxi-driver was very generous; he carried Gustad and Sohrab to Khodadad building and from there he took Gustad to Madhiwalla Bonesetter. It was Major Bilimoria who insisted on going to that bonesetter, and he took the responsibility of Gustad's treatment. If it had not been for Jimmy's taking him to the bonesetter, he would be a complete cripple. He was now almost like any other healthy man, without crutches or stick, or terrible heaving-swaying walking. Gustad reflected, "What would I have done that day without Jimmy? . . . that was the amazing thing about him, he was always there when needed—call it coincidence, call it friendship, that was Jimmy's way." (60)

The third section of the chapter relates how Gustad replied to Major Bilimoria's letter at midnight when everybody was asleep. It is clear that Gustad felt obliged to him and so he decided to accept his proposal though there was risk in accepting a packet on behalf of somebody who did not even disclose his address. Writing the letter was a ritual for him; he searched for a holder to fit a nib—the process became obsolete after the ballpoint pen came in vogue—and then wrote on an 'uncrumpled sheet.' To write with nib-holder was a part of tradition for Gustad who sincerely felt that in the name of modernity all that was our heritage had been discarded. And hence, people are not showing respect to others which was also a part of our tradition. Gustad felt:

> No one wrote with them (the nib-holders) any more, not even in schools. But at one time that was how children made the transition from pencil to ink. This was the bloody problem with modern education. In the name of progress they discarded seemingly unimportant things, without knowing that what they were chucking out the window of modernity was tradition. And if tradition was lost, then the loss of respect for those who respected and loved tradition always followed. (61)

Chapter 5

Chapter 5 starts with Dilnavaz's conversation with Ms. Kutpitia who had asked Gustad to keep quiet when he was charging at Sohrab the night before. In the early morning (water-tap time),

Dilnavaz awoke automatically and was surprised to see Ms. Kutpitia beckoning her upstairs. Her surprise increased when she found the old lady express her concern for Sohrab who reminded her, as she said, of her nephew Farad. Dilnavaz had never seen Farad, but she had heard how Ms. Kutpitia had dedicated her life to motherless Farad, and how the boy met with an accident and died, leaving her aunt miserably alone. Ms. Kutpitia verified the facts that earlier Sohrab had much interest in I.I.T., but after being qualified in the entrance examination he lost interest in it. She explained the matter as a case of 'jaadu-mantar': "Somebody has fed him something bad. In his food, or in a drink." (63) Dilnavaz was sceptic at the beginning, and masked her feeling politely. But she was tempted to believe in what Ms. Kutpitia said; it simplified and explained the mystery. Ms. Kutpitia also wanted to know if she knew somebody who would be profited by Sohrab's failure. Dilnavaz could not think of anyone, but she shivered with the very idea of stealing one's brain for someone else. Ms. Kutpitia further enlarged the list of causes behind Sohrab's change of mind: it could even be an evil mixture he stepped on in the street. She also had remedies in her stock. She advised Dilnavaz to start with lime; she explained the process and the precise gestures required. Her superstition is further explicit in her observation that she had taken the wise decision by not attending the dinner. For, all was spoilt by quarrelling, and the power also went off. Her final interpretation was that the chicken slaughtered in her house was very unlucky. The curse of the death-scream had stayed under her roof. Though Dilnavaz was apparently not affected by the superstitious belief, her anxiety for her son had already made her mind soft which could not remain rational for a long time.

The second section of the fifth chapter focuses on the mind of Sohrab, who had special knack for arts, though he could show his proficiency in science subjects, too. He also got up in the morning, though at night he had lain awake, "agonizing over the hurt, the confusion, the harsh words." "The seed of Sohrab's troubles had germinated long ago, long before last night, when his parents discovered how easily things came to their first-born, at home, in school, at work or play. There seemed to be nothing Sohrab could not do, and do well. Whether it was arithmetic, or arts and crafts, or moral science, he bagged several prizes each year on Prize Distribution Day. Regularly, there were awards for elocution and debating. In the interschool drama competition, the play he acted in walked away with the trophy. His exhibits in the school science fair finished first. And before long, Gustad and Dilnavaz were convinced their son was very special." (64-65) Thus, when Sohrab showed any interest in model airplanes, it was interpreted as an indication of his successful career as an aeronautical engineer. Similarly, his tinkering with mechanical things was interpreted as suggestive of his scientific genius. Even his failure in the art of entomology—he attempted to preserve moths and butterflies—was not allowed to be his failure. Gustad gladly shouldered the blame with his confession that he had brought petrol instead of carbon tetrachloride, and could not get the proper drying agent Sohrab wanted. But Sohrab noted that his father had never dreamt of an artist-son, though his success in the field of arts was not negligible. For example, Sohrab was very proud of his homemade production of *King Lear* in Khodadad Building. He was Lear, producer, director, costume designer, set designer and whatnot. He also wrote an abridged version of the play knowing that none would sit more than an hour. It struck him curiously that his parents had never thought of acting as his possible career: "It was never: my son will paint, my son will act, he will write poetry. No, it was always: my son will be a doctor, he will be an engineer, he will be research scientist." (66) And gradually, the dream of I.I.T. took shape and took hold of their imagination. It became the Promised Land. "It was El Dorado and Shangri-La, it was Atlantis and Camelot, it was Xanadu and Oz. It was the home of the Holy Grail. And all things would be given and all things would be possible and all things would come to pass for he who journeyed there and emerged with the sacred chalice." (67) Sohrab's frustrated anger that was let loose the night before, was not therefore a new one.

Ever since he had found his father obsessed, he developed anger which was expressed whenever he found the father boasting of his son's success.

That morning Sohrab saw the two letters on the desk and his mother asked him of Bilimoria's letter. After Gustad woke up, she complained to him that he had started concealing matters. Gustad said that he only wanted to think about the content in secret, without any suggestion from others. Thereon Dilnavaz was sorry that she was taken for nonsense. Gustad explained why he had decided to help Bilimoria. Sohrab commented that his decision was right, but he also apprehended that Bilimoria might have joined some underground communist party. He said,

> I was just thinking about Jimmy Uncle and your friends talking politics. He always used to say, "Only two choices: communism or military dictatorship, if you want to get rid of these Congress Party crooks. Forget democracy for a few years, not meant for a starving country." . . . Imagine if Jimmy Uncle is planning a coup to get rid of our corrupt government. (68)

Gustad enjoyed Sohrab's advice, but was careful to conceal his approval. And so, he called Sohrab's talk "idiotic-lunatic" and observed that what Jimmy said was just a way of talking. Sohrab also said that he was joking, but the fact of corruption still remained. He questioned, "what about the leaders who do wrong? Like the car manufacturing license going to Indira's son." (68) Gustad was not yet talking to his son directly. Addressing Dilnavaz he said, "He [Sohrab] may be a genius, but let me teach him something. Whatever you read in the paper, first divide by two—for the salt and pepper. From what is left, take off ten percent. Ginger and garlic. And sometimes, depending on the journalist, another five percent for chilly powder. Then, and only then, will you get to the truth free of 'masala' and propaganda." (68) As Sohrab said that he had learnt it from a college friend whose father worked at the testing centre, Gustad became serious and told him directly that he should keep clear of the college friends and their idiotic-lunatic talk. "Be grateful this is democracy," he said, "If that Russia Walla was here, he would pack you and your friends off to Siberia." (69) Gustad now came back to the initial bone of contention between the father and the son. He advised Sohrab to forget his college friends and the simple B.A. degree. Dilnavaz motioned to Sohrab to follow her and took him to the kitchen. She now tried the lime method as per Ms. Kutpitia's instruction. Sohrab protested, but Dilnavaz somehow managed, appealing to him that he would not be hurt in the process and his brain would be healthy. Though Sohrab found it funny, he obeyed his mother who had intelligence enough not to mention Kutpitia's name before him. And surprisingly, everything Ms. Kutpitia said seemed imbued with deep wisdom to Dilnavaz.

The third section of the fifth chapter projects Gustad in his office. His mood was still off, and at lunch-time, he did not go to the stairwell where the 'dubbawalla' deposited the tiffin boxes. He decided to let his lunch return home uneaten, and without the pencilled note to Dilnavaz which, over twenty-one years, was the one constant in their lives. Dinshawji approached his table and offered him his sandwiches which he carried in his briefcase every morning. Gustad refused to take sandwich and both of them started walking. They usually enjoyed the lunchtime in canteen. Everyday in the canteen, over lunch, their regular group told jokes. No linguistic or ethnic group was spared by them; they even did not spare themselves. Invariably, Dinshawji was the star performer. He could store everything he once heard. Sometimes, instead of jokes, they had a song-session, and Gustad was a master-singer in those sessions. Sometimes they were also engaged in passionate argument about matters that concerned the community. Despite the attractions of the stairwell Dinshawji stuck to Gustad and both of them emerged under the hot sun. They were chatting on several things including the suffering of the commuters in trains. Dinshawji never kept secret his disgust for the Shiv Sena who demanded that Maharashtra was for the Maharashtrians. Dinshawji and Gustad decided to walk down Vir Noriman Road. At the corner a pavement artist sat cross-legged beside his crayon drawings of gods and goddesses. He got up now and started to collect the coins left by the devotees.

The difference between Gustad and Dinshawji is clear in their conversation. Unlike Gustad who is rather tolerant and remains aloof from direct politics, Dinshawji gets involved in politics and criticizes the Shiv Sena vehemently. He says,

> Wait till the Marathas take over, then we will have real Gandoo Raj. All they know is to have rallies at Shivaji Park, shout slogans, make threats, and change road names. . . . Why change the names? . . . Names are so important. I grew up on Lamington Road. But it has disappeared, in its place is Dadasaheb Bhadkhamkar Marg. My school was on Camac road. Now suddenly it's on Lokmanya Tilak Marg. I live at Sleater Road. Soon that will also disappear. My whole life I have come to work at Flora Fountain. And one fine day the name changes. So what happens to the life I have lived? Was I living the wrong life, with all the wrong names? Will I get a second chance to live it all again, with these new names? Tell me what happens to my life. Rubbed out, just like that? (74)

Dinshawji suffered from nostalgia and he was also afraid of the rising provincialism. His anger was the direct result of identity crisis. Gustad's personal problem—a mixed one arising out of his son's adamant behaviour and the request of a long-lost friend—is thus in contrast with Dinshawji's crisis in maintaining Parsi identity, a crisis that also affects Gustad who had chosen to remain silent on the matter.

Their conversation was interrupted as an accident took place in front of them. A man on a Lambretta was hit by a car going in the opposite direction. The man fell down beside the pavement, and a trickle of blood oozed from his mouth. Dinshawji wanted to go to the man, but suddenly Gustad was overcome by nausea and dizziness and held on to Dinshawji's arm. Dinshawji diagnosed the condition as the result of his skipping the lunch and took him to a nearby restaurant where they ate 'samosa' and coffee. Gustad now told Dinshawji that the man on Lambretta was the taxi driver who had helped him on the day of his accident, and he felt sorry that he could not help him in his need. Dinshawji asked him not to repent as it was not his fault that he had become ill. Their conversation again turned to politics; Dinshawji referred to the Bangladesh war and criticized America for supporting Pakistan who was then engaged in slaughtering people in Bangladesh. He said, "Where is . . . America now? Not saying one word. Otherwise, if Russia even belches, America protests in the UN. Let Kosygin fart, and America moves a motion in the Security Council." (76) Gustad explained to him why Pakistan was strategically so important to America. Russia was very friendly with Afghanistan, and if Pakistan too, would become close to Russia, then Russia's road to the Indian Ocean would be clear. And America must resist it. As it was his habit, Dinshawji used slang language to express his anger. Lunch time being already over, the two friends returned to their office.

The fourth and the last section of the chapter describes Gustad's fresh problem at home. He was told by Dilnavaz that their younger son Darius was after a girl about whose father Mr. Rabadi had complained to her. Gustad recalled the feud between him and Mr. Rabadi over the latter's pet dog and interpreted his complaint as an extension of that feud. Yet, when Darius returned home, he asked him not to meet Mr. Rabadi's daughter so that no further complaint might come from that idiotic person. The chapter ends with a focus on the inconveniences caused by flies and mosquitoes and also by the bad smell of urine coming from the other side of the compound wall that had been continuously used as public lavatory.

Chapter 6

Gustad's waiting for the Major's reply to the letter he had written to him and the reaction in his family after the letter reached comprise the next chapter. The refugee problem because of the Bangladesh War is also foregrounded. In the background of India's conflict with Pakistan, the problems faced by the Parsi community are also referred to.

The first section starts with Gustad's expectation of the Major's letter and is followed by a conversation between Gustad and Roshan who wanted a rupee from his father to join the raffle in their school. The prize was a long and beautiful imported doll from Italy, she said. Asked by her father she also told that the half of the raffle money would go for the new school building and the other half would be spent in helping the refugees. On her father's further query she told that the refugees were people who had run away from East Pakistan and come to India because the people from West Pakistan were killing them and burning their homes. To answer little Roshan's question why West Pakistan was killing the people in East Pakistan, Gustad said, "Because it is wicked and selfish. East Pakistan is poor, they said to West, we are always hungry, please give us a fair share. But West said no. Then East said, in that case we don't want to work with you. So, as punishment, West Pakistan is killing and burning East Pakistan." (81) Referring to the 'meanness' of Pakistan Gustad turns to the topic of his 'ungrateful' boy for whom he had gone to so many institutions including Parsi Punchayet Education Fund, R.D. Sethna Trust, Tata Scholarships and Wadia Charities for Higher Studies, and the boy now said that he was not interested in I.I.T. Dilnavaz was also at a loss, as Ms. Kutpitia's prescription of using lemon on Sohrab had failed to work. Sohrab's insistence on doing a B.A. course was useless for Gustad who now explained his son's behaviour in terms of betrayal. All his hopes of gaining social status through Sohrab's job secured through his I.I.T. degree being belied, Gustad was sad and angry. His anxiety about Jimmy Bilimoria's letter that had not yet come added to his misery. The bitter mood increased his irritation caused by a swarm of mosquitoes.

In his depressed mood Gustad recalled the past days when the water supply was generous and the milk from Parsi Dairy Farm was both creamy and affordable. After the tall structures around the Khodadad building rose up, the setting sun was first to be blotted. The black stone wall, six feet high, around the building was the sole provider of privacy particularly for those who practised 'kusti' in the early morning. The Parsis badly needed that wall which could shelter them from the non-Parsi eyes. But the wall turned to be an open-air toilet, thanks to the increasing number of people and became hellish for the residents of the building. The sense of insecurity felt by the Parsis is also apparent from Darius's fear to be ridiculed by his classmates. The children were asked to take old newspapers to their school. "Darius said he would prefer *The Times of India* because his friends would make fun of the Parsi *bawaj*i newspapers. Gustad would have none of that. [He said] 'You should be proud of your heritage. Take the *Jam-E-Jamshed* or nothing at all.'"(83) Darius had little intention to be proud of his heritage and so he decided to go to the neighbours.

The second section of the chapter describes incidents that took place a week later. Much to her joy Roshan won the first prize in the Annual School Raffle and a letter was sent to her father for taking the big Italian doll from the school. Gustad was unable to hide his disgust after he finished the letter. But he had to change his face for Roshan's sake and had to hire a taxi to bring the doll that was so delicate and long that no other vehicle could be used for the purpose. Before going to the school Gustad made a phone call to the principal in order to know when she would be available for delivering the doll. And Ms. Kutpitia being the only person in the building who had the telephone facility, Gustad had to go to her flat. The old lady refused to take the rose that Gustad had sent for her through Roshan, and took thirty paisa for the phone-call. She also reminded Gustad that "old age and sorrow comes to everyone some day." The writer thus creates an opportunity to throw further light on the old lady. The lame Tehmul is also brought on the scene. He came running to hand over a bill to Gustad who became apprehensive for the poor fellow who had once been recruited by the Shiv Sena for distributing racist pamphlets and were on the verge of being beaten up by a group of South Indian people. That day he was saved by Gustad who cautioned him not to accept things from strangers. Tehmul's child-like simplicity is expressed in her eagerness to touch the doll Gustad brought from Roshan's school. Another character, Cavasji, a man in his late eighties, is also introduced through his curses and grumblings. Leaning his ancient "white-maned" head outside the window, Cavasji would reprimand the sky and register his displeasure with the "Almighty's grossly inequitable way of running the universe": "To the Tatas You give so much! And nothing for me? To the Wadias You give, You keep on giving! You cannot hear my prayers? The pockets of the Camas only You will fill! We others don't need it, You think?" (87)

The third section renders Gustad's short encounter with Tehmul and the arrangement for shelving the doll. Gustad found that Tehmul held thirty copies of a petition and he asked him to give each paper to every tenant of the building. The tenants were required to read and sign, and so Gustad advised Tehmul to speak slowly so that all of them would understand what he said. The doll was so big that it needed a separate showcase in which it could stand. For the time being, Dilnavaz wanted to keep it flat on the bottom shelf in her cupboard. Roshan did not like the idea at all; but there was no alternative. The doll would not fit in on the shelf. To keep it there it was to be undressed. At the time of undressing the big doll, Tehmul entered the flat. He touched it, caressed it and watched it with a fascinating look; as Dilnavaz was undressing it, "a trickle of saliva started its descent from one corner of his mouth."

The fourth section is about the long-awaited letter from Major Bilimoria in which the Major requested Gustad to collect a packet from a book-stall in 'Chor Bazaar.' To make the stall more specific, a copy of *Complete Works of Shakespeare* would be displayed there. Gustad was requested to open the book to *Othello,* end of act one, scene three, where Iago gives advice to Roderigo. The line 'Put money in thy purse' would be underlined in red. If everything would be found accordingly, Gustad must have reached the right place and the Major's man was to hand over the parcel then. Gustad was to take the parcel at home and follow the instructions given in a note. About his own activity Major Bilimoria wrote that he was working with RAW (Research and Analyzing Wing) and was very busy. Dilnavaz was much concerned with 'Chor Bazaar' and commented that the place was not nice. Gustad laughed at her fear and said that it was not in the least a place for thieves. Even foreign tourists would go there frequently. Having read the letter she found fault with everything. The business of going to Chor Bazaar and searching for Shakespeare seemed mysterious and she could not understand what the Major had to do with Research work. Gustad explained to her what he knew and for the rest he had a ready answer, "a friend cannot be let down." As Sohrab entered the room, he also wanted to know where he intended to go. Gustad was still angry with him and tried to ignore him. But Sohrab expressed his views clearly: "I am surprised Major Uncle joined RAW. . . . Our wonderful Prime Minister uses RAW like a private police force, to do all her dirty work. . . . She sends men from RAW to spy on opposition parties, create trouble, start violence so the police can interfere. It's a well-known fact. . . . What about the chemical election? Only RAW could have done that. She made a real mockery of democracy." (92-93) Gustad protested, saying that all that was rumour. Sohrab continued to stick to his views, but Gustad was not in a mood to think over the matter as he was already prejudiced against him. As it is usually noted among the minority, they like to support the central government as they suffer from a sense of insecurity. Gustad, too, supported the central government and expressed his concern for the national interest. He said, "The enemy was at the border, that Pakistani drunkard Yahya was cooking something in partnership with China, and fools like her son went around saying rubbish about the Prime Minister." The conflict between the father and the son hardly revealed any hope of being removed, much to Dilnavaz's helplessness. She had already applied the lemon formula as per Ms. Kutpitia's prescription and failed. The differences of attitude in the Noble family are thus made distinct and the suspense in regard to the packet gets thickened.

Chapter 7

The seventh chapter is crucial from the point of view of the plot, as it centres on Gustad's search for the bookshop wherefrom he was to get the packet sent by the Major. The first section shows how Gustad managed a half-day leave on Friday from Mr. Madan, the manager of the bank, telling a lie that he had developed problem with his leg that had been fractured in an accident eight years ago, and therefore he was to see the physician on Friday afternoon. Gustad started limping lest there be any doubt in any one's mind that he did not tell the truth. Details of his conversation with the manager and also with Dinshawji are recorded. Though middle-aged, Dinshawji had the habit of flirting with girls, and he was found clowning around Miss Laurie Coutino's desk. She was the new typist in the bank and Dinshawji had succeeded in getting acquainted with her. Forsaking his natural flair for humour, he tried to be dashing and flamboyant. The result was "a pitiful spectacle of cavorting and capering" during which he looked ludicrous but could not understand. Gustad was embarrassed for his friend and intervened. He asked Dinshawji not to disturb Miss Laurie so that she could do her work well. Though Dinshawji followed Gustad, he was not happy to be interrupted. But Gustad was able to get his mind distracted and this incident shows his attitude to his friends. Though he had only a few friends, he always tried to help them and hence, it was not surprising that he would go to Chor Market in search of a mysterious packet only to oblige his long lost friend.

The second section of the chapter is all about Gustad's search for the bookshop displaying the complete volume of Shakespeare. As he went along the market, his eyes were attracted towards a set of Meccano which took him to his happy childhood days when his father, still active and the owner of a prestigious bookstore, purchased a Meccano set for him. To the delight of parents and grandparents, various models such as fire-engine, crane, racing car etc. emerged from little Gustad's room.

His greatest triumph was a drawbridge that could be raised and lowered. During the bankruptcy, the Meccano set was lost with everything else. "The word [bankruptcy] had the sound of a deadly virus, the way it had ravaged the family." (101) Affected by nostalgia, Gustad moved from one shop to other and could not resist purchasing three beautifully bound books for six rupees. Those were *Great Dialogues of Plato, Encyclopedia of Religion and Ethics*, Vol. 7, and Henry Gray's *Anatomy of the Human Body.* Gustad was so engrossed with the idea of a small bookcase, full of good books, that he even decided to visit the Chor Bazaar regularly. At last he found a store at the rear of which he noticed *The Complete Works of William Shakespeare,* bound in red cloth with gold lettering.

The third section is about Gustad's verification if that was the right place and then, his conversation with the 'taxi driver' who had helped him at the time of accident. He opened the volume to *Othello* and turned to the end of act 1 and found the words underlined in red. Being sure that he came to the right place he looked up and saw a man with a white turban watching from the shadow of the near-by tea-stall. As the man came out of the shadow, Gustad observed that the turban was not a turban at all, but a heavy bandage of white surgical gauze. As the man came nearer, Gustad recognized him. He was none other than the taxi-driver who was riding a Lambretta and was hit by a car the day Gustad was walking with Dinshawji during lunch break. The man addressed him as Mr. Noble and they shook hands joyfully. Gustad asked his name as he did not have the opportunity to be formally introduced to him. His name was Ghulam Mohammed, he said. It is learnt that Major Bilimoria and Ghulam Mohammed had long association, but they would often pretend to be strangers to each other for safety. Both of them were army men and Ghulam Mohammed was once rescued by Bilimoria who was known in the army as Bili Boy. After the order of retreat was given, Ghulam Mohammed could not return as he lay wounded in the hills. Bilimoria went alone to look for him and rescued him. From that day Ghulam Mohammed was ready to do anything for him; his friend was Ghulam's friend, and his enemy Ghulam's enemy. They had their tea together and Ghulam gave him an address for contacting him. Gustad received the packet from Ghulam and his three books were also packed. He took a bus and reached home. At the gate Tehmul was waiting and he carried the book parcel to his flat.

Chapter 8

The chapter starts with Dilnavaz's conversation with Ms. Kutpitia who had prescribed a ritual with lime for removing Sohrab's stubbornness which she explained as working of some black spell that is evil power. Ms. Kutpitia's explanation was that the black spell had gone so deep and strong inside Sohrab that lime could not pull it. In that case, she suggested, another human being was to be used for pulling the spell out. Earlier she told that after sunset one lime had to be rubbed around Sohrab's head seven times and then the lime was to be thrown in the sea. Now she prescribed that instead of throwing the lime, its juice would have to be given to someone for drinking. In that case the spell would go inside the body of the person who drank the juice. Dilnavaz did not like to do any harm to others and so she could not think of any person. But Ms. Kutpitia immediately suggested the name of Tehmul. When Dilnavaz shrank from the idea, Ms. Kutpitia told him that Tehmul did not possess much brain to start with, and hence it would make no difference to him. Moreover, one should be happy that for the first time Tehmul would do something good for another person. Dilnavaz was free from hesitation after this counselling and squeezed the juice of the used lime and added salt and sugar in the juice.

As she was waiting for Tehmul, Roshan came and told that she had loose motions. Dilnavaz had stored some common medicines and gave her one. She also found Tehmul soon and gave him the juice. Tehmul liked the drink and asked for more. Dilnavaz assured him that she would give him later. She also asked him to keep quiet as Roshan was sleeping. Tehmul obeyed her, putting his finger on his mouth. As Gustad entered the compound, he gave him the instruction promptly: "quiet quiet. Roshan is sleeping."

Gustad was in a good mood as he entered with the packets. First he brought out the books and kept them on the desk. Dilnavaz was irritated and called him crazy for bringing books. Gustad did not mind and went on describing what had happened in Chor Bazaar. Dilnavaz found no cause for excitement in Gustad's encounter with Ghulam. Rather she was irritated to learn that he had drunk tea from a roadside stall. As he was already informed by Tehmul, Gustad asked about Roshan. He was satisfied that Dilnavaz had given her two pills of Entero-Vioform. Here is the occasion to go back to the past days when they learnt about common medicines from their family physician Dr. Paymaster. The doctor purchased a closed-down dispensary when he started practice, but he did not bother to change the board outside that read the name of one Dr. R.C. Lord. He did not mind if the patients referred to him as Dr. Lord. As his practice grew and he made some money he changed the board outside, displaying his own name. This change proved to be an enormous blunder, as the patients did not like to be treated by some unknown Paymaster and insisted on the return of the good old Dr. Lord. They refused to listen to any explanation or be examined by the 'new' doctor. And a few patients, who were treated by Dr. Paymaster, complained that the medicine did not cure as before. Dr. Paymaster learnt a new lesson that a doctor's name was infinitely more important than his skills, and he brought back the old signboard. In connection with Dr. Paymaster's subscription of foreign journals, the foreign exchange regulation act of the government is mentioned and the author has a scope of commenting on the corrupt politicians.

> Like everything else about the government, foreign exchange regulations involved convoluted rules and tortuous procedures, and Dr. Paymaster decided to spare himself the agony. After Lal Bahadur Shastri became Prime Minister upon Nehru's death, it seemed for a while that the stagnant waters of government would at last be freshened and vitalized, despite the sceptics who said that

> such a short man would not be able to command respect on the world stage. Then along came the twenty-one-day war with Pakistan in which he fared much better than Nehru had in the war with China, and silenced the unbelievers. . . . Some even claimed it was the new Prime Minister's supporters who poisoned Shastri, so that her father's dynastic-democratic dream could finally come true. Whatever the truth, once again the government was in chaos. Streamlining foreign exchange regulations ranked very low on the country's list of priorities. (114)

The link between this observation and the story of the Gustad family is that Dr. Paymaster could no more purchase any foreign magazine and remained unaware of new medicinal names. And when it was found that the doctor was repeating the same medicines for the treatment of diarrhoea, cough and such other common diseases of the children, Dilnavaz stopped going to the doctor and herself prescribed medicines. She even became so confident that she began to prescribe those medicines for other children in the building. Gustad did not however approve of these "neighbourly prescriptions," but Dilnavaz took it to be her duty.

As Dilnavaz wanted to see what the Major had sent in his packet, Gustad tried to tear it with his penknife. Tehmul was then seen outside the window, waving a bunch of papers. Gustad drew near him and learnt that he was to sign the copy of petition. After he signed the copy, Tehmul took it back and returned happily. Gustad, then, tried to open the packet, working the penknife through the plastic cover. And much to their surprise, new bundles of currency notes came out. As Gustad's eyes fell on the window, he found Tehmul gaping at the little hill of money. He shut the window immediately though it did not sound well that some outsider should know about the money.

The third section of the chapter describes Gustad's attempt to shut Tehmul's mouth. First he offered him one rupee to keep the money matter secret. Tehmul wanted two rupees, and Gustad paid him that too. And at the same time he frightened him with his knife. Catching his nape in one hand, Gustad moved the knife across his throat from ear to ear and told him that if he would tell anybody about the money, the knife would work on him. Tehmul was really afraid and said that he would not tell anybody about the money. Gustad watched him go and was sorry that he had to frighten the poor fellow. But it was the only way; for nothing remained in Tehmul's mind except fear. Coming back to the room he checked the first and the last serial numbers of the hundred rupee notes and understood that the packet contained ten lakh rupees. Immediately, Dilnavaz requested Gustad to return the money. Gustad recalled that the Major wrote about a letter that contained instructions for further activities. They found the letter in which Gustad was instructed to deposit the amount in the account of some Mira Obili. Gustad said that the Major was trying to save the poor Bengalis being murdered by Pakistan. Dilnavaz was exasperated at his child-like behaviour. She strongly opposed the idea of depositing that much amount. That would be dangerous and illegal, she reflected, one that might take his job. Gustad continued to sympathize with Jimmy who had to do dangerous things in RAW. Dilnavaz reminded him that Jimmy had willingly accepted that job of secret service, knowing that to be dangerous. But Gustad had a job in a bank and he was to support his family with his salary. He should think beforehand what would happen in case he were to lose his job. Gustad began to put the package together reluctantly. She also helped him stack the bundles. As he grumbled that he had given the Major word, she reminded him that to ask for a favour without telling the nature of the favour is not nice. She chalked out a plan to get an escape from the trouble. If Gustad would write to the Major that he had been transferred to some other department and was therefore unable to deposit the amount, he would get an alibi to return the money. Gustad also supported the idea. At this time Sohrab entered the room and was astonished to see the heap of notes. Having read the letter Sohrab reflected that the work would be risky. He also noted that Mira Obili was an anagram of Bilimoria. He jokingly said, "Jimmy Uncle says this is Government money, right? So let's spend it on all the things Government is supposed to do. Wouldn't it be nice to fix the sewers in this area, install water tanks for everyone." He could not complete his sentence when Gustad sprang from his chair without warning and aimed a powerful slang at him which, however, got missed. Shaken and bewildered, Sohrab turned to his mother and complained that he was only making a joke. The mother quietly reminded him of Gustad's anxiety for Sohrab's career and the boy left the room, trembling with emotion. Gustad began to grumble remembering all the tit-bits he had done for the boy in the midst of utter poverty and how the boy was now returning him. As it was already late for going to Chor Bazaar, they had to keep the money in some secret place. Gustad thought of returning the money to Ghulam Mohammed who had given him his address.

The fifth and the last section of the chapter starts with Gustad's anger as he learnt that Darius had brought bundles of newspapers from Jasmine whose father had complained to the Noble against Darius. He warned the boy not to have any further contact with their family and gave full attention to the mosquitoes. Suddenly he remembered a unique way of getting relieved from mosquitoes he had seen in a hotel in his childhood and decided to try that method. He placed a round shallow dish under the bulb and filled it with water. When the surface grew still, the bulb's reflection steadied and shone brightly. Then the mosquitoes started to dive in leaving the real bulb. After sometimes Gustad changed the water in the dish and was happy to get relieved of the insects. That night Sohrab refused to come to the dinner table. Two days later, Sohrab packed a few of his things and left home. At the time of leaving he told his mother he had made arrangements to live with some of his college friends. Dilnavaz wept and tried her best to make him understand that his father only wanted the best for him, but he could not be dissuaded. In the evening Gustad learnt what had happened. Though he was hurt, he said the harsh words did not concern him.

Chapter 9

The chapter starts with Sohrab's concern for Roshan's enervating diarrhoea and the forbidding package kept in the dingy 'choolavati' and the two things "swirled like the whirling wind-tossed leaves fallen in the compound." The third thing—Sohrab's leaving home—he pretended to neglect. Much to his concern Gustad learnt from their neighbour Inspector Bamji that Tehmul was talking some nonsense about a mountain of notes in Gustad's flat. Bamji also said that if his nonsense reached the wrong ears, that might cause trouble. Thieves might be tempted for the imaginary money. Gustad decided to warm Tehmul again. He was further shocked when another neighbour, Mrs. Pastakia, congratulated him for winning a lottery. He got some relief at the weekend when Dilnavaz announced that Roshan was better and he prepared the note for Ghulam Mohammed who was to be back in Bombay by that time.

The second section describes Gustad's frustration as he could not trace Ghulam. He repeatedly went to the House of Cages, the place from where Ghulam was supposed to receive his notes, and learnt that he had collected his messages. And that was all. No word came from Ghulam. In the meantime monsoon arrived in full force, and the newspaper told that the refugees were still coming, and their number was predicted to be ten million by the next month. Gustad's thought is followed by a fine description of rainfall. The torrents of rain took Gustad to those horrifying days after the accident when Major Bilimoria shouldered all the trouble of carrying him to the Bonesetter Madhiwalla who cured him. That night after the recollection of his past days Gustad had a deep sleep. He also had a nightmare of losing his job after being caught red-handed with all the bank notes by the manager Mr. Madan.

The third section is all about the headless bandicoot that had been thrown into Gustad's vinca bush. The crows gathered in the compound from miles around. Gustad was first to notice it after his prayer and then he asked Dilnavaz to have a look at the scene. It was horrifying for her to see the cleanly severed head beside the body. It was sure that a sharp instrument of human design was used, but the cause of such a decapitation could not be traced. The watchman was called and was accused of not being vigilant. The watchman tried to convince Gustad that the previous night he was moving along the compartment in his long raincoat and cap. As Gustad said that he had not heard any banging of stick, the watchman replied that the noise of rain and thunder drowned the sound of his stick. Gustad asked him to make harder sound henceforth and warned him to be vigilant throughout the night.

The third section of the chapter relates a similar incident on the following Sunday. This time it was a cat, brown with patches of white, whose head was severed from the body and attracted hosts of crows who were flapping and pecking, sometimes attacking one another. The watchman was called this time by Tehmul who was much excited at the incident. The watchman got panicked as Gustad threatened him by saying that his pay would be held. Inspector Bamji returned home at that time and came to the spot. He commented that someone must be having some grudge against Gustad and wanted to harass him through the skilful use of his knife. He also said that if the watchman were more alert, that type of harassment could be avoided. The watchman begged for one more chance and that was granted. The Noble began to suspect everybody until Gustad noted a piece of paper, folded and inserted snugly between two adjacent branches, as though in a letter-holder. He found two innocuous lines written in pencil which seemed to be a child's rhyme in Gujarati and meant, "Stole the rice of Bilimoria, we'll take a stick and then we'll beat ya." There was no doubt now about the meaning of the two decapitated carcasses. Gustad was threatened for not depositing the money of Bilimoria. As he thought later, it was the work of Ghulam who had threatened him for not depositing the money as per the Major's instruction.

Chapter 10

The tenth chapter starts with Gustad's disappointment at the behaviour of Major Bilimoria who threatened him in a savage way, probably through Ghulam. He was so much affected by the feeling of an incomprehensible betrayal, that he felt that some vital part of him had been crushed to nothingness. He sat with a scrap of paper before him. "Years of friendship swam before his eyes and filled the piece of paper; it taunted him, mocked him, turned into a gigantic canvas of lies and deceit. What kind of world is this, and what kind of men, who can behave in such a fashion?" (141) He felt trapped by Jimmy whom he had taken to be his best friend and was deceived. He wishes he could spend the rest of his life in his grandfather's arm-chair. Gustad's solitary thoughts were disturbed by Dilnavaz's arrival who was surprised to see that Gustad had finished his prayer so soon. The habit of sharing all with her, a habit that had developed during the twenty-one years of his married life, was so powerful that he could not block out of his voice the brokenness he felt. He handed her the scrap of paper containing the rhyme. She read it and suggested that they should immediately go to the police with the money and disclose everything. Gustad resisted the temptation to join in her way of thinking. He told that the local police had no power over RAW. He further said that they were dealing with heartless people who were like poisonous snakes. They could very well cut the heads of Darius and Roshan instead of the bandicoot and cat. He told her that only one way was left: he was to deposit only one bundle a day to avoid suspicion. He assured her with the remark that after twenty-four years of service in bank, he knew the place and procedures inside out. After calculation they found that it would take one hundred days. He said that he would write to him, telling what he would do with the money. Gustad seemed to be a shattered man. First, his hopes had been destroyed by Sohrab, and now he was trapped by one who was like a brother to him.

The second section of the chapter describes how Gustad put ten thousand rupees in his briefcase and carried it while going to his bank the next day. The air-raid siren, that was introduced recently, started its keen lament as Gustad got off the bus. The siren reminded him thát it was already ten o'clock and he should have been by his desk. With ten thousand rupees in his briefcase, Gustad was tense as he walked with the crowds. After he reached the office, he stopped by Dinshawji's desk and asked Dinshawji to meet him outside in the lunch break. He had decided to disclose the secret to Dinshawji and during the lunch break he told him everything, starting from Major Bilimoria's letter about the guerrilla operation to the money package from Ghulam Mohammed. But he left out the episode of the bandicoot, the cat and the rhyming couplet. Instead, he emphasized how their effort would help the Mukti Bahini's liberation struggle, which Dinshawji found very stimulating. "The more enthusiastic he became, the worse Gustad felt at having to dupe his sick friend who was now willing to break banking laws and jeopardize his job and pension this close to retirement." (144) Dinshawji was so inspired at the end that he was even ready to join a bayonet charge against Pakistani soldiers. He also revealed the secret plan of America that wanted a war between India and Pakistan so that it could help Pakistan to defeat India. And after defeat in the war Indira was to lose the next election. And America wanted that, for Nixon did not like her friendship with Russia. As the lunch break was coming to its end, Gustad handed over the money in an envelope to Dinshawji to deposit it in the account of Mira Obili. By three o'clock Dinshawji moved around Laurie's desk. He was singing a song and insisting that she should dance with him. Gustad was worried for Dinshawji, for his ailing appearance and constant effort to hide pain, and also for his embarrassing ways and the demise of his self-respect. Next day at lunch, while passing the packet of money to Dinshawji, Gustad asked him not to draw others' attention by moving around Laurie. But Dinshawji said that the safest way was to behave in this way, so that others would not think that he might be serious. So Gustad let him continue in his way, and was happy to see that the deposits were going on.

The third section describes Roshan's illness and her treatment. Early in August, after Gustad had taken twenty seven bundles for deposit, there was an unexpected doorbell and Dilnavaz was alarmed. Much to her surprise she saw Roshan, accompanied by one of the school nuns. Roshan did not feel well that day and went to bathroom several times at school and so the teachers decided to bring her back home. Roshan insisted that his father should be informed so that he would return early and take her to the doctor. Dilnavaz went to Ms. Kutpitia's flat to telephone Gustad. This time the old lady refused to take thirty paisa as it was an emergency call for Roshan's illness. She also suggested a prescription as she had little faith in medical science. She said, "When a laughing-playing child like Roshan suddenly becomes sick, there can be other reasons. Such as evil eye. And doctor's medicine is no prevention or cure for that. There are special ways." (149) She also prescribed a thread with a big knot at the end in which a yellow lime and seven green chillies were to be strung together, and the thread was to kept hanging over the door. It was like a protection, she explained, and each time Roshan walked under it, the evil eye would lessen. Dilnavaz agreed to prepare the talisman immediately, and also informed that Sohrab had not yet returned home. Ms. Kutpitia asked Dilnavaz to keep patience. She also prescribed another remedy, a more dangerous one that required Tehmul's nails. Equipped with the old lady's knowledge, Dilnavaz returned to her flat. Roshan was assured that her father would come early and closed her eyes.

The fourth section of the chapter describes Gustad's encounter with Mr. Rabadi who again told Gustad that his son had stolen his newspapers. Gustad could no more tolerate this insult, and so collected all the old newspapers he had in his flat and dumped them outside Mr. Rabadi's flat. Then he took Roshan to the doctor. In the meantime, Dilnavaz had enough time to call Tehmul for giving him the lime juice. And when he came, she told him that his nails were big enough and needed trimming. She took her nail-cutter and cut the nails of his dirty fingers and also the toes. Then following Ms. Kutpitia's instructions she threw all the nail clippings on the glowing coal. She also sprinkled a pinch of turmeric and cayenne powder on the black molten mass. "Now the smell grew worse. A harsh pungency was added to the terrible fetor. Coughing and choking, she opened the window and stood by it, tears running down her face, till Tehmul's nails vaporized completely and became one with the firmament." (154) Dilnavaz's sense of sin is explicit in her thoughts: it seemed to her that Tehmul said mummy as he must have remembered his mother's touch when Dilnavaz was cutting her nails. Her eyes were also filled with tears at the thought of his imminent loss of intelligence. But her mother's instinct got the better of her humanity, as she was obsessed with the well-being of Sohrab.

Chapter 11

The chapter is an instance of distracted way of narration. The theme of the chapter is Gustad's taking Roshan to Dr. Paymaster's chamber. But before the arrival of the doctor on the scene, the entire locality along with the categories of patients the doctor had to deal with, are described in detail in half-humorous tone. The first section starts with how many buildings in the neighbourhood had been changed in recent years. Earlier, the locality had a poor look with its abundance of dust; it was still dusty, but was changed into an overcrowded, bustling hub of commerce. "Crumbling, leaky warehouses and rickety-staired, wobbly-balconied tenements had been refurbished and upgraded, from squalid and uninhabitable to squalid and temporarily habitable. The sewer system remained unchanged, broken and overflowing. Water supply continued to be a problem. So did rats, garbage and street lighting." (155) Gleaming new signboards featuring everything that is needed in household and in factories changed the appearance of the locality altogether. The enterprising individuals who are ready for servicing motor cars, repairing refrigerators, fans and what-not, changed the activity of the place which no longer retained its previous look.

The narrow sordid footpaths which were covered with black rubber strips, the waste products of the factories, were disgusting and frightening as one could easily mistake a six-foot strip of black rubber for a snake, particularly in the month of August when the snake charmers would come with their snakes for the occasion of 'Naga Panchami.' Though many things changed in that neighbourhood, four establishments resisted the change and survived. The first two were the cinema houses, located at the crossroads not far from the beach. When a new film arrived, it roused the neighbourhood; the black-marketeers and scalpers began buzzing around the halls, like the mosquitoes in the Khodadad building. Price ratios could keep soaring, depending on the stars and number of songs on the sound track. The black-market usually slowed after the first mad rush. One of the cinema halls was renovated, and the other had no choice but to follow suit. Gustad remembered that he had taken his family to see a film based on an epic in one of the renovated cinema halls. The third establishment in the locality, a brothel house called House of Cages, did not change and continued its basic business. The author takes a long diversion this time, taking the readers through Gustad's memory, describing the grotesque stories which Gustad had once heard from Peerbhoy Paanwalla who had his stall outside the House of Cages. The dispensary was the fourth establishment in the locality that had never altered its function. Dr. Paymaster had well adjusted himself to his locality. The patients and their ailments fell into four distinct groups. First, there were the victims of workshop injuries. The patients belonging to the second group were 'by-product' of the cinema industry; they were patients of sunstroke and dehydration as a result of long queuing in the sun, or persons having bruises at the time of purchasing ticket. The House of Cages provided the third group of patients who needed periodic check-ups as required by the municipal licensing authorities. The fourth group was made up of families like the Nobles and Dr. Paymaster looked forward to them.

Having delivered details of Dr. Paymaster's neighbourhood and the nature of his patients in the first section, the author describes the meeting of Gustad and Paymaster in the second section of the eleventh chapter. After greeting Gustad and Roshan he asked if they would take some cold drink or tea. Gustad politely refused and described Roshan's problem of loose motions going on for a few days. The doctor wanted to know why he was late to come and when he learnt that she had been given Entero-Vioform and Sulpha-Guanidine, he commented that those were medicines and not to be gobbled like sweets. While examining her he asked about her school and she told him of the big Italian doll in her wedding dress. The doctor, who was famous for making jokes with his patients, proposed that he would marry the doll. Roshan giggled at the idea of music to be arranged during the wedding. Diagnosing the disease he said that it was not the case of diarrhoea, but of some intestinal virus. He gave medicines for seven days and asked to come next week. Dr. Paymaster believed that politics, economics, religious problems, domestic strife, all could be dealt with methodically. It is necessary to diagnose the disease first through observations of symptoms, and then medicine has to be prescribed. He also believed that just as some diseases of the human body were incurable, there were also diseases of countries, of families, of theological dogma, that had fatal outcomes. He diagnosed the condition of East Pakistan as incurable: "East Pakistan is suffering from a diarrhoea of death. . . . East Pakistan has been attacked by a strong virus from West Pakistan, too powerful for the Eastern immune system. And the world's biggest physician is doing nothing. . . . Only the complete intravenous injection of the Indian Army·will defeat this virus." (164-65) The doctor's metaphorical use of language brings into focus the setting of the novel.

The third section describes Dilnavaz's reaction after she heard the doctor's diagnosis. She had repeatedly told that the drinking water should be boiled. But Gustad did not pay heed to this and observed that potassium permanganate was enough. It was now her turn to shout at him. When Gustad said that it was for her convenience that he had asked her not to boil, for, she had to be awfully busy in the morning for storing water, Dilnavaz became furious and expressed his grudge in raised voice. She accused Gustad for not lending a helping hand to her household work, and also for indulging his sons. When he asked angrily if it was his fault that Sohrab did not join the I.I.T., or Darius was wasting time with a girl, she answered that he had spoilt the boys from the very beginning, supplying them with everything they wanted, never saying 'no' to their undue demands. As they were shouting, Roshan came and standing at the door, started to sob. She said that she did not like them fighting. Both the parents assured her that they were only discussing family matters, as the elders were supposed to do. The section comes to an end with the end of the quarrel, thanks to Roshan's intervention.

The fourth section describes the rather funny incident of Mr. Rabadi's lifting the newspapers kept in front of his flat by Gustad and burning them. He was unable to lift the lot in his arms, and insisted that his wife should help him. She was all for selling them, but Mr. Rabadi wanted to show Gustad that keeping papers in front of his flat would not lessen his son's guilt. While carrying the lot, they ran into Inspector Bamji, and Mr. Rabadi brought an accusation against Gustad saying that Gustad had made a trap for killing him by keeping heaps of papers in front of his flat. He dropped the papers close to the bushes; then he struck and dropped a match. He clarified the matter to the Inspector who had nothing to say. The fire drew the attention of others, and Gustad, too, was attracted by the fire and came down to the bush. He was amused to see that Mr. Rabadi had been provoked to such length. As he came back to his flat, he found that the mosquitoes, maddened by the smoke, descended in blind fury. He wanted to use the method of keeping dish full of water in front of the bulbs to remove the mosquitoes, but found that the drum was empty.

Chapter 12

The twelfth chapter starts with Gustad's financial problem caused by Roshan's disease. The doctor had changed her prescriptions four times within a fortnight, and also ordered blood tests, stool tests and barium X-rays. Gustad had to sell his camera to pay the bills. He was much worried about her and yet he tried his best to keep his feelings secret. He proposed to bring out the Italian doll out of the cupboard and to get it dressed so that the doll would give company to her. Roshan was excited with the idea and Gustad assured her to do the job after coming from office. He also sang her favourite song to please her. That day he went to the bank with the thirty-ninth bundle of money. It started raining when he reached Flora Fountain. From the bus stop he could notice the bank building, washed up by rain. As he reached the bank, he was surprised that Ms. Laurie touched his elbow from behind and wished him. She wanted to have a private talk with him, and it was decided that they would meet during lunch time. As usual, Dinshawji was engaged in humorous talk with others as office hour had not started yet. Gustad opened his briefcase and casually handed over the bundle of money, informing that he had some work during lunch time. Dinshawji felt that Gustad must have some secret work. The first section ends with Gustad's growing anxiety for Laurie's secret talk.

The second section is about the proposed meeting of Gustad and Laurie. They went to a restaurant nearby, and as the ground floor was crowded they went upstairs and were allotted a private room. Gustad felt rather uneasy for it was clear from the behaviour of the waiters that the privacy of such rooms was meant for some sordid purpose. However, they ordered food and talked without hesitation. Laurie said that she had wanted to talk to the manager, Mr. Madan, but later decided to talk to Gustad. Gustad became more surprised than ever and learnt much to his concern that she had serious charges against Dinshawji. He had already apprehended the possible result of Dinshawji's flirting with Laurie and had asked him to control himself, but he paid no heed to his warning. Laurie explained how she had taken Dinshawji's humorous talk casually; but one day he used slang and without understanding what he meant, she openly appreciated what he said. Recently she found out what exactly he had meant and felt awkward in the presence of other colleagues who had enjoyed the slang that day and must have developed a bad idea about her character since then. Laurie clearly said that whenever she found men laughing, it seemed to her that they were discussing her. It became difficult for her to come to work, and she even thought of resigning. Gustad found her really upset and tried to appease her. Laurie also asked him if Dinshawji was in secret service. That she had not believed it was clear from the way she said it while laughing. But Gustad was alarmed with the thought that Dinshawji's depositing the money had no more been a secret, and he might have to face trouble for that. Gustad tried his best to assure that Dinshawji would never upset her again. He also drew her sympathy by telling that he was seriously ill and that he was to retire after two years. Though Gustad did not disclose his feelings to her, his mind was filled with anger at the 'idiotic-lunatic nonsense' of Dinshawji.

In the third section Gustad is seen on his desk, kneading his forehead. It was becoming too much for him to bear all sorts of sufferings and anxiety. Roshan's sickness, Dilnavaz's blaming him, Jimmy's treachery, Sohrab's betrayal, Dinshawji's stupidity and lastly, Laurie's complaint—all this had been torturing his mind, threatening to crush him altogether. As Dinshawji came close, Gustad could not control himself any more. He slammed his fist on the desk and made a great sound. Addressing Dinshawji as stupid fool, he said that he had made the blood in his brain boil. Dinshawji was hurt, and Gustad asked him to see him at six o'clock. When they met after office, Dinshawji smiled weakly and Gustad asked him to take his cup of tea which might be the last thing he would ever enjoy. They walked past the traffic of vehicles and human beings and came to a tea stall. While waiting for their tea Gustad burst the bomb, giving details of what Laurie had told him about Dinshawji. He wanted to use the words as deadly as knife. Dinshawji's pale countenance lost its last trace of colour. Gustad said mercilessly that there was more; he told that Laurie had not believed in his secret service, but if Mr. Madan could ever learn about the ten lakh rupees and guerrillas, there would be no way to escape. Dinshawji acknowledged that he was stupid, and asked him what he should do next. Gustad asked him to stop making fun. Thereon Dinshawji wanted to know if people would be inquisitive about him after he changed his behaviour. Gustad said that he would tell everybody that Dinshawji was seriously ill and then people would find it quite natural that he stopped making fun and nobody would be suspicious of him.

The fourth section records Gustad's attempt to get the compound wall of the Khodadad building painted by one pavement artist whom he had seen in Flora Fountain. Before the artist started his work, the whole wall was washed. The artist had a B.A. in World Religions before he transferred to the School of Arts. Thus he developed an interest in painting gods, saints and prophets of different religions. Hinduism alone, with its number of gods and saints, could provide him with sufficient subject matter, but he liked to include a variety in his drawings and was gratified with the idea of promoting tolerance and understanding in the world. Gustad was impressed by his learning and his ideas. The artist first painted a portrait of Trimurti, a blending of Brahma, Vishnu and Shiva, the Hindu gods of creation, preservation and destruction. Then followed representations of Crucifixion, Jumma Masjid, Moses descending with the Ten Commandments, Ganapati Baba and others. Within a few days the wall filled up with gods, prophets and saints and people stopped making nuisance by the side of the wall. As a result the sting in the air was gone, and the number of flies and mosquitoes began to diminish. The chapter ends with a reflection on the artist who became restless after completing the paintings on the wall. "Now, however, his old way of life was being threatened. The agreeable neighbourhood and the solidity of the long, black wall were reawakening in him the usual sources of human sorrow; a yearning for permanence, for roots, for something he could call his own, something immutable. Torn between staying and living, he worked on, ill-at-ease, confused and discontented. Swami Dayananda, Swami Vivekananda, Our Lady of Fatima, Zarathustra, and numerous others assumed their places on the wall, places preordained by pavement artist; together, they awaited the uncertain future." (184)

Chapter 13

The first section of the chapter starts with some hope in Gustad's mind about Roshan's recovery. In office, while handing over the bundle of money to Dinshawji, he noted a swelling in his stomach and also noted that he was dragging himself painfully to bathroom. He had totally renounced his clowning and Gustad thought that Dinshawji must be worse for giving up his games. That he was responsible for forcing him to abandon his comic ways gnawed at his conscience. He was also aware that he had been using Dinshawji for personal cause. In the evening when he returned from bank, he was happy to see that the people were respecting the wall, and somebody had even left a small bunch of flowers in front of the drawing of Saraswati. His happy mood disappeared as he entered his flat and learnt that Roshan's condition had become worse. The anxiety about the daughter made the parents restless and they started quarrelling on the issue of who was responsible for her illness. As a result, Gustad went out for the doctor without taking his tea and even a glass of water.

The second section creates suspense as Dinshawji entered Gustad's flat, with a newspaper under his arm and a bulky envelope in his hand. Dilnavaz was afraid that he might start his silly jokes, and greeted him rather stiffly. But she found that the man was completely changed. In a shaken voice he wanted to talk to Gustad, and was almost on the verge of weeping when he learnt that he was out. He only said that he had a very important work with him. His voice melted Dilnavaz's resistance and she asked him to be seated. She immediately sent Tehmul to the bus stand to see if Gustad was still there waiting for bus. Tehmul went and returned very soon to inform them that Gustad had already gone. Dinshawji's distress was so acute that Dilnavaz could not let him leave. Dinshawji thanked her and began to wait for Gustad. In the meantime, his timid whispers had reached the back room and awakened Roshan. She came to him with her doll to enjoy. He told the girl that she was not at all sick. She smiled and fussed with the doll's veil. He asked her to sing a song and she sang softly the prayer, "Two little eyes to look unto God," performing each line with all the actions taught by her teacher in school. Dinshawji clapped when she finished the prayer. Inspired by his clapping, she sang another song. Dilnavaz now asked her to stop singing lest she felt tired. After the session of song was over, they started playing games with their hands spread flat on the teapoy. Though Dilnavaz did not like that she should play, they continued playing and Dinshawji's acting even made Dilnavaz laugh. After sometime, Roshan went to bed smiling and her doll remained on the sofa. Dinshawji's anxiety and nervousness returned after Roshan left.

The third section describes Gustad's conversations with Dr. Paymaster who was not in a good mood that day. After listening to Gustad, he expressed his doubt that they might not have followed his prescriptions. Gustad felt hurt at such comments of the doctor. When he left with a new list of pills he began to grudge: "How dare he say such things! Taking advantage, just because he knows me for so many years. What does he think of himself? First virus, now colitis. Easy to keep throwing out new names. Doctors think everyone else is stupid." (191) On his way back he met Peerbhoy Paanwalla who informed him that Mr. Mohammed had come there in the morning and that he was looking very worried and upset. He also offered Gustad a 'paan' and Gustad had to buy it against his will. The rest of the third section makes clear the causes of Dinshawji's sudden arrival in Gustad's place. After Gustad reached his flat, he was shown the newspaper brought by Dinshawji. There was news entitled 'CORRUPTION

RIPE IN RAW' which read that Jimmy Bilimoria, an officer of the RAW, had been arrested by the CBI and city police on charges of fraud and extortion. He was so much surprised that he uttered 'impossible' after going through the first sentence. Dinshawji asked him to read the entire column and he learnt about Bilimoria's confession that he had perpetuated the fraud in order to expedite aid to the guerrillas in East Pakistan. The charge against Bilimoria was that some months ago in New Delhi he had telephoned the State Bank of India, impersonating the Prime Minister's voice and had instructed the cashier to withdraw sixty lakh rupees from the bank's reserves for delivery to a man who would identify himself as Bangladeshi Babu. The next he had identified himself as Bangladeshi Babu and took delivery of the sixty lakh rupees. Delivering the report, the reporter raised some basic questions about the Bank's mode of working and also about the viability of the Prime Minister's direct call to the Bank asking for money. The reporter wrote, 'Was the Chief Cashier so familiar with Mrs. Gandhi's voice that he accepted the instructions without any verification whatsoever? If yes, does it mean that Mrs. Gandhi has done this sort of thing frequently?' They felt at a loss in regard to their future activities. They had already deposited more than half of the money as per the Major's instruction and the rest was still hidden in Gustad's kitchen. Though Gustad became desperate, Dinshawji remained calm and suggested that the first thing they would have to do was to think about the money. Gustad said that he would burn the money. Dinshawji neglected such erratic suggestion and said that first of all, they should stop depositing further and for the money that had already been deposited, Gustad should contact Ghulam Mohammed, if he too was not in jail. Gustad knew that Ghulam was still free and he decided to contact him. Dinshawji and Dilnavaz began to discuss the corrupt ways taken up by the Congress party, but Gustad was annoyed as he felt tricked by the Major. The chapter closes with Dinshawji's departure.

The fourteenth chapter starts with an elaborate description of Gustad's journey to Mr. Mohammed's place. On the way he crossed the Aarey Colony milk booth where he found three boys and one girl, all in tattered clothes, examining the used bottles. The booth attendant shouted at them, but with little effect. As Gustad reached the corner, the attendant leaped out from the rear and caught the little girl by the sleeve of her frock. He started beating the girl and as he lifted his hand for the third blow, Gustad grabbed his collar from behind and the shock made him lose his grip. The girl ran to a safe distance and all the four urchins were happy. The booth attendant explained how they were used to making nuisance the entire day and the customers tried to avoid his booth. Gustad did not argue with him. Instead, he asked for one bottle of milk for the girl. After taking a few sips she called the boys to share. When Gustad told her that the milk was for her, she replied that they were her brothers and they also liked milk. Then Gustad bought three more bottles for the boys and waited while they drank. After finishing the milk they disappeared in the rush of movie-goers, and Gustad came to Peerbhoy to enquire about Ghulam.

Peerbhoy told that Ghulam was on the top floor of the House of Cages. Gustad entered the building hesitantly. The place was filled up with cheap perfume smells. A radio or record player somewhere was playing an old film song. The women were waiting for customers. Gustad glanced quickly at them while passing. The rooms that came in his view were sordid. The luxuries that are found in the stories about such places were missing. As Gustad entered Ghulam's room, he found the man polite and courteous as ever. He referred to the newspaper report and confirmed the news of arrest, and said that everything printed in the paper was not correct. Gustad wanted to know why Jimmy had sent him ten lakh rupees to deposit. He also made enquiry about the cat and the huge rat thrown in his bush, with their heads cut off. Without showing any emotion Ghulam replied that he had nothing to do about rats and cats. About Jimmy he told that he had enemies, and that the whole story had been cooked up at the very top to cover their wrong doings. He also said that he was not in a position to answer his question about money. As he asked Gustad to trust Jimmy, Gustad said that he had already trusted him too much. Ghulam then explained that Jimmy's life was in danger. At this time, screams and shouts drowned the record, and the two men came to the landing. Much to his surprise Gustad saw Tehmul approaching the women, trying to grab at a breast or to reach inside a skirt, and the women in turn shook him by the ear, pulled his hair and clipped him on the head. He held out a round cigarette tin that jingled but there was no taker. Gustad shouted at Tehmul, asking him to stop. Tehmul stopped immediately, and the women also stopped teasing him as they were scolded by Ghulam. Gustad and Ghulam finished their talk. Ghulam asked Gustad to withdraw the amount he had deposited. Gustad told him of the difficulty of depositing and withdrawing that big amount. Ghulam retorted, "Better than bones being broken," and Gustad got confused about the person whose bones were referred to. Ghulam further said that the money should be returned in thirty days. Gustad reacted with his remark that it was impossible to do the job within thirty days, as he could withdraw only one bundle a day. Ghulam suggested him to withdraw two at a time. Otherwise, he said with a smile, he would have to rob the bank. Gustad tried to protest again, but the man was hard as steel. He said that things would go badly for all of them if money was not deposited on time. They fixed the delivery date and Gustad returned. He learnt from Peerbhoy that Tehmul had left.

The second section, a short one, displays the influence of superstitious belief and of black magic on persons like Dilnavaz who are anxious about their children. Dilnavaz had no faith on black magic when she was happy with her three children. It was her anxiety for Sohrab who did not agree to join the I.I.T. after qualifying the entrance and who even left home after his haughty encounter with his father that led Dilnavaz to believe in Ms. Kutpitia's promise of easy solution through a sort of black magic. She also went to the old lady, whom she now considered wise, for Roshan's illness. When her prescription of lime and green chilly failed to work on the girl, Dilnavaz rushed to her again. Ms. Kutpitia examined the used lime and chillies and commented that the lime had turned as hard as a rock and as black as devil; the chillies also remained "all still green as Satan's emeralds instead of turning red." She explained all this as the work of the devil's evil eye, and the poor girl had to tolerate the full force of the evil. Dilnavaz was so much engrossed with the 'logical explanation' of Roshan's illness that she stuck to Ms. Kutpitia's prescription. The old lady also gave an explanation of Roshan's relapse: "Inside the child, two forces are attacking: evil eye, which is unintentional; and something else, something dark, something deliberately inflicted. Now, when the evil eye is crushed, the child recovers. Then the dark force arises and the child is sick again. (She picked up the lime and said) This black stone reveals the dark force." (206) She, then, gave two chunks the size of pigeon eggs to Dilnavaz and dictated the procedure of what to do with the chunks for curing Roshan. She also suggested another process for Sohrab's return. And Dilnavaz, a twentieth century lady, who was aware of current incidents and was in the habit of reading newspapers, believed in those superstitious ideas and followed the prescriptions of the old lady.

The third section of the chapter starts with Dinshawji's advice that Gustad should comply with everything Ghulam Mohammed had said. Gustad was afraid of the idea of withdrawing two bundles a day, but Dinshawji asked him not to worry over the matter. Dinshawji started the task of withdrawing two bundles a day confidently and quietly. Each evening he passed two bundles to Gustad who took home those bundles and stuck them back into the black plastic under the unused 'choolavati' in the kitchen. Gustad was full of admiration for the cool courage and good sense of Dinshawji. The appearance of the buffoon could no more be traced in that responsible and broadminded man. One morning Gustad noticed that the rose plant, the vinca and the 'subjo' bush had been hacked to the ground. Every stem, every branch had been slashed off, chopped into little pieces. He did not call the watchman this time; for he knew that it was

Ghulam Mohammed's bloodless reminder. After Dinshawji had withdrawn the entire money from the fictitious account, Gustad could know that he had been seriously ill. He collapsed in the office and was sent to Parsi General. Mr. Madan granted Gustad's request to accompany Dinshawji. Gustad remained in the hospital ground for some time after leaving Dinshawji inside. He noted a butterfly flitted among the flowers and recalled that Sohrab had one such in his collection. He wondered that he had not forgotten anything about Sohrab.

The fourth section, a brief one, describes Dilnavaz's performance on the lumps of alum given to her by Ms. Kutpitia. As per her direction, Dilnavaz threw the lumps on the hot coals and they fused into a single blob. The blob bubbled and frothed, making a hissing, gurgling sound as it perched viciously atop the coals. It was done in front of Roshan who watched with interest till the seething activity ended. She was then asked to go to bed, and Dilnavaz collected the remnant and rushed to Ms. Kutpitia who was delighted to see the result. Ms. Kutpitia placed the indeterminate mass on the telephone table and inspected it. She asked Dilnavaz to look at it without seeing it so that she could decipher different meanings in it. Ms. Kutpitia was, however, dissatisfied with Dilnavaz's lack of imagination. Finally she guided Dilnavaz in such a way that she could decipher a dog. And when Dilnavaz questioned how a dog could send evil things, Ms. Kutpitia impatiently said that the alum shape would only give clues. She suggested that the culprit might be a man with dog. Obviously, Dilnavaz came to the conclusion that the culprit was none other than Mr. Rabadi who was always in conflict with Gustad.

The fifth section shows how the compound wall became totally changed after the artist had painted pictures of gods and saints on it. While coming back home from office, Gustad found a fragrance in the air near the wall and learnt that someone had offered an incense stick to goddess Laxmi. He also learnt from the painter that he had received enough money from the people in the locality. He confided that he was going to save up to buy new painting supplies. He had decided that henceforth he would paint in oil and enamel only. Gustad was surprised at the vast knowledge of the painter who unfolded one story after another—the stories behind Mount Mary, tomb of Haji Ali and other places of religious importance. Inspector Bamji, who also came there at that time, thanked Gustad for taking initiative in changing the compound wall. He also gave the information that some residents had grumbled that a Parsi Zarathosti building's wall should not be decorated by pictures of Hindu gods and goddesses. Gustad replied that the artist had also drawn Zarathost Saheb, Meherji Rana and Dustoorji Kookadaru. The inspector appreciated the inclusion of saints belonging to different religions. "A good mixture like this is a perfect example for our secular country. That's the way it should be." (214) The chapter ends with the news that Roshan's Italian doll was stolen.

Chapter 15

The first section of the chapter describes Gustad's conversation with Ghulam who was paid the entire amount that Dinshawji had withdrawn before he was admitted to hospital. Gustad asked Ghulam to count the money. And Ghulam looked hurt. Gustad knew that he was hypocrite and vicious like cobra spreading its hood. He said that the need of their friendship was over. Ghulam sighed and showed him a newspaper that carried the news that three different magistrates in three days were trying to dispose of Bilimoria's case. Ghulam angrily said that the people at the very top level were involved. Gustad retorted that Bilimoria had lied to him from the beginning and so he did not know whom he should trust. Ghulam looked pained again and said that the Major was hurt with the thought that Gustad had thought himself betrayed by him. Ghulam also gave him a letter in which Bilimoria requested Gustad to go to Delhi and see him in jail so that he could tell him the long complicated story of his arrest. Having read the letter Gustad expressed his unwillingness to go to Delhi. After Ghulam's repeated request he told that he would think about the matter and then got away from his place.

As Gustad entered the compound, Tehmul came running to him with a letter from the landlord who thanked his tenants for signing the petition against road-widening. He promised to keep them aware of the lawsuit. The chapter ends with Gustad's musing that the court work was slow, that they would be old or even die before the issue of any court order.

The second section describes Gustad's spending time with Dinshawji in the hospital. He brought Dinshawji up to date on bank news and personalities. To amuse him, he narrated Mr. Madan's row with an employee, or described what Laurie had worn to work. After the subject exhausted, Gustad told him that the money had been returned to Ghulam and he also showed him the Major's note. When Gustad asked his opinion about the major's note, Dinshawji found it difficult to give opinion, but said that if he were in Gustad's place he would go. Gustad was happy to do something for him. He raised the head a little, winding the handle of the bed. He also served him food and as Dinshawji's hand shook terribly, he took the spoon and began feeding him. Dinshawji forced him to take half of a mutton cutlet that was served to him. Gustad found that Dinshawji's wife never turned up during the visiting hour and so, to give him company, he visited the hospital regularly and particularly on the Sunday afternoons. The next half of the section describes Gustad's sudden encounter with his friend Malcolm in the Crawford Market where he went to buy the Bovril for Roshan. The two old friends put down their shopping baskets and shook hands all over again. They were so much overwhelmed by the chance meeting that they could not talk sensibly for sometime. Then they exchanged news and caught up in some way on their decades of separation. Malcolm was still single and had fulfilled his early ambition of earning his living by music. Malcolm was touched by his friend's troubles—illness of daughter and Dinshawji, and Sohrab's leaving home—and wanted to take him to the place of Mount Mary where Gustad could pray for his children and for his friend. Gustad had heard of the miracle of Mount Mary from the pavement painter and agreed to go there that afternoon, feeling that Dada Ormuzd was telling him to go there.

The third section is all about the two friends' visit to Mount Mary. Gustad told Dilnavaz that he was going to Dinshawji, and felt guilty that he was using up the sick friend's afternoon visiting hour. On the way to Mount Mary there were hawkers engaged in pushing sale. But Malcolm did not allow Gustad to buy candles from them. Besides candles, there were rosaries, holy pictures, plastic Jesuses, pendant-size silver crosses on silver chains, crucifixes, framed photographs of Mount Mary, souvenirs of Bombay etc. Gustad was surprised to see the wax products—fingers, hands, elbows, arms, legs and other parts of two sizes, child and adult, along with complete male and female figures—which were displayed in neat rows for sale. Malcolm explained that the suffering people would offer up those parts of the body which troubled them. He said humorously, "Think of it as a repair shop. Mother Mary is the Mechanic for all sufferers. She mends everything." (227) Malcolm picked out a female child's torso and gave it to Gustad for Roshan; for Dinshawji he selected the full male body of wax, in case the cancer had spread all over the body. A male head was also taken for Sohrab. And Malcolm insisted on buying a hip for Gustad. Gustad had to pay the money; for, otherwise, the offerings would not work. They also purchased four candles and went inside the hot crowded church. The candles were lit and Gustad sincerely prayed for all except himself.

After the offering was made, the friends sat on a dry boulder. They talked fondly of old days. Gustad remembered the sonata that Malcolm used to play with his father. Malcolm told that the sonata was the last movement of Cesar Franck, and it was his father's favourite. Even in his death bed when he could not even remember his name, this sonata was always in his mind. He could only make sounds with his mouth, no speech. And yet, he would keep humming the last movement. Gradually, their conversation shifted to the present, to politics and the state of the nation. Malcolm said, "Indira has visited every country in

Europe, they all say they sympathize. But nobody does a damn thing to make Pakistan behave decently. What is left but war?" (230) After sometime, Malcolm left and Gustad stayed there for a while, gazing at the horizon. The sea was calm and the tidal bustle could only be perceived near the shore. He had an intense feeling and he could not say if it was joy or sadness. The sun sank in the ocean, its journey done for the day. Gustad also thought of his journey of life; the past days crumbled in his memory. As the waves proceeded and covered the rock on which they sat, he went home.

Chapter 16

In the first section of the chapter, Ghulam Mohammed came to Gustad's flat to see him. Gustad had not yet arrived and Dilnavaz had the idea that he was with Dinshawji in the hospital. Ghulam wanted to wait for Gustad in the compound, but Dilnavaz asked him to stay inside so that he could warn Gustad at the door. As she was waiting for Gustad in the kitchen, Tehmul came with the news that there was a phone call for Gustad who was to receive it at Ms. Kutpitia's flat. Dilnavaz did not like to leave Ghulam alone in the flat and wondered who might phone on Sunday. Gustad soon arrived and was briefed at the door. He asked Dilnavaz to receive the phone call and himself started talking with Ghulam. Ghulam opened his briefcase and took out a newspaper. He showed the paper to Gustad, indicating an article entitled 'Sentencing Soon in Rupees-for-Raw Case.' It was written that the defendant's request for a retrial was denied. The head of the special investigation team, who had asked for more time to conduct a thorough review of the evidence, was killed in a car accident and his replacement brought the investigation to a rapid conclusion. Gustad read the paper and returned. Ghulam requested him to go to Delhi and see the Major. Gustad did not agree and tried to sound hard as he said that the Major had lied to him and had used him for his selfish purposes. Ghulam tried his best to appease him and persuaded him to see the Major. He also said that the visit would take only three days. He also handed Gustad reservation ticket to Delhi. At last, he accepted the ticket and agreed to go.

Dilnavaz returned with the telephone message that Dinshawji was no more. She did not understand how it was that Gustad had known nothing about Dinshawji who became unconscious in the late afternoon. Gustad had to confess that he had not gone to the hospital, but to the church. He briefly narrated what had happened after meeting Malcolm and went out for the hospital. He was very sorry for leaving Dinshawji, wondering why he had not gone to the hospital on Sunday afternoon. Gustad approached Dinshawji's bed and found that he lay with a sleeping look. It was astonishing that he was beside Dinshawji's bed and he could not see him. Or, it might be that Dinshawji was observing everything from above and laughing at him. The various tubes and other apparatus that had clung to his body were withdrawn and it seemed that he had never been ill. Gustad was affected by strange thoughts: "Were the tubes removed carefully, the way they were inserted: skilfully by steady hands? Or just yanked out—the useless wires of an old broken radio, like my Telerad. And then the tubes thrown away in the rubbish, like the coils and transformers and condensers littering the pavements outside the repair shops." (238) The rude and callous behaviour of Dinshawji's wife Alamai, whom Dinshawji would refer to as his vulture at home, made it clear that his married life was indeed very unhappy. "No children and a wife like Alamai, thought Gustad, and yet such a sense of humour. Or because of it. His domestic vulture. He almost broke into a smile again as he recalled the favourite line: 'No need to take me to the Tower of Silence when I die. My domestic vulture will pick up my bones clean ahead of time.'" (239) Alamai was accompanied by a "pasty-faced young man" called Nusli whom he introduced as her nephew who had been adopted by late Dinshawji as their son. It was difficult for Gustad to tolerate the selfish, bad mannered woman for a long time and so he waited in the compound for the arrival of 'hearse,' the van used for carrying the dead to the Tower of Silence. He sat on a bench under the trees and recalled the childhood days of happiness. He remembered his mother bidding him goodbye standing outside a mosquito net while he was inside observing her through the gauze-like material. "Her voice came clearly, but she looked so insubstantial behind the enveloping veil, far away, beyond his reach, and he was alone, under the canopy of white, entombed in his mosquito-free mausoleum. It had been such a long journey, and he fell asleep." (242) That picture of his mother remained locked up in his mind forever and he liked to remember her that way. He also remembered his father, who always tried to cheer him up when he was a child, and then he became bankrupt and the spirited man was totally shattered. Gustad came back to the present world with the thought that death can choose to be prompt or fashionably late. Dinshawji had not waited for death till his old age. Very soon nothing would remain of him, but his memories.

After the 'hearse' from 'Bombay Parsi Punchayet' arrived, the body of Dinshawji was taken inside. Gustad accompanied Alamai and her nephew to the Tower of Silence. She seemed to be a shameless hypocrite. Her sudden cry of wailing appeared funny. Gustad felt that Dinshawji would have enjoyed this. "His domestic vulture, finally singing her torch song." (245) The second section gives detailed descriptions of the ritual after the dead body was taken to the prayer bungalows. Alamai was given the option of four-day prayer at upper 'bungalee' and one-day prayer at lower 'bungalee.' She chose one-day prayer as she explained that she could not stay there for four long days. The time for the funeral next afternoon was scheduled, and Alamai agreed to have the announcement in the morning newspaper *Jam-E-Jamshed.* The prayer of 'dustoorji'—the verses of the ancient Avesta-mingled with the sounds of night. "Steadily, from the trees and bushes rose the voices of night and nature, and from all the lush vegetation that grew here on the hill, around the Tower of Silence. The murmuring of leaf-hoppers and tree-dwellers, winged and crawling ascended Doongerwadi, up towards the Tower of Silence. Their murmuring blended with the sandalwood and *loban* and prayer music floating forth from the room with the oil lamp, and Gustad understood it all." (248)

The third section is very small, describing Gustad's return to his flat after the prayer of 'dustoorji' was over and also his reaction after hearing the prayer. Gustad told Dilnavaz that he saw Dinshawji smiling while the prayer was going on. Dilnavaz did not oppose him, but said that prayers were indeed powerful, able to put a smile on Dinshawji's face and in Gustad's eyes. Gustad expressed his wish that at the time of his departure from the world there should be smile on his face and also in her eyes. The clock was still silent signifying that Gustad was experiencing the bliss of 'still time.'

Chapter 17

This chapter is all about the Parsi funeral rituals which were observed after the demise of Dinshawji. The manager issued a memo which included employee's names under two headings: Funeral 3.30 p.m. and Uthamna Ceremony—Tuesday 3.00 p.m. Mr. Madan also attended the funeral and offered Gustad a ride in his car. There was a large turnout at Doongerwadi. Though relatives were few, many friends and colleagues attended the funeral. The overflow was accommodated in a pavilion adjacent to the 'bungalee,' along with the non-Parsis. Looking over the gathering, Gustad realized that Dinshawji had brought laughter into the life of almost every person sitting there silently. Gustad was allotted place in the first row and Mr. Madan also sat there. All the Parsi rituals were followed. First, there was the ritual of the dog. The Doongerwadi dog was led to the bier, the *char-chassam* dog, which, with his preternatural eyes, would contain the *nassoo*, the evil of death, and assist the forces of good. Suddenly, Alamai stood with her arms raised and began to wail addressing the dog that did not bark. Women hastened to calm her and Gustad shook him at the pathetic exhibition. The 'dustoorjis' waited patiently until silence was restored, and then continued with the Ahunavad Gatha. The rest of the prayers proceeded without interruption. At the conclusion, they invited Alamai to place 'loban' and sandalwood on the 'afargan' fire. She seemed quite calm now. After family members and relatives finished their obeisance, the other mourners filed past for the 'sezdoe.' While they bowed and touched the ground three times, the room suddenly grew dark. The sunlight streaming into the prayer hall was blocked by four shadows. The 'nassasalers' had arrived. They stood in the doorway, waiting to carry the bier to the Tower of Silence.

The professional pall-bearers were all clad in white from head to foot. They also put on white gloves and white canvas shoes. People moved aside to give them a wide berth, fearful of contact. The approach to the well of vultures was for men only. The women lined up on the verandah. Alamai requested Gustad to take Nusli with him up the hill and Gustad called him. Every man from the bank had decided to take the last walk with Dinshawji, and many of them were weeping. They went up the hill and Gustad remembered how he had covered the road earlier, with the bodies of his parents and grandparents. The 'nassasalers' halted near the stone platform. They uncovered the face for the last time so that the mourners could bid farewell to Dinshawji. Then the four men carried the bier again and climbed the stone steps to the door leading inside the Tower. They entered and pulled it shut behind them. The mourners could see no more, but they knew that the four men would now place the body on a 'pavi,' and without touching his flesh they would tear off the white cloth using their special hooked rods so that he could be exposed to the creatures of the air. "Overhead, the vultures were circling, flying lower and lower with each perfect circle they casually described." (254) The chief of the carriers clapped three times as a signal to start the prayer for Dinshawji's ascending soul. While they prayed, the vultures descended in great numbers. The high stone wall was lined with them and their serpent-like necks and bald heads rose incongruously from their plumage. The ritual came to its end when the mourners made their last stop for washing their hands and faces and performed 'kusti.'

The second section of the chapter describes Gustad's experience in the railway station and boarding the train bound for Delhi. He had already requested Mr. Madan to grant him leave for two days, and the manager did not ask him why he was taking leave; for, he took it for granted that Gustad would attend Dinshawji's family. It was unlucky for Gustad that the railway had been on strike since midnight and he could not avail his reservation done for him by Ghulam. In the beginning, however, Gustad felt relief as he could cancel the trip with clear conscience. But as it was announced that one unreserved train bound for Delhi would run, Gustad's conscience compelled him to board it. He had to pay rupees ten to a coolie for keeping a seat in one compartment. The compartment was crowded and Gustad had little conversation with the fellow travellers. Gustad ate the sandwiches that Dilnavaz had given him in a packet and became engaged in introspection: "Would this long journey be worth it? Was any journey ever worth the trouble? Then his thoughts were of Dinshawji. Random thoughts, crossing decades of their lives. . . . How he made people laugh. At lunch and tea-breaks. Even during working hours, one-liners every now and then. Yes, to be able to make people laugh was a wonderful blessed thing. And what a long journey for Dinshawji too. But certainly worth it." (260)

In the third section the camera shifts from Gustad to Dilnavaz. Growing anxiety and Ms. Kutpitia's influence made her more and more superstitious. In the wake of Gustad's early-morning departure, one incident after another followed and she interpreted them as 'disasters.' The milk boiled over; she burnt the rice; kerosene overflowed the funnel when the stove was being filled. She was in actuality much worried about Gustad and wished he had not decided to go to Delhi. But she knew that Gustad would never get peace unless he found the truth. And there was no other way to know what actually had happened but to go to Delhi. All the same the thought of Gustad entering a jail, even as a visitor, was frightening. Besides, she had not yet done what Ms. Kutpitia had prescribed for Roshan's illness. She could not understand why the old lady always asked her to be patient about Sohrab. As she was thinking about all this, Mr. Rabadi, accompanied by his dog Dimple, rang the Noble's door bell. Mr. Rabadi repeated the charge brought against Darius that he was after his daughter. As the two were exchanging haughty remarks, Darius emerged from the back room and Mr. Rabadi asked her to inquire whether Darius had been with his daughter. Dilnavaz asked him to leave the place, but he did not. Darius, then, heaved the door shut and Mr. Rabadi was heard threatening them. He would lodge two complaints to the police station, he said. Asked by Dilnavaz, Darius said that the girl needed some help to learn bicycling and he helped her as others had got tired in carrying her only one round. Dilnavaz pleaded him not to have any contact with that girl, as her father was a real crackpot. Dilnavaz also came to an easy solution as it suddenly came to her mind that Roshan's health and wealth were 'used' to make Rabadi's daughter so fat. Whatever Ms. Kutpitia had said, seemed sensible to her after she could explain to herself where exactly Roshan's health and weight were going.

The fourth section of the chapter again focuses on Gustad's journey. After midnight Gustad was offered the luggage-rack for sleeping by the young man who had managed it from the coolie for twenty rupees. He told Gustad that he had slept enough and would like to sit in Gustad's seat. Gustad readily agreed to sleep on the luggage-rack as his limbs had started aching at every point. He slept, half-dreaming and half-imagining that he was in a coup with Dilnavaz. He got up in the morning and drank tea. He also offered the 'luggage-rack' man a glass of tea. The chapter ends with an image, familiar with the railway passengers in India: Gustad anxiously returning the glass having taken a few hurried sips after the train had started to move, and the 'chai-walla' getting it back while running along the side of the train on the platform.

Chapter 18

The first section of the eighteenth chapter records Gustad's experiences in Delhi. He used the lavatory in the waiting room of the railway station. The ice-cold water of Delhi's December morning stung sharply. But it was wonderfully invigorating after the tiring journey. Leaving the station he got into the auto-rickshaw which carried him to the gate of the jail where Bilimoria was imprisoned. At the reception area he consulted the note Ghulam Mohammed had given him and asked for Mr. Kashyap. After half an hour he was asked inside and he learnt from Mr. Kashyap that the Bilimoria was ill and had been taken to the hospital section. However, Gustad was escorted to Bilimoria's bed and he had to cross smelly wards. Though the usual time allotted to visitors was half an hour, Gustad was allowed to stay there for four hours. The room where Bilimoria was kept, was stifling and its single window was bolted shut. Gustad found that only a shadow of Major Bilimoria, the strong man who had once lifted Gustad and carried him to the bonesetter, was lying on the bed. Gustad moved cautiously to the foot of the bed and watched him. As Jimmy's eyes fluttered open and looked at Gustad, he tried to utter his name, but could not. Gustad was alarmed by his condition and his feelings towards him totally changed. "Anger, accusations, demands for explanations emptied from Gustad's mind. Only a monster could harass a broken man for answers. He would wait, listen to what Jimmy wanted, comfort him, and offer his help. Everything else had to be forgotten. And forgiven." (268) And Gustad listened to the Major and learnt about the corruption at the top level. Having joined the RAW, Bilimoria found that Indira Gandhi, the P.M. of India, had been using it as her own private agency. He had no idea that he would be asked for spying on opposition parties, ministers and for black-mailing them. With much difficulty to utter words, the Major broke off, gasping. After taking water he again started speaking. When East Pakistan was being attacked by the West Pakistan and swarms of refugees were coming to India, Bilimoria was called in an interview by the P.M. In her calm and confident voice she asked him to take the charge of training and supplying the 'Mukti Bahini' in East Pakistan. He went there to train the tough fighters and felt that without money no proper help was possible. After he had sent his report to P.M.'s office, one day he was asked to go to her small private office where he was instructed how to meet the chief cashier of one S.B.I. branch and ask for sixty lakh rupees. He was asked to introduce himself as Bangladeshi Babu. After he got the money from the bank, she tried to trap him. Jimmy closed his eyes and could not utter any more, as the injection was gripping his tongue. Gustad let him sleep for sometime and went downstairs to have tea and snacks in the canteen.

The second section is all about Dilnavaz's preparation of a sort of paste as per Ms. Kutpitia's prescription. First she sliced the lemons and chopped the chillies which were used for making 'taveez,' and then proceeded to grind it all to a fine paste. The paste was mixed with milk and different kinds of spices ground together. A teaspoonful of mouse dropping was also put in the mixture. The final ingredient, a spider's round white egg-case, was also collected and mixed. Dilnavaz was so much obsessed with Ms. Kutpitia's assurance that she could remove all the troubles faced by Dilnavaz, provided she prepared perfect medicines as prescribed by her, that logic and rationality ceased to work. Following the old lady's instructions she put the pan containing the paste on the stove, and the carefully preserved alum shape was crumbled and added. And then she waited for the opportunity to throw the entire paste on Mr. Rabadi's head from the balcony. Mr. Rabadi's roar resounded through the compound, but Dilnavaz was happy that there was no evidence that his scalp had been anointed by her. Having performed this ridiculous act, she felt that Ms. Kutpitia would be proud of her. She began to believe sincerely that the 'medicine' worked immediately as Roshan did not like to sleep any more. She rushed to the old lady and requested her to do something for Sohrab's return. This time she was given a shoe-box with a lizard inside it and was directed to keep the box under the bed where Sohrab used to sleep.

The third section takes the readers again to the jail hospital. Bilimoria said that Indira Gandhi had called him again to tell him that she had enemies everywhere and if they would learn that she had telephoned for the money, she would be in trouble. He was then asked to write a few lines that he had imitated Indira Gandhi's voice and took the money with the intention of helping the 'Mukti Bahini.' He was assured that he would have no trouble and like an idiot he believed that. When he went to Bangladesh, he found that the money had not reached there. Having investigated the matter he came to know that the money he had disbursed for supplies was intercepted by P.M.'s office and was rerouted to a private account. Ghulam had also investigated the matter that time on his behalf, and they tried to finish him off on his Lambretta. Bilimoria confessed that at this stage he was frustrated with the ways of the politicians and thought that there would be no harm if he would put aside ten lakh rupees and distribute the amount among his dear ones. And so he decided to send ten lakh rupees to Gustad. Gustad gently asked him why he had not told him the truth. Bilimoria said that he knew Gustad's principles and was afraid that he would not have agreed to do the job in case he knew the truth. But Bilimoria was mistaken to think that they would not bother about ten lakh rupees. He was arrested and then, they started a case based on his confession. And after the amount was paid, every thing ran well and he was taken to the hospital for treatment. Bilimoria asked Gustad's forgiveness and Gustad said there was nothing to forgive. He also said that he had heard of corruption but had never imagined that corruption could reach that level. Having heard the Major's confession, Gustad left him and went back to Bombay. He heard that the war with Pakistan had started.

Chapter 19

The first section of the chapter is about the ludicrous way of making black magic with the lizard in a shoe-box that had been kept under the bed on which Sohrab used to sleep. Ms. Kutpitia asked Dilnavaz to bring Tehmul with her and she did so and felt helpless as she could not understand what was going to happen. The old lady asked them to enter her flat and much to Dilnavaz's surprise the two locked doors in her flat were opened. In the faint light of the dim, dust-coated light bulb, the shadowy chambers covered with dust and cobweb created an eerie stillness. Those were the rooms of Ms. Kutpitia's nephew Farad and of her brother, the father and the son who had died in the car accident on the mountain road. The books, the dresses, the furniture and everything else remained as they had been before. Ms. Kutpitia took the shoebox from Dilnavaz's hand and placed it on Farad's desk, opening the lid just a crack. As the lizard poked its snout, she promptly whacked it over the head with the ruler. She pinched the lizard's wriggling tail between her thumb and finger and snipped off about two inches of the appendage with a pair of blunt, rusty scissors. Like regular cotton wick, the tail was inserted into a wick-holder, dipped in oil. She then asked Dilnavaz to stand outside and asked Tehmul to watch the fun. The idiot boy was much excited to see the fun as the wicker-tail was lighted. He was shouting "twistingburningtwistingburning" for five minutes and was then asked to leave the place. The practice was meant for bringing Sohrab home through making Tehmul lose his mind. No one noticed that the lizard tail had wriggled its way out of the glass and fell on the tattered exercise books on the table.

The second section focuses on Gustad's return. Before he entered his flat, he examined the compound wall and found that everything in crayon had been erased and done over in oil. It was indeed a miraculous transformation of the wall that had been stingy and full of mosquitoes. Now, the passers-by were regularly offering sandalwood, flowers and incense sticks. Some new paintings also attracted his attention. The last painting was that of Dustoorji Baria, known for his miracles and for solving all sorts of problems besides spiritual ones. Gustad did not like that the photograph and the suggestion for painting had been given by Mr. Rabadi. The painter also told that Inspector Bamji had asked him to stop that painting, and said that he was no holy man but a disgrace to the Parsi society. At that time Mr. Rabadi had also come there and began to argue with the Inspector.

Gustad asked the painter what his own view was. The painter said, "I don't like to weaken anyone's faith. Miracle, magic, mechanical trick, coincidence—does it matter what it is, as long as it helps? Why analyze the strength of the imagination, the power of suggestion, power of auto-suggestion, the potency of psychological pressures? Looking too closely is destructive, makes everything disintegrate. As it is, life is difficult enough. Why to simply make it tougher? After all who is to say what makes a miracle and what makes a coincidence?" (289) Through the painter's observation a tolerant view of life is offered. The section ends with the incident of fire; smoke was seen emerging from Ms. Kutpitia's flat.

The third section describes the loss caused by fire. It was miraculous that Ms. Kutpitia's flat had come through largely unscathed. It was affirmed that divine intervention had come to the rescue. Some ascribed the good fortune to the wall which attracted the people who uttered their invocations that created endless vibrations of a propitious nature. Inside Ms. Kutpitia's flat, the damage was confined to the locked rooms. The precious grief-nurturing reminders of her beloved nephew and brother had perished. Dilnavaz found that Ms. Kutpitia rather enjoyed the sympathetic attention of people who had decided to forget her reputation for meanness and crankiness. It was tacitly accepted now that a person so providentially delivered from the jaws of fiery death must have forces of goodness on her side. It was however no great matter of puzzlement for Ms. Kutpitia that the fire died in such a docile manner.

As war was declared and people had to be prepared for blackout, Gustad expressed satisfaction that he had not removed the blackout papers pasted during the war with China. He had to do some mending and Darius helped him in the work. Gustad also decided that underneath the huge four-poster bed would be the air-raid shelter for resisting the worst result of war. The chapter ends with Gustad's chatting with Inspector Bamji on the war.

Chapter 20

The chapter starts with public awareness about the necessity of maintaining rules and directives concerning air raids and sirens. In the bank, Mr. Madan issued guidelines about this. The instruction list reminded Gustad of Dinshawji who would have had a field day in the canteen, mimicking Mr. Madan. Now there was no joke in the canteen. Everyone was talking about the grim, gruesome stories of what was happening across the border. Details of the USA intervention and its Seventh Fleet on the Bay of Bengal were discussed in newspapers and in public places. When Gustad returned home, he felt that Cavasji's blood-pressure was high again, for he was crying out that if any bomb was to fall, it should fall on Tata Palace or on Birlas and Tatas. He was, however, not allowed to shout keeping his head outside the window, violating the blackout rule. His son came and gently led him away, shutting the papered-over window.

The second section is about Gustad's discovery that Tehmul had stolen Roshan's doll and had used the big doll for satisfying his sexual desire. Gustad was by nature vigilant and while inspecting if all the tenants of the Khodadad building had obeyed the instructions for black out, he found that light was coming through the window of Tehmul's flat. He went there and found that the idiot was lying naked on the bed with the doll. Gustad was angry as well as embarrassed. Tehmul started to blubber, his tears mixing with sweat. Gustad asked him to put on his dress and then sent him to wash his hands. The scene sickened him and he began to hate the idiot. Tehmul was still weeping and wanted to tell that the women in the House of the Cages did not entertain him. Gustad's anger began to ebb slowly, as he felt that Tehmul had a child's mind and a man's urges; shunned by the prostitutes, he turned to the doll in despair. He began to pity the idiot and decided that he would not take away the doll. He wished he had the power of miracles, the power to cure Tehmul's ills and restore to him all the rights and virtues of mortals.

The third section describes Gustad's conversation with Dr. Paymaster who was happy to learn that Roshan was well. Soon, their talk was diverted to politics, to Bangladesh war and to the inefficiency of local municipality. Gustad also found that Peerbhoy Paanwalla had changed the theme of his stories and people demanded his stories that expressed some patriotic emotions. He also introduced a new product (paan) called Patriotic Paan: instead of folding betel leaves into their usual triangles, he made little rectangular trays of each leaf; then he filled them with all the ingredients used in 'paan' and arranged the colours in three horizontal bands, saffron, white and green. Having returned to the compound, he saw Tehmul searching something in darkness. With the help of the torch carried by Gustad, he found the little beaded bracelet from the doll's wrist. Gustad was touched by his blissful smile and God-like simplicity.

The fourth section gives the information that the war came to an end and the black papers used during blackout were no more needed. Newspapers continued to analyze the war—the crucial battles and the reactions of the Bangladeshis after the arrival of the first Indian troop in Dacca. Gustad read whichever paper he could borrow in the canteen and Dilnavaz glanced over Ms. Kutpitia's copy of 'Jam-E-Jamshed' each morning. The chapter ends with the news of Bilimoria's death of a heart attack, the information that Gustad saw in a newspaper.

Chapter 21

The first section of the chapter describes how the people in Dr. Paymaster's neighbourhood were ready for the march to the municipal ward office in protest against the corruption and negligence of the municipality. Dr. Paymaster was not much willing to join the march in the beginning. He tried to point out that the municipal corruption was only a microcosmic manifestation of the greed, dishonesty and moral turpitude that flourished in the country's centre; it was like bad smell which would disappear as soon as the gangrenous government at the centre was removed. But his neighbours said that they could not hold their breath forever and so they had to do something to remove the stink. Hence, Dr. Paymaster shut his dispensary and joined the march. It was decided that the 'morcha' would start near the House of Cages and take two hours to reach the municipal office where a 'gherao' was to be conducted. The waiting crowd applauded the doctor who acknowledged the cheers with a half-hearted wave.

The second section starts with Dilnavaz's reading *Jam-E-Jamshed* where she got the news of Bilimoria's funeral to be held that morning. She informed Gustad of the incident who decided to attend the funeral at Doongerwadi. Gustad wondered who could have arranged the funeral and felt grateful to whoever it was. Through Gustad's presence in the funeral meeting where debate was raging between the reformist and the orthodox camps, Mistry found another occasion to highlight the orthodox Parsi views in regard to their age-old practice of letting the dead body be devoured by vultures. While going back, Gustad noticed a taxi waiting in the shade of a tree and recognized the driver, Ghulam Mohammed. The mystery of who arranged the funeral was resolved immediately.

The third section, a very small one, focuses on Malcolm Saldanha, the piano player, who was now an employee in the municipality and who, in spite of his hatred of his job, was happy with the regular salary. He was going through the instructions given to him that day while drinking his cup of tea. Suddenly the project's location attracted his attention: 'Khodadad Building.' The section thus ends with suspense in regard to the municipality's plan about the building.

The fourth section describes Sohrab's arrival in the flat during office time. Whenever he would come to see his mother occasionally, he chose the time when Gustad was supposed to be in office. That day he learnt that his father had gone to attend the funeral of Major Bilimoria. Dilnavaz requested Sohrab to talk to his father nicely. She tried her best to convince him that his father always loved him and that he had been changed a lot during the recent time. Much to her happiness she found Sohrab agree to her proposal.

The fifth and the last section of the chapter focuses again on Gustad who was now conversing with Ghulam. Gustad found him weeping; he had seen many sides of the man: jovial, threatening, callous, cajoling, sarcastic, emotional. But never had he found him emotional earlier. Ghulam said in a voice of slight complaint that the Parsis did not allow the outsiders like him to join the funeral meeting. Gustad felt guilty. He also asked Ghulam why he had not informed him of the funeral personally. Ghulam had no answer, but he offered to drive him home. While driving the taxi, Ghulam hinted on taking revenge on the persons responsible for Jimmy's death.

Chapter 22

The first section makes it clear that Malcolm was in the charge of breaking the compound wall of the Khodadad Building. When Malcolm broke the news to the pavement artist, he crumpled. He gathered up his paints and brushes, box and belongings, and dropped them in the compound. There he sat, cross-legged, without any energy. Reluctantly, Malcolm gave orders for the workers to proceed. The workers demarcated the requisite areas first and found that the 'neem' tree fell within the municipality's latest land acquisition. Two men were dispatched to cut down the tree. In the meantime, the 'morcha' entered the lane shouting "Municipality's bullying will not do." As the marchers drew abreast with the wall, a fresh vitality animated their slogans. Suddenly, one of the 'morcha' directors signalled the column to a halt. He began to give a speech on why they had halted there: "what better place than this sacred wall of miracles to pause and meditate upon our purpose? The wall of gods and goddesses. The wall of Hindu and Muslim, Sikh and Christian, Parsi and Buddhist! A holy wall, a wall suitable for worship and devotion, whatever your faith! . . . Let us pray that in the spirit of truth and non-violence we will defeat our enemies!" (326) The procession roared its approval, surging towards the wall. The municipal workers stood clear as queues formed before each portrait. As it was known that the wall was going to be broken, the crowd expressed their disbelief first, and when the news was confirmed, the people fell on the municipal workers. "Wall destroyed! The words percolated through the 'morcha' and trickled through the crowds of bystanders. Wall destroyed?! Disbelief turned to indignation, then to outrage that surged through the congregation and swelled into a tidal wave, making the ground tremble as it galloped for the shore. 'Impossible!' said the wave with ten thousand mouths, raging and rumbling. The wall of gods and goddesses cannot be broken! We will see that not one finger is raised against the deities! We will protect them with our blood if need be!" (326). The situation was fast deteriorating. Malcolm said that he had not made the decision and that he was just to follow the order of his bosses at the municipality. The very word 'municipality' was loathsome to them, as they were protesting against the corruption of municipality. Fighting was inevitable then.

The second section starts with Gustad's arrival at the gate of the Khodadad Building. At that time the offended workers reached for crowbars and pickaxes. The policemen, who were appointed for guarding the procession heading towards the municipality, shuffled their feet and gripped their lathis, making a show of alertness. The sub-inspector sent a message to the police station asking for more police. Gustad saw that Tehmul was nearby and was very excited. He asked the idiot not to be near the marchers. The members of Khodadad building came out and much to his surprise Gustad noted Sohrab who fleetingly met his father's eyes and then turned away. Gustad asked Inspector Bamji if he could do anything in this situation. He answered that he never interfered when off duty. It was learnt that the municipal authority was not in the mood of retreating and the section ends with Inspector Bamji's observation: "Net practice is over. Now the test match begins." (332)

The third section describes direct attack through throwing of stones. For Tehmul it was an immense game of 'catch-catch' with a thousand players and he trembled with excitement. "He clapped his hands with glee as a rock landed by the gate. What fun it could be to catch one. With his own hands. What fun. Just like the children catching the tennis ball. So much, so much fun." (332) Gustad saw him running to catch a flying brick, and before his cry reached Tehmul's ears, the idiot was struck. The brick caught him on the forehead, and Gustad heard the crack. Tehmul dropped without a sound. Gustad ran to him and grabbed the unconscious body. Sohrab ran to call Dr. Paymaster who was in the 'morcha.' The doctor examined and found him dead. Tehmul's brother was out of station and the Tower of Silence was informed by Ms. Kutpitia. The body could not be kept on the gate for a long time, but the idea of carrying the heavy body two floors up was daunting. Without a word Gustad carried the body. With a single mighty effort he took the body upstairs and put it on the bed. Sohrab gazed at his father with fear and admiration. After keeping the body on the bed, Gustad recited the Yatha Ahu Varyo and Ashem Vahoo repeatedly. He recited as much for Tehmul as for Jimmy and Dinshawji. He also recited for all the dear ones who had departed. And then he heard the voice of Sohrab who called "Daddy." Gustad went up and put his arms around Sohrab and hugged him tightly.

The last section describes the process of demolition—the crunching, grating, rasping as men with shovels trampled through the gravel. The pavement artist awoke from the trance of despair. He rose and went to Gustad to thank him for giving hospitality. When Gustad asked him if he had any plan about his future destination, he said, "Where does not matter, sir. In a world where roadside latrines become temples and shrines, and temples and shrines become dust and ruin, does it matter where?" (338) At the time of going he left the oil paint which he bought, ironically, to make his painting permanent. Perhaps he realized that the idea of permanence was absurd. Gustad left the sun-flooded compound and entered the flat. The novel ends without displaying any reaction of Dilnavaz.

Such a Long Journey as Parsi Fiction

The rise of Parsi fiction is a common feature in the literary scenario of postcolonial India and Pakistan. A galaxy of Parsi writers—Dina Mehta, Firdaus Kanga, Keki Daruwalla, Bapsi Sidhwa, Rohinton Mistry and Boman Desai—have enriched the English literature in Indian subcontinent during the last three decades of the twentieth century. Some of these writers have settled in America and Canada, and yet they express their concern for the Parsi community to which they belong. The word Parsi, meaning a native of 'Pars' (now in southern Iran), is an ethnic term. The religion of the Parsis is Zoroastrianism, founded by Zarathustra around 2000 B.C. The date is however disputed, as some historians claim that it was founded in 7000 or 8000 B.C. while others view that it was around 600 B.C. Whatever be the exact time of Zarathustra, his followers continued to practise the ancient monotheistic religion long after they had been forced to leave their original land after the conquest of Iran by Arab. A group of Parsi refugee arrived on the western coast of Indian subcontinent in the eighth century. They landed in the port of Sanjan in Gujarat which was then ruled by King Jadhav Rana. Their priest (Dastur) appealed to the king for permission to settle there. They were allowed to settle in Gujarat with five conditions imposed on them. They adopted the Gujarati language; their women were to wear sari; their men were to handover weapons; they were to venerate the cow and their marriage ceremonies were to be performed at night only. Proselytizing was also strictly prohibited. The Parsis followed these instructions and began to live in India as a secluded community.[1] Though they did not merge in the mainstream, loyalty to the ruler of the day became a characteristic trait of their community.

During the colonial period they were the first to learn English language and could hold a prestigious position in the national scenario. The rise of Parsi novel is a direct outcome of their English language education at an early stage. As the Parsis could maintain their distinct identity in an alien land, thanks to their rich heritage, it became obvious that they would project this distinctness in their fictions.

The Parsis are thus an ethno-religious minority in India who live mostly on the western coast, and specifically in Bombay. In Pakistan the Parsis have settled mostly in Karachi and Lahore. According to the 1997 census report given by the Government of India, about 75-80,000 Parsis are living here. Though the total population of the Parsis is insignificant, their active participation in the social, cultural, political and economic life, particularly during the colonial period, is worth mentioning. Eminent jurist Nani A. Palkiwala observes, "History affords no parallel to the role of Parsis in India. There is no record of any other community so infinitesimally small as Parsis, playing such a significant role in the life of a country so large."[2] In several sectors such as shipping industry, aviation, banking, catering, canning and dairy products, the Parsis have shown their excellence. Luminaries such as Rustomji Jivanji Gorkhodu, a close associate of Mahatma Gandhi, K.F. Nariman, Dadabhai Naoroji, Sir Dinshaw Eduljee Wacha, and Pherozeshah Mehta, to mention a few, played prominent roles in Indian freedom movement. The Parsis are also marked for their self-honour and that is why they have never demanded any reservation in jobs or entrance examinations, though they have always maintained a strong sense of group identity. When their sense of honour was jolted, it is not unnatural then, that they would try to mend it.

With this background of the Parsis in the Indian subcontinent, the postcolonial writers in English belonging to the Parsi community are writing fiction which reflects their distinctness. These are (i) inclusion of their religious rituals and functions which they have retained so far against all sorts of odds, (ii) their sense of honour as well as insult, for being treated as the 'other,' (iii) their hopes and aspirations along with their attempts to retain the glory that they had once received. Rohinton Mistry's novels have all these qualities, and in addition to these he also expresses the quality of self-scrutiny. The superstitions of some Parsi people are critically analyzed. Some traditional rituals such as cremation of the dead body are also analyzed and discoursed. Feminist and subaltern issues in the Parsi community also emerge in his novels.

Such a Long Journey projects the life-style and problems of one Parsi family living in a Parsi colony. Gustad, the protagonist of the novel, is introduced through his morning prayer:

> The first light of morning barely illumined the sky as Gustad Noble faced eastward to offer his orisons to Ahura Mazda. The hour was approaching six, and up in the compound's solitary tree the sparrow began to call. Gustad listened to their chirping every morning while reciting his 'kusti' prayers. . . . Gustad Noble eased his prayer cap slightly. . . . The black velvet of the cap contrasted starkly with his cinereous sideburns. (1)

Gustad's prayer is described in detail. The way he put on 'kusti' and uttered his prayers would give a non-Parsi a clear idea of Parsi ritual:

> Gustad finished retying the 'kusti' round his waist and noted with satisfaction that the two ends, as usual, were of equal length. He raised and lowered his shoulders to let his 'sudra' settle comfortably around him. . . . He turned his face to the sky, eyes closed, and began reciting the Sarosh Baaj, silently forming the words with his lips. . . . There was nothing he disliked more than to permit a break in his morning prayers. Bad manners, that's what it was. He would not rudely interrupt when talking to another human being, so why do it with Dada Ormuzd? (15)

Ahura Mazda or 'Wise Lord' is the absolute, omnipotent, eternal God proclaimed by Zoroaster or Zarathustra. Ahura Mazda is both the creator as well as the judge on the day of the last judgment. Zarathustra preached the monotheistic religion of the One Supreme God, Ahura Mazda. His message is positive, life-affirming and based on strong moral stand. According to him, the whole universe is dominated by two primal forces, Good and Evil—'Spenta Mainyu' and 'Angra Mainyu'—and an individual's duty is to make a choice between the two. The supreme God Ahura Mazda combines with Spenta Mainyu to become the principle of good represented as 'Ohrmazd.' Gustad's prayer to Ahura Mazda and to Dada Ormuzd, his strong moral stand as is manifested in his decisions, his participation in all the formalities in the Tower of Silence—all these are specific Parsi activities that have enriched the novel.

Gustad's hesitation in buying beef from Crawford Market may be interpreted in terms of the prohibitions imposed on the Parsis in the eighth century. The Parsis were asked to venerate the cow and due to this condition, traditional Parsis still do not eat beef, though there are no religious taboos against the eating of beef. Gustad would eat beef but he did not like to be exposed as eater of beef outside his community. So he was anxious that while carrying the raw meat from the market, meat juices must not drip from his basket, causing the vegetarians' protest.

> Gustad alone, with his meagre wallet and worn basket lined with newspaper to soak up meat juices that could start dripping in the bus, causing embarrassment or, worse still, angry protests from vegetarian passengers. Throughout the trip he felt anxious and guilty—felt that in his basket was something deadlier than a bomb (21)
>
> Gustad therefore felt relaxed when he stopped shopping at Crawford Market.
>
> By this time, he had lost touch with Malcolm, and was spared embarrassing explanations about the tenuous, tangled connection between his desertion of Crawford Market and the sadhus' nationwide protest against cow slaughter. It was easier to remain the silent, unknown apostle of beef. (26)

Gustad's belonging to minority community is repeatedly referred to in the course of the novel. His friend Malcolm, who had taught him how to buy beef, always said: "Lucky for us that we are minorities in a nation of Hindus. Let them eat pulses and grams and beans, spiced with their stinky asafoetida—what they call 'hing.' Let them fart their lives away. The modernized Hindus eat mutton. Or chicken, if they want to be more fashionable. But we will get our protein from their sacred cow." (23) Gustad's faith in Zoroastrianism is also asserted. When Malcolm would take him to church on Sundays on their way to Crawford Market, Gustad was on his guard, conditioned as he had been from childhood to resist the call of other faiths. "All religions were equal, he was taught; nevertheless, one had to remain true to one's own because religions were not like garment styles that could be changed at whim or to follow fashion." (24) A comparison of Zoroastrianism with the existing religions in India is also done in the course of their conversations. When Malcolm told Gustad that Christianity had come to India over nineteen hundred years ago, with Apostle Thomas landing on the Malabar coast among the fishermen, long before the Parsis came on the western coast, Gustad retorted,

> That may be, but our prophet Zarathustra lived more than fifteen hundred years before your Son of God was even born; a thousand years before the Buddha; two hundred years before Moses. And do you know how much Zoroastrianism influenced Judaism, Christianity, and Islam? (24)

Critics have pointed out the possible influences of Zoroastrianism on Judaism and Christianity in the following theological concepts which are shared by all the three religions:

1. Belief in one supreme and loving god.
2. The concept of Heaven and Hell and individual judgment.
3. A strict moral and ethical code and a belief in the ultimate triumph of good.
4. The messiah to come for the final restoration.
5. The concepts of resurrection, final judgment and life everlasting.
6. The Zoroastrian origin of words like Satan, Paradise, pastor and amen.[3]

When Gustad told Malcolm of the possible influences of Zoroastrianism on other monotheistic religions, he must have had the above list in his mind. The theological concepts mentioned above are matters of common discourse among the Parsis.

The novel contains scattered remarks usually uttered by the minorities or thrown at them by the majority group which together give the novel a look of Parsi fiction. For example, Dinshawji described how the 'goondas' shouted while breaking the thick glass of the windows in the bank: "They were shouting 'Parsi crow-eaters, we'll show you who is the boss." (39) Gustad's wife Dilnavaz was always amused by the sight of a short tail of hair growing from the centre of the milkman's head otherwise perfectly shaven. "She knew it was a Hindu custom in some particular caste, she was not exactly sure, but couldn't help thinking that it resembled a grey rat's tail." (3) Gustad asked Parsi Punchayet Education Fund, R.D. Sethna Trust, Tat Scholarships, Wadia Charities for Higher Studies—all Parsi organizations—for financial help to get Sohrab admitted to the I.I.T., and much to his disappointment Sohrab refused to enrol himself in I.I.T. Gustad was so disappointed, because he had dreamt of a bright future for his eldest son and hoped that once Sohrab would come out as an I.I.T. engineer, the whole family was likely to be elevated to a higher status and they would no longer be treated as 'other.' Sohrab's refusal was thus a great blow to Gustad and he could not forgive him. That the entire family was treated as culturally 'other' becomes clear from Darius's refusal to take copies of *Jam-E-Jamshed* when each student of their school was asked to bring five old copies of newspapers from home. He said that he would prefer five *Times of India*'s because his friends would make fun of the Parsi 'bawaji' newspapers. The novel also presents some conversations which are concerned with the Parsi customs.

> Sometimes the hour went in passionate argument about matters that concerned the community, such as the Tower of Silence controversy. When the bank clerks and tellers debated the reformers' proposal to introduce cremation, tempers flared and there were

> bitter personal attacks. But Dinshawji would manage to end matters on a light note, saying things like: 'Better that my dear domestic vulture eats me up than the feathered ones. With her I have a guarantee—she at least won't scatter pieces of my meat all over Bombay.' (72)

Besides such scattered remarks which concern the Parsis exclusively, there are occasional remembrances of things past, both of the golden old days shared by the Parsi community in India, and also of prosperity of the Noble family in the past days. Gustad was affected by nostalgia when he bought only one live chicken from the market and carried it in his basket. He remembered how his father would usually buy more than one, and was always accompanied by a servant for carrying things. The loss of the book store had turned Gustad's father into a broken and dispirited man. Gustad worried deeply as his father visibly shrank. He did the best he could do as breadwinner of the family. But his meagre income could never raise the status of the family. With a low social status he became more conscious of his position as culturally 'other.'

> No future for minorities, with these fascist Shiv Sena politics and Marathi language nonsense. It was going to be like the black people in America—twice as good as the white man to get half as much. (55)

It was quite natural that the minorities, who are negligible in number, become terrified at the rise of fanaticism. A common Parsi's anxiety is best revealed through Dinshawji's humorous remarks. Remembering the contribution of the Parsis to the banking system in India, Dinshawji said,

> What days those were, *yaar*. What fun we used to have. Parsis were the kings of banking in those days. Such respects we used to get. Now the whole atmosphere only has been spoiled. Ever since that Indira nationalized the banks. (38)

Dinshawji was aware of the changing political scenario that was the ultimate cause of the changed status of the Parsis in India. With his traditional sense of obeying the ruler in the country

Gustad was rather hesitant to use strong words of criticism against the central government. But Dinshawji brought direct charges against the Prime Minister:

> She [Indira Gandhi] is a shrewd woman, these are vote-getting tactics. Showing the poor she is on their side. . . . Remember when her pappy was Prime Minister and he made her president of Congress Party? At once she began encouraging the demands of separate Maharashtra. How much bloodshed, how much rioting she caused. And today we have that bloody Shiv Sena, wanting to make the rest of us into second-class citizens. Don't forget, she started it all by supporting the racist buggers. (39)

He even attributed the bad manners of 'dubbawalla' to the rise of communal parties such as Shiv Sena.

> What to do with such low class people? No manners, no sense, nothing. And you know who is responsible for this attitude—that bastard Shiv Sena leader who worships Hitler and Mussolini. He and his 'Maharashtra for Maharashtrians,' nonsense They won't stop till they have complete Maratha Raj. (73)
>
> Dinshawji further expressed his concern using his characteristic use of slang:
>
> 'Wait till the Marathas take over, then we will have real Gandoo Raj. . . . All they know is to have rallies at Shivaji Park, shout slogans, make threats, and change road names. . . . Why change the names? . . . Hutatma Chowk!' He spat out the words disgustedly. 'What is wrong with Flora Fountain?' (74)

A fearful family man, Gustad had always tried to remain free from controversies. He was never vocal about the demands of minority people, but his anxiety was always there. He chose to be safe when fanatics were concerned. He remembered how a peaceful rally turned to be violent.

> Like all riots, it had started with a peaceful rally. A vast congregation of sadhus wielding staffs, tridents, and various other equally sanctified religious instruments, staged a demonstration outside Parliament House to protest against cow slaughter. Familiar with modern trends in political campaigning and public relations, they also brought along a herd of cows. Slogans were raised, banners

> unfurled, curses showered on Government personnel: drums, bells, horns, cymbals added to the clamour; and the gentle creatures in their midst began lowing nervously. The wrath of the gods was invoked upon the murderers of sacred Gomata, and suddenly, quite inexplicably, the gathering turned violent. (221)

The comic-serious tone of the description fits in with the mood of the novel that projects serious matters through ironic statements that provoke laughter. Though the Parsis like to be confined to their community, they also have a strong urge to be recognized as Indians. Thus when Dinshaw sang songs to please Roshan in the party and Gustad proposed that he should be called poet laureate, Dinshawji said, "Laureate-baureate nothing. I am a son of mother India. Call me Kavi Kamal, the Indian Tennyson!" (47)

Rohinton Mistry has given an elaborate description of the rituals which are observed after the demise of a Parsi man. Gustad attended the dead body of Dinshawji on the way to the Tower of Silence and remained in the prayer bungalows till the function was over. He also attended the funeral ceremony of Bilimoria. Through Gustad's participation in rituals and his observations of prayers Mistry has described the tit-bits of the Parsi culture in the novel. The dead body is taken to the prayer bungalows in a special van known as *HEARSE*. Before the prayer starts, the dead body has to be cleansed in the traditional method which is known as *suchkaar* and ablutions. After cleansing the body it is covered with white cloth and laid on the marble platform. The priest first lights a lamp and then holds a sliver of sandalwood, dipped in oil, to the flame. Then the priest starts prayer. As Gustad observed that everything proceeded efficiently, he was astonished at the routine work. "It was as if Dinshawji died everyday." The soft prayer was soothing.

> The *dustoorji* prayed beautifully. Each word emerged clear and full-toned, pure, as if shaped for the first time by human lips. And Gustad, lost in his thoughts, began to listen. It sounded so soothing. Such a wonderful voice. Soft, smooth, rich as velvet

> The dustoorji was not praying loudly, yet, little by little, in ever-increasing circles, his voice touched every point of the prayer room. . . . A dim bulb burned outside on the verandah. . . . Inside, the oil lamp cast its soft glow on Dinshawji's face moved in waves with the movement of the flame. On his face light and shadow played like little children, touching it gently, now here, and now there.
>
> The prayers filled the dark room slowly. Slowly, the prayer sound was the dark room. And before he was aware of it, Gustad was under its gentle spell. He forgot the time. . . . He listened to the music, the song in a language which he did not understand, but which was wonderfully soothing. All his life he had uttered by rote the words of this dead language, comprehending not one of them while mouthing his prayers. But tonight, in the dustoorji's soft and gentle music, the words were alive; tonight he came closer than he ever had to understanding the ancient meanings. (247-48)

The description quoted above is not just a record of Parsi ritual, but a revelation of a spiritual experience gained through the music of an ancient language that has an enchanting power over the soul. As the soul is enchanted by the verses of the ancient Avesta, the human soul feels that the incantations merge with the sounds of Nature. "And as the notes and syllables were intoned, they mingled with the sounds of night. Steadily from the trees and bushes rose the voices of night and nature, and from all the lush vegetation that grew here on the hill, around the Tower of Silence." (248) Here is a new understanding of the impact of an age-old religion that had taught man lessons of adaptability and broadness of mind. As Zoroastrianism sees no difference between man and nature, it dictated that after death the human body would directly merge into nature through the process of being eaten up by vultures.

Mistry makes an elaborate discussion on the topic in the form of a debate raging between the reformists and the orthodox while describing the funeral of Major Bilimoria. There are complaints against the Parsi practice of using vultures for eating up dead bodies. It is said that pieces of human flesh left by the vultures fall on the balconies and roofs of buildings and cause nuisance. Mistry presents a discussion among the Parsis in regard to this rumour. The bereaved insisted that the Punchayet do something about it. They said that the vultures should be properly trained, or more vultures should be brought for consuming the entire flesh inside the well. The reformists wanted to bring a change in the process. "The orthodox defence was the age-old wisdom that it was a pure method, defiling none of God's good creations: earth, water, air and fire. Every scientist, local or foreign, who had taken the trouble to examine the procedure, using modern hygienic standards, sang its praises. But the reformists, who favoured cremation, insisted that the way of the ancients was unsuitable for the twentieth century. Such a ghoulish system, they said, ill became a community with a progressive reputation and a forward-thinking attitude. The orthodox camp (or vulturists, as their opponents called them) countered that reformists had their own axe to grind in legitimizing cremation—they had relatives in foreign lands without access to Towers of Silence. Moreover, the controversy was a massive fraud cooked up by those who owned shares in crematoria, they charged." (317) There is in fact no end to this controversy. And Mistry did not project his own views on the issue. He only offered a realistic picture of the Parsi community, of the conflicts and differences among the Parsis on their funeral process.

Such a Long Journey centralizes the Parsi community as do Firdaus Kanga's *Trying to Grow*, Farrukh Dhondy's *Bombay Duck* and Bapsi Sidhwa's *The Crow Eaters.* All these works display their authors' consciousness of their community through the protagonists who belong to the community. In *Such a Long Journey*, the Parsi enclave 'Khodadad Building' emerges as the background and all the residents of the building are Parsis whose presence beneath the narrative structure of the novel is strongly felt. Their way of life, distinct from the majority, their anguish at the changing pattern of communal relationship and their nostalgia for the good old days are exhibited in such a way that they emerge as Parsis on personal level and as human beings of flesh and blood on a broader level. A graphic description of certain customs and rituals related to the Parsi community happily merges with the Indian sensibility expressed in the novel. Thus the novel with its vast canvas of Indian life including Indian politics is a Parsi novel as well as an Indian novel representing the ups and downs in the life of an average Indian.

NOTES

1. Eminent Parsi literary critic Nilufer Bharucha observes, "These unequal conditions provided fertile breeding ground for feelings of ambivalence and alienation from the host country. This ambivalence and alienation became exacerbated during the colonial period, when the Parsis were among the first to embrace English language education and become the most westernized Indian community. Most Parsis, thus felt bereft at the end of the Empire and the resultant loss of the special/elite status they had enjoyed during the colonial period. Several migrated to the west in the 1950s and 60s." 'The Parsi Voice in Recent Indian English Fiction: An Assertion of Ethnic Identity,' V. Sarang and N. Bharucha, ed., *Indian English Fiction* 1980-1990: *An Assessment* (Delhi: B.R.), p. 358.
2. *We the Nation: The Lost Decades* (New Delhi: UBSPD, 1994), p. 317.
3. In a presentation made to Vision TV of Canada on 26 May 1995, Keki B. Shroff showed how Zoroastrian ideas have played a vital role in the development of western thought. The list of common beliefs was presented by him.

Structure of *Such a Long Journey*

The structure of a novel is often used in the sense of 'form' and thus becomes synonymous with the plot in a novel. Structuralist critics, on the other hand, conceive of a literary structure on the model of the systematic way that a language is structured. In the present context, structure of a literary work means, to quote R.S. Crane, a rendering of all its component materials and parts into "a beautiful and effective whole of a determinate kind."[1] That is, the chapter seeks to investigate whether Rohinton Mistry's emphasis on Parsi sentiments as well as contemporary reality and his postcolonial stand as a writer merge happily with the story, or to be specific, with the plot that starts with some rising problems and end with denouements.

Such a Long Journey has a traditional plot-pattern. Despite occasional use of remembrances of things past, it maintains the chronological method of describing incidents. It begins with Gustad Noble's early Morning Prayer—he offered his orisons to Ahura Mazda displaying 'kusti' prayer—and with the awakening of the tenants in Parsi enclave 'Khodadad Building' who became engaged with their daily activities. The mood of happiness prevailed till the Noble family made arrangements for a family celebration. Gustad lived with his wife Dilnavaz and three children. The older ones were sons, Sohrab and Darius, and Roshan, the youngest child in the family, was their only daughter. Sohrab had qualified in the I.I.T. entrance much to his father's gratification, and Gustad purchased a live chicken to celebrate his success as well as Roshan's birthday. Gustad's purchasing live chicken was prompted by nostalgia. His father had a big book store in the city and he had enjoyed a prestigious position. He could therefore afford to go to Crawford Market for live chickens, accompanied by servants. For Gustad, a mere bank clerk, it was luxury and he felt humiliated to carry the chicken home. Yet he took the trouble because Sohrab had created new hopes in his mind. The prospect of his being an engineer meant that Gustad's marginalized condition in the society was coming to an end, that the family would once again be honoured. Moreover, Roshan was his most favourite child and he had always wanted to do something special for her. But the joyous mood was over as Sohrab refused to be enrolled as a student in the I.I.T. and behaved rudely with Gustad in the presence of his friend Dinshawji, who was the only guest in the celebration party. Gustad's conflict with his eldest son aggravated and it ended in Sohrab's leaving home. This was the first problem that Gustad had to face. The other two problems were also common family problems; Roshan had to suffer for a long time for some problems in the intestine, and Darius developed an infatuation for the daughter of their neighbour Mr. Rabadi who visited Gustad's flat repeatedly to complain against Darius. The first two problems were seriously taken by Gustad and Dilnavaz who tried their best to get relieved of the problems and suffered till the end of the novel when these were solved. Dilnavaz's involvement in black magic, as she was prompted by the old dame Ms. Kutpitia residing in the 'Khodadad Building,' is closely related to these problems from which Dilnavaz wanted badly to be relieved.

But the outer problem, with which Gustad's life was entangled, was related to the contemporary political scenario. In the beginning of the novel, Gustad remembered his friend Major Bilimoria who had lived in Khodadad Building and who was like his own brother and yet who left the building suddenly without telling him where he was going. Much to Gustad's grief, Bilimoria had not even written to him explaining his behaviour. Suddenly, he was surprised to get a letter from Bilimoria who requested him to receive a parcel on his behalf, though everything was kept in the dark. Bilimoria only wrote that he was not at liberty to tell him all the details except that it was a matter of national security. He only referred to his secret work with the government after leaving the army. After much thought, Gustad replied to Bilimoria expressing his willingness to accept the parcel. In his second letter Bilimoria wrote that he was working for RAW and also hinted at India's war with Pakistan. He also gave full instructions about how Gustad would collect the parcel from a book-stall in Chor Bazaar. In the manner of a detective story, it was written that Gustad would have to find out which bookstall had displayed *Complete Works of Shakespeare*. And in order to be absolutely certain that he had reached the right shop, he was to open the book to *Othello*, end of Act I, scene iii, where Iago gives advice to Roderigo. If the line 'Put money in thy purse' was underlined in red, it was sure that the shop was the right one. Though there were fears to be in a false position, Gustad stuck to the point that "a friend cannot be let down." Mistry describes Gustad's adventure in detail and maintains suspense effectively. Another surprise was waiting for Gustad after he found out the right shop. The man who carried the parcel was none but the taxi-driver who had carried him home after his hip was broken in a road accident long ago and whom he had seen few days back on a Lambretta that was crashed by a car. The man was still bandaged for the wounds he received during the accident. Gustad expressed his gratitude that had been due for a long time and took tea offered by him. He learnt that his name was Ghulam Mohammed who still remembered Sohrab who had accompanied Gustad on the day of the accident.

The real trouble started after the parcel was opened and the instructions given inside were read. The parcel contained ten lakh rupees and Gustad was instructed to deposit the amount in the account of some Mira Obili. Dilnavaz was so afraid that she asked Gustad to return the money as soon as possible. Gustad also thought of returning the money. But the immediate problem was to keep the money in some secret place. Gustad and Dilnavaz chose a rejected oven in the kitchen and kept the money, wrapped in black plastic, inside it. Yet the matter was leaked out by the idiot, Tehmul, who saw the heaps of money from outside the window and told others about what he saw in spite of Gustad's instruction not to tell anybody about the matter. Gustad was relieved that though persons like Inspector Bamji had known about it, they never believed in Tehmul's utterances. Gustad's problems increased as he could not find Ghulam Mohammed. He left notes to the address given to him by Ghulam on the day of money transfer, but got no reply. The money was with him causing continuous tension. To add fuel to the fire, someone flung a big rat with its head severed from his body in the bushes in front of his flat in the dead of night, and after a few days a cat was flung in the same spot in a similar way. Gustad could understand that all this was done by Ghulam only after he received a paper in which someone was threatened for stealing Bilimoria's rice. He understood that he had no other way but to deposit the money as per instruction. At last he consulted his friend Dinshawji who came forward to help him knowing that the money was meant for the 'Mukti Bahini.' It was decided that every day Gustad would bring rupees ten thousand in a packet and Dinshawji would deposit the amount. It was going on much to Gustad's anxiety. Gustad's anxiety ran parallel with the nationwide anxiety and security measure for the war with Pakistan. "For several weeks the threnodic siren had been wailing every morning at exactly ten o'clock: a full three-minute warning, followed by the monotonic all-clear. . . . Like some gigantic bird of mourning in the skies above the city, circling, diving and wheeling, it drowned the traffic noises." (143) It was also the time when Gustad had to tackle the problems at home, paying repeated visits to Dr. Paymaster for Roshan's treatment. A new turn came to the plot when it was published in the newspaper that Major Bilimoria had been convicted for impersonating the P.M.'s voice while telephoning the chief cashier in a branch of SBI, and for taking sixty lakh rupees. It was a bolt from the blue for Gustad, and also for Dinshawji whose ideals of nationalism were shattered. The two friends now decided to stop depositing money. Gustad went to see Ghulam to the place the address of which he had with him. Ghulam insisted on the speedy return of the money. Thereon Gustad told Dinshawji about Ghulam's demand and Dinshawji was ready to take the risk of withdrawing the money part by part. He had been ill for a long time, and it was a coincidence that he was hospitalized after the entire money was withdrawn. Gustad returned the money to Ghulam who now behaved properly and also requested Gustad to see Bilimoria in Delhi jail. Gustad turned down the idea this time, but after Ghulam went to his flat with the same request and also with tickets for Delhi, Gustad decided to go to Delhi and see Bilimoria. His conversation with Bilimoria who was seriously ill and was kept in jail hospital, clarified the entire matter and the link between Gustad's problem and the political scenario was established.

It came out from Bilimoria's confession to Gustad that he had been trapped by Indira Gandhi who used him for taking sixty lakh rupees from the bank, presumably for helping the 'Mukti Bahini,' and actually for meeting her selfish interest. When Bilimoria could know that the money he gave was re-routed by PM's office, he felt frustrated at the corruption in the highest place. Ghulam was employed by him that time for investigating and verifying the matter, and there was an attempt at his life. Ghulam's 'accident' is thus explained by Bilimoria as outcome of a murder plan by the corrupt politicians and the plot of the novel takes a cohesive form. The mystery of ten lakh rupees was also solved when Bilimoria confessed that after being convinced that the huge amount taken for helping the 'Mukti Bahini' in Bangladesh was consumed by the P.M., he decided to take aside ten lakh rupees for his friends like Gustad who were actually in need of money. Bilimoria had no family of his own and there was no cause to disbelieve him. Bilimoria thought that having received fifty lakh rupees, the P.M. might neglect ten lakh rupees. But this did not happen; he was arrested for ten lakh rupees and was pressurized in jail through torture for returning that ten lakh rupees immediately. This also explains why Ghulam was so keen on getting the money back and threatened Gustad in various ways. Bilimoria hoped that once the money was returned he would also be set free after four years. This hope was also shattered as he died in hospital. The plot is thus skilfully woven; the personal problems of Gustad and the external incidents of Bangladesh War that offered scope for corruption happily merge together. And this happy blending served Rohinton Mistry's purpose of taking revenge on Indira Gandhi for besmearing the Parsi community through the Nagarwala case of 1960s. Mistry felt that the story was waiting to be told by the side of historiographical account which might have been just peripheral or must have excluded it deliberately to please the centre of power, and he centralized it in his narrative.

The major problem faced by Gustad in the novel—there was real fear of his being caught with the huge amount for which he could even lose his job—was solved after he could return the money and the mystery came to light after Gustad met Bilimoria in jail. Among the minor problems faced by Gustad, Roshan got cured after going through a long process of treatment under Dr. Paymaster, and Sohrab also came back home. For Sohrab's return Dilnavaz performed some black magic prescribed and supervised by Ms. Kutpitia who was known in the neighbourhood as the old witch. Dilnavaz's concern for her son led her to believe in what the old woman said. She explained that Sohrab had developed something wrong in his brain and if another person was made ready on whom that wrong thing could be thrust, Ms. Kutpitia knew how to transfer the wrong thing from Sohrab's brain to that person's. Tehmul, the idiot, was chosen for transfer and Ms. Kutpitia actually performed something funny with a lizard in her own room in the presence of Tehmul. And very soon Tehmul was killed, as he went to catch a flying brick during the conflict between the police and the 'morcha' people. Gustad was so moved by the death that he alone carried the heavy body of Tehmul to his brother's flat and began to recite prayer, placing the right hand on Tehmul's head. He was as if in a trance and just at this time Sohrab entered the room, calling 'father.' Gustad turned around and hugged him tightly. Sohrab had already learnt of the troubles Gustad had undergone and was asked by his mother to behave properly. The incidents of the day brought him close to his father, but the reunion of the father and the son over the dead body of Tehmul comes out as a direct outcome of Ms. Kutpitia's black magic. The readers are intrigued by the author and fail to understand what he is up to. In a tricky way, the author only makes casual remarks such as "Or coincidence. But what did it matter, the result was the same. Besides, was there a person alive who, at one time or another, did not find it difficult to disbelieve completely in things supernatural?" (275) Mistry keeps a blank space in his novel intentionally; after the performance of the magic by Ms. Kutpitia, Dilnavaz is totally forgotten. The readers eagerly wait for Dilnavaz's reaction after Tehmul's death, at the cost of which, according to Ms. Kutpitia's demand, Sohrab's return was possible. But Dilnavaz never appeared after Tehmul's death and it is not learnt how shocked she was. Leaving the matter to the readers' imagination, Mistry winds up the plot. At the end of the novel Gustad's crisis is over. He is relieved of fear after returning the money to Ghulam, and his lost faith in humanity is restored after he learns the truth from Bilimoria. It is so painful for him to know that his friend Bilimoria was involved in a fraud case. The truth about Bilimoria restored peace to his mind. Of course, he had to accept that corruption at the highest place was not a mere rumour. Gustad's development as a human being is evident in his dealings with Tehmul. He even found in the idiot's face a blissful smile and thought that "Tehmul's picture would fit right in among the others upon the black wall." (309) With this realization Gustad could now ignore in which college Sohrab was going to be admitted. The loss of two faithful friends—Dinshawji and Bilimoria—taught him some basic truths of life. The apparently irrelevant incidents such as details of prayers and Gustad's feelings towards nature are not irrelevant in reality—these are introduced to highlight Gustad's heightened consciousness. Mistry tried his best to present an integrated whole and he succeeds.

Rohinton Mistry's innovative way of integrating India's war with Pakistan into Gustad's private life deserves praise. There are also attempts to link the outside incidents with the personal ones. The year of India-China war (1962) was also the year of Roshan's birth. Gustad's terrible accident also took place that year. It is remembered that Dinshawji's gall-bladder operation and the death of India's Prime Minister Lal Bahadur Shastri took place at the same time (197). Dr. Paymaster had the tendency to relate diseases to political troubles. He believed that politics, economics, religious problems, domestic strife, all could be dealt with methodically: one is required to observe the symptoms, make the diagnosis, prescribe medicine and offer the prognosis. But he also believed that just as some diseases of the human body were incurable, there were diseases of countries, of families, of theological dogma, that had fatal outcomes. He made a humorous comment while relating Roshan's disease to Bangladesh War: "Sometimes, of course, even a case of diarrhoea can be worrying. Look at East Pakistan—a patient with a simple sickness, but very difficult to cure. A patient in critical condition, needing the intensive care unit." (164) Dr. Paymaster's intuition is revealing and helps one understand the structure of the novel. In *Midnight's Children,* Rushdie made an elaborate study of contemporary Indian history, relating his characters to the major historical events of their time. Rohinton Mistry's characters are not however related to political incidents in the same way. But there are attempts to relate some political events to personal ones. Gustad's problems ran parallel with India-Pakistan conflicts that resulted in Bangladesh War. Gustad's personal problems and their cure are coincidences, but his trouble with the money was directly related to Bangladesh War. If there were no Bangladesh War, there would be no refugee problem and the occasion of raising funds for 'Mukti Bahini' would not arise. And in that case there would have been no problem for Gustad. Rohinton Mistry's clear and unbiased visions, his analysis of the political tensions and his capacity to delve deep beneath the surface have enabled him to project almost a flawless structure.

The compound wall of the Khodadad Building serves as a symbol that is closely related to the plot of the narrative. At the beginning of the novel there was apprehension that the wall would be broken for broadening the road. The owner as well as the tenants of the building gave a joint petition to the municipality against the proposal, and yet the wall was broken all of a sudden, after it had been decorated with portraits of gods and saints belonging to all the religions. In the very first chapter Gustad expressed his concern over the matter.

> A notice was pasted to the pillar, while a shining black oil puddle marked the spot where the lorry had stopped. The official document from the municipality bulged in places with glue and air bubbles. . . . What was the need to widen the road? He measured the ground with hurried strides. The compound would shrink to less than half its present width. . . . More a prison camp than a building, all cooped up like sheep or chickens. With the road noise and nuisance so much closer. (16)

Gustad consoled himself with the thought that it was just a proposal and nothing would come of it. He was sure that the landlord would not give away half of his compound for the 'fair market value' that the municipality offered. Gustad was right in thinking that the landlord would oppose. When Gustad was tortured by the problems of one lakh rupees and of Roshan's illness, Tehmul showed him thirty copies of petition letters to be signed by the tenants which together would be submitted by the landlord. Gustad was assured that the municipality would no more be able to widen the road and so he invited the pavement artist to paint portraits of gods and saints on the wall. And when the compound wall took the shape of a roadside shrine, the municipality labourers came with government order to break the wall. In the last chapter of the novel, the mishap that took Tehmul's life was caused by an encounter between the police and the municipal labourers on the one side and the 'morcha' people protesting against the Municipality on the other. The breaking up of the compound wall helps the author to wind up his narrative.

> The workers had started chiselling out the mortar between the stone slabs. . . . The labourers set up a vigorous chant, full of muscle and vitality. . . . A truck of gravel and sand was being unloaded. . . . Crunching, grating, rasping as men with shovels trampled through the gravel. The sound made Gustad freeze for a moment. . . . Presently, the first huge block of black stone, the one with the Trimurti, was levered off with crowbars and sent crashing to the ground. (338)

The compound wall is thus integrated with the development of the plot and adds charm to the narrative.

Finally, the role of the pavement artist and the journey motif, made explicit in the title, epigraph and also in some scattered remarks, are happily blended with the structure of the novel. Gustad had invited the pavement artist for painting some portraits on the compound wall of the Khodadad Building that had continuously been made dirty by the people in the locality. The project worked wonderfully. The compound wall was first cleansed and then the pavement artist painted portraits of gods, goddesses and saints taken from different religions. Instead of using the side of the wall as a lavatory, the people began to worship the gods and saints painted on the wall. The stink was replaced by the fragrance of flowers and incense sticks offered to the gods and saints. And the pavement artist also received some money from the people and started replacing the crayon painting with oil painting. But his idea of bringing permanence was foiled after the municipality workers started breaking the wall for the acquisition of the land by the municipality. This plan of the municipality, again, was designed long ago and the owner of the house had submitted petition, duly signed by all the tenants, in protest against this plan. Tehmul was given the charge of distributing the papers to each tenant for signature and he had the occasions to visit Gustad in his flat for this reason. And Tehmul had to die at the time of breaking the wall. All the incidents are thus perfectly linked to the structure of the novel which becomes enriched with ideas. The destruction of the wall develops the idea that nothing is permanent in this world and so the pavement artist left the material for oil painting when he started his journey again. When Gustad asked him where he was going, he said, "In a world where roadside latrines become temples and shrines become dust and ruin, does it matter where?" (338) As Gustad told him that he forgot to take the box containing materials for oil-painting, he said, "I have taken everything I need for my journey. My box of crayons is in here." (339)

The journey motif, made explicit through his last remarks, is suggestive of Gustad's spiritual journey towards the fulfilment of human feelings and also of the journey of the Parsis who left their land in the eighth century.

NOTE

1. *The Language of Criticism and the Structure of Poetry* (1953; ch.1). A leader of the Chicago school of criticism, R.S. Crane revived and developed the concept of form in Aristotle's *Poetics*.

Contemporary History in *Such a Long Journey*

The famous philosopher Friedrich Nietzsche (1844-1900) observed, "The historical sense in our time forms a sixth sense, pervading the philosophy, history and culture of modern era."[1] A serious author of twentieth century could not avoid this historical sense. Moreover, history made up by the historians is often found insufficient and not real, because the historians are hardly provided with the freedom and scope necessary for truthful representation of events and characters. The political interruption is always there, compelling the historians to curtail that portion of his writing which goes against the interest of the concerned political leaders or heads of the states. Hence, Ezra Pound said, "Our knowledge of the past is marred by the omissions of the most vital faces."[2] The duty of a serious novelist is to supply those missing faces not, however, in a direct way that is the prerogative of the historians, but in an indirect way, mixing it up with imaginary events and situations. Rohinton Mistry uses history in his fiction both through direct comments of his characters and through supplying the missing faces in the form of imaginary characters. His historical sense is so intense that after migrating to Canada, he continued to write about India, focusing on the contemporary history, apprehending that the writers in India were forced to reject some facts under repressive regime.

Such a Long Journey is set in the early Seventies when India had to be involved in war with Pakistan that led to the creation of a new country, Bangladesh. Indira Gandhi was the Prime Minister of India at that time and there were rumours about her secret activities which could not be officially proved. Through the feelings and apprehensions of some Parsi characters Mistry reveals those secret activities and through an imaginary character Major Bilimoria, he reconstructs the fraud case in which a Parsi gentleman Mr. Nagarwala was involved and for which the entire Parsi community felt humiliated. Mistry also brings in some historical events through the recollections of the characters. In the first chapter of the novel, Mistry introduces the flat of the protagonist Gustad Noble and refers to India's war with China in 1962.

> The room was dark like the others in the flat, with blackout paper taped over the glass panes of the windows and the ventilators. Gustad had put it nine years ago, the year of the war with China. How much happened that year, he thought. Roshan's birth, and then my terrible accident. . . . What a dreadful year 1962 had been. And such a humiliating defeat, everywhere people talking of nothing but the way the Chinese had advanced, as though Indian army consisted of tin soldiers. To think that till the very end both sides had been proclaiming peace and brotherhood. Especially Jawaharlal Nehru, with his favourite slogan, 'Hindi-Chinee bhai-bhai,' insisting that Chou En-lai was a brother, the two nations were great friends. And refusing to believe any talk of war, even though the Chinese had earlier invaded Tibet, positioning several divisions along the border. (9)

The duplicity of the political leaders and their greed are also rudely exposed. Fund-raising at the time of war or any natural calamity is a common practice in India, but it is never made clear to the public how the amount raised through collections from the poor and the underpaid is spent. Mistry ironically renders the practice of fund-raising by the Indian politicians.

> Teams of fund-raising politicians toured the neighbourhood. Depending on which party they belonged to, they made speeches praising the Congress government's heroic stance or denouncing its incompetency for sending brave Indian jawans, with outdated weapons and summer clothing, to die in the Himalayas at Chinese hands. Every political party unleashed flag-emblazoned lorries to crisscross the city with banners that were paradigms of ingenuity: weaving together support for the party and support for the soldiers,

> while fund-raisers shouted themselves hoarse through megaphones, exhorting people to be as selfless as the jawans who were reddening the Himalayan snow with their precious blood to defend Bharat Mata. (10)

The novel also reveals that some of the articles received from the people as donation to war-fund, were displayed in the Chor Bazaar.

Explaining his views on writing novels based on his own experiences, V.S. Naipaul wrote that for every kind of experience there is a proper form. "Fiction works best in a confined moral and cultural area, where the rulers are generally known; and in that area it deals best with things—emotions, impulses, moral anxieties—that would be unseizable or incomplete in other literary forms."[3] This observation is applicable to *Such a Long Journey* in which Rohinton Mistry expresses his personal emotions and impulses in regard to the leaders in India through his created characters who share the same ancestry and background with the author. Naipaul reminded his readers: "Tolstoy used fiction to bring the siege of Sebastopol closer, to give it an added reality."[4] Mistry also adds an added reality by inserting the strong emotions of the characters which add an extra dimension to dry historical facts. He writes,

> The country's beloved Panditji, everyone's Chacha Nehru, the unflinching humanist, the great visionary, turned bitter and rancorous [after the Chinese War]. From now on, he would brook no criticism, take no advice. With his appetite for philosophy and dreams lost for ever, he resigned himself to political intrigues and internal squabbles, although signs of his tyrannical ill temper and petulance had emerged even before the China war. His feud with his son-in-law, the thorn in his political side, was well known. Nehru never forgave Feroze Gandhi for exposing scandals in the government; he no longer had any use for defenders of the downtrodden and champions of the poor, roles he had himself once played with great gusto and tremendous success. His one overwhelming obsession now was, how his darling daughter Indira, the only one, he claimed, who loved him truly, who had even abandoned her worthless husband in order to be with her father—how to ensure

> that she would become Prime Minister after him. This monomaniacal fixation occupied his days and nights, days and nights which the treachery of Chou En-lai had blighted for ever. (11)

This is not just a record of facts, but the strong sentiment of the Parsi community, humiliated and belittled at the hands of a corrupt government.

Lal Bahadur Shastri, who became India's Prime Minister upon Nehru's death, is however praised in the novel. It was hoped that the stagnant waters of the government would at last be freshened and vitalized, despite the sceptics who said that such a short man would not be able to command respect on the world stage. In the 1964 war with Pakistan he fared much better than Nehru had in the war with China. After Shastriji's untimely death there were rumours that it was not natural death. But no historian could ever report that rumour, as it was not 'official' news. Rohinton Mistry's concern was the whole of cultural-political-social condition of India and that is why he includes the rumour in his novel.

> While the crowds cheered, Shastri boarded a plane for Tashkent where Kosygin had offered to negotiate a peace between India and Pakistan. The night the Tashkent Declaration was signed, Shastri died on Soviet soil, less than eighteenth months after he became Prime Minister. Some said he had been killed by the Pakistanis, and others suspected a Russian plot. Some even claimed it was the new Prime Minister's supporters who poisoned Shastri, so that her father's dynastic-democratic dream could finally come true. (114)

India's war with Pakistan becomes bright and real as the details of the war were told as stories by Major Bilimoria, an ex-military man, to the children, Sohrab and Darius. For the young listeners, the stories quickly acquired the status of legend, with their Major Uncle the legendary hero who fought so well that the cowardly Pakistanis turned tail and ran.

Wars with China and Pakistan were past history as per the novel's setting. The incidents in the novel are set in the Bangladesh war. Dinshawji expressed the apathetic attitude of the big brothers, America and Russia towards the suffering of the poor Bangladeshi people in his characteristic way:

> Have you seen all the pictures in the newspaper? Bloody butchers, slaughtering left and right. And look at the whole world, completely relaxed, doing nothing. Where is *maader chod* America now? Not saying one word. Otherwise, if Russia even belches, America protests at the U.N. Let Kosygin fart, and America moves a motion in the Security Council. (76)

When Sohrab commented that Indira Gandhi used RAW like a private police force, sending men from RAW to spy on opposition parties and to create trouble, Gustad refused to accept his remarks as truth. Those were mere rumours, he said. And he was sorry that his son was spreading rumours at a time when the enemy was at the border. "That Pakistani drunkard Yahya was cooking something in partnership with China, and fools like her son went around saying rubbish about the Prime Minister." (93) Ironically, Gustad realized through his own experiences that whatever Sohrab had told and whatever had been written on the pages of the newspaper, were all true. The sufferings that Gustad had undergone after accepting Bilimoria's packet of money and the information he gathered from Bilimoria's confession changed his attitude to Indira Gandhi. A historian has no such opportunity to show how the common people lost faith in the existing system of governance. But a novelist has, and that is why a novelist is empowered to enrich his fiction with what Naipaul called 'an added reality.' Gustad's fear that if he would not deposit the amount, the lives of his children were at stake, changed his attitude to RAW immediately. He said to Dilnavaz, "We are dealing with heartless people—poisonous snakes. It could have been Roshan and Darius instead of the bandicoot and cat. . . . I suppose we should be grateful to Jimmy for that." (142) Gustad's criticism of the government institutions is not therefore his biased view, but the result of his experience.

Gustad's conversation with Bilimoria in jail is all about Indira Gandhi's corrupt practice. And this is revealed not by a reporter but by a victim of that corrupt practice and is therefore more convincing than any report in newspapers. Bilimoria said,

> 'She [Indira Gandhi] was using RAW like her own private agency. Spying on opposition parties, ministers . . . any one. For blackmail. Made me sick. Even spying on her own cabinet. . . . Bribes, thievery . . . so much going on, Gustad. RAW kept dossiers. On her friends and enemies. Where they went, who they met, what they said, what they ate, what they drank.' Jimmy broke off, gasping. Despite his condition, his fondness for rhetoric would not let him trim the story beyond a certain point of leanness. . . .
>
> 'Soldiers slaughtered thousands of demonstrators. Refugees came. . . . My superior told me our government will help guerrilla movement. Rightaway I said I was interested. So Prime Minister's office called me for interview. . . . What close control she keeps on RAW. Strong woman, Gustad, very strong woman . . . very intelligent. . . . She put me in charge. Training and supplying the Mukti Bahini.' (270-71)

Bilimoria could not complete his statement in one try. He was very weak and there was the effect of injection. He became delirious for sometime and then again he started. While working in Bangladesh he understood that money was the main thing for the soldiers and so he had no doubt in the Prime Minister's intention when she told him to see the chief cashier in a State Bank and introduce himself as Bangladeshi Babu. Bilimoria was instructed not to disclose his RAW identity. He did what he was asked to do and received sixty lakh rupees. The Prime Minister again called him to her office and said that she had enemies everywhere who would gather information that she collected money and who would not bother to see if the money was spent for good purpose. They would destabilize the government and the country would suffer as a result, she said. Bilimoria was then asked to write on a paper that he had imitated the P.M.'s voice and received the money for helping the 'Mukti Bahini' in Bangladesh. She also assured him that there was nothing for him to be afraid of, and he agreed like a fool. He also confessed that after he could know that the money was not used for the Mukti Bahini, he was disappointed and frustrated. He then put aside ten lakh rupees for helping his poor friends and for that he was convicted. Only after that ten lakh rupees were returned, he had the hope of being released after four years. Gustad had already learnt from Ghulam that there was no hope of his release and soon after Bilimoria was dead. Such a gruesome story records the actual incident that is always bypassed in history.

Historians hardly record anything that goes against the contemporary regime. Thus if a historian is entitled to write a history of the time of Indira Gandhi, he may not write how the new rules introduced in her time were criticized by the common people. But it was part of Mistry's plan that the entire political atmosphere of India at that time should enter into the corpus of his text. Indira Gandhi's nationalization of banks was directly criticized by Dinshawji.

> "What days those were, *yaar*. What fun we used to have." Dinshawji touched the corners of his lips to wipe the foam. "Parsis were the kings of banking in those days. Such respect we used to get. Now the whole atmosphere only has been spoiled. Ever since that Indira nationalized the banks."
>
> Gustad topped up Dinshawji's glass. "Nowhere in the world has nationalization worked. What can you say to idiots?"
>
> "Believe me," said Dinshawji, "she is a shrewd woman, these are vote-getting tactics. Showing the poor she is on their side. *Saali* always up to some mischief. Remember when her pappy was Prime Minister and he made her president of Congress Party? At once she began encouraging the demands for a separate Maharashtra. How much bloodshed, how much rioting she caused. And today we have that bloody Shiv Sena, wanting to make the rest of us into second class citizens. Don't forget, she started it all by supporting the racist buggers." (39)

Indira's financing of her son's Maruti car manufacture and the secret of Swiss bank account are also introduced in the way of discourse.

The wretched condition of the country is also exposed through the views of other characters. Dr. Paymaster said,

> Imagine that our beloved country is a patient with gangrene at an advanced stage. Dressing the wound or sprinkling rose-water over it to hide the stink of rotting tissue is useless. Fine words and promises will not cure the patient. The decaying part must be excised. You see, the municipal corruption is merely the bad smell, which will disappear as soon as the gangrenous government at the centre is removed. (313)

Corruption in government institutions is a reality in India and Mistry exposes that reality in his novel. Gustad's experience in the railway station is one example. Through Gustad's sensitive reactions to his surrounding an intimate view of life is rendered that also provides a holistic picture of perceived reality. A post-colonial writer, Mistry has a clear of view of his responsibility to art. He achieves a fusion between fact and fiction that attracts the readers' attention to contemporary history. He accepts those parts of history which he thinks necessary for exposing the kind of reality targeted by him. *Such a Long Journey* ends with the construction of Bangladesh as an independent country which also brings relief to Indian society. A vast canvas of Indian life in the background of certain explosive chapters of Indian politics is viewed and reviewed in the novel.

In her article 'Writing the Diaspora' Uma Parameswaran writes that among several characteristics and qualities of the literature of the Indian Diaspora, she has noticed a peculiar quality: "the Diaspora writers seem to set their works in India, rather than in their new homeland." She also writes, "I have always valued the interconnections between literature and society."[5] Mistry's novels approve of her remark. In *Such a Long Journey,* he sought to reveal the contemporary Indian history, particularly those hidden portions that had been evaded by others. In the beginning of the novel, 'history' gets transmuted through the gaps in the narrative; but as the narrative proceeds 'history' becomes a part of it. Mistry dares to project history in a naked manner (Indira Gandhi is mentioned by name) and connects it with the fictional character (Major Bilimoria) in such a way that the readers get confused for sometime to decide if they would take the narrative as non-fiction. But ultimately there is no doubt that it is a great work of fiction that includes vivid portraits of personalities, panoramic sweeps of Indian cities and life-style.

NOTES

1. "Beyond Good and Evil," *The Complete Works of Friedrich Nietzsche*, ed. Oscar Leuy (Edinburgh: Edinburgh University Press, 1923), p. 167.
2. "Some Recent Directions in American Cultural History," *American Historical Review,* LXXIII, Feb. 1968, p. 200.
3. 'Reading and Writing, a Personal Account,' *Literary Occasions* (Picador, 2003), p. 24.
4. *Ibid.*
5. "Writing in Diaspora," *The Atlantic Literary Review*, Vol. 1, No. 2, p. 164.

Characterization in *Such a Long Journey*

Rohinton Mistry is a skilful artist who has developed the art of character-sketch and has raised it to a height that is hardly surpassed. In most cases he follows the dramatic method of introducing the character through his/her activities and through the conversation in which the character takes part. This method is integrated with elements of interior monologue which help the creation of life-like characters. *Such a Long Journey* projects a good number of characters most of whom belong to the Parsi community. Only two characters, Malcolm and Ghulam Mohammed are from outside the Parsi community. Malcolm is Christian and Ghulam, Muslim. Hindus are not at the centre of the narrative, though they make their appearance as guest artists in such characters as the milkman who is noted for the tuft of hair in the middle of his shaven head.

Character of Gustad Noble

Gustad Noble is the protagonist of the novel *Such a Long Journey.* A middle aged, god-fearing man, Gustad is very fond of his family. He passed his childhood almost luxuriously. His father was the owner of a prestigious book-shop in the city of Bombay, but he lost everything when he was hospitalized leaving the sole responsibility of the business to his brother who came to be a nuisance. Gustad had to try hard to support his family from an early age. His parents did not survive long. When the novel starts, he is a tenant in a two-room flat in Khodadad Building where he lives with his wife Dilnavaz, two sons Sohrab and Darius, and only daughter Roshan. The narrative moves forward with Gustad's problems which are wound up towards the end of the novel.

The characteristic features of Gustad's character at the beginning of the novel may be stated as follows. An out-and-out Parsi, Gustad observed the Parsi rituals in detail. Though broadminded, he never deviated from his faith, as he believed that one's religion is not like one's dress that may be changed. His dreams and aspirations were quite modest and he was rather upset when those modest aspirations were denied by fate. He loved his children sincerely and his hip was broken when he tried to save his eldest son from an accident. He had much hope on his eldest son Sohrab who, he imagined, would save the family from the humiliating condition and so he was much disappointed when Sohrab refused to be enrolled in I.I.T. Gustad was a good friend. He accepted Bilimoria's proposal of depositing ten lakh rupees only out of gratitude for his old friend who had once helped him a lot. He had a strong moral sense and he was dutiful. The illness of Roshan was disheartening to him and he repeatedly went to Dr. Paymaster for her treatment.

Gustad was very fond of books. In his small cabinet he kept some old books which had been rescued from his father's bankrupt book-store. Whenever he would open that cabinet of treasure, "the rich, timeless fragrance rose from the precious pages, soothing his uneasy confused spirit." (53) He was even tempted to purchase books from Chor Bazaar where he went to search for the packet sent by Bilimoria. A simple man by nature, Gustad liked to believe others. And whenever he was disillusioned, he received rude shocks. Thus he was much shocked when Bilimoria left Khodadad Building without telling him anything. But whenever he received Bilimoria's letter requesting him to help, he helped him readily though it was risky for him. A friend's word cannot be let down, he said. When it came to his notice that Bilimoria was involved in a fraud case and was arrested, it took no time to change his mind. Yet he went to see Bilimoria in a jail in Delhi only to know the truth. He believed in whatever he heard from the ailing Bilimoria. And his faith in P.M. was shattered forever. Gustad's sincere love for Dinshawji, who took the risk of depositing ten lakh rupees for his sake, and for his good old friend Bilimoria who once saved his life, became explicit in his feelings when he attended the funeral parties for both his friends.

Gustad's personal problems were solved at the end of the novel. He got relieved from the crisis that was related to Major Bilimoria. Roshan recovered and Sohrab came back home. But in the meantime he had undergone a sea-change. Earlier he was rather selfish, concerned only with his own status. He aspired that Sohrab would become an engineer and the position of the family would be raised. Sohrab's refusal hurt him so much because he had been concerned only with his own aspirations, not with Sohrab's. He felt that his family was treated as the 'other'; he had not thought of other people who were inferior to him in all respects. But after he had gone through some experiences—particularly the shock of Dinshawji's death and of Bilimoria, and the spiritual experience while attending the prayer at Dinshawji's funeral—Gustad was totally changed. Gustad's change is perceptible in his attitude to Tehmul. Tehmul always liked Gustad who had never misbehaved with him, as other tenants would usually do. But Gustad had not developed any special feeling for him in the beginning. But the night he found Tehmul with Roshan's big doll and felt that the poor fellow was actually an adult with a child's mind, his mind was filled up with sympathy for the idiot. Tehmul's blissful smile seemed to Gustad to be God-like. "The rays played upon his beaming face, upon the innocent joy he displayed for the rusty old torch's meagre light. Sadness and affection filled Gustad's heart. In this pose, with his blissful smile, he thought, Tehmul's picture would fit right in among the others on the black wall." (309) When Tehmul was killed while trying to catch a brick, Gustad was so shocked that he forgot his surroundings. He alone carried his body to his brother's flat, and putting his hand on Tehmul's head began to pray.

> With covered head he sat, placing his right hand upon Tehmul's head. Tehmul's hair felt stiff under his fingers, matted where the blood had dried. He closed his eyes and began to pray softly. He

> recited the Yatha Ahu Vayo, five times, and Ashem Vahoo, three times, his bloodstained hand resting light as a leaf on Tehmul's head. . . . Tears began to well in his closed eyes. . . . Yatha Ahu Varyo and Ashem Vahoo, and the salt water of his eyes, as much for himself as for Tehmul. As much for Tehmul as for Jimmy. And for Dinshawji, for Pappa and Mamma, for Grandpa and Grandma, all who had to wait for so long. (336-37)

Just at this time Sohrab came to him and the father and the son were united. Gustad's essential human dignity as well as the capacity to behold celestial bliss in terrestrial matters is revealed in his gestures. Gustad's long journey along the path of life elevated him to that height where his own sorrows and aspirations merged with those of others.

Major Bilimoria

Major Bilimoria is a combination of fact and fiction. Though a fictitious character, Bilimoria is easily recognized as a reconstruction of Mr. Nagarwala who became known all over India for being involved in a notorious fraud case. He was accused of imitating the voice of Prime Minister while asking for money on phone from a cashier in a bank. Bilimoria in the novel was also accused of imitating the voice of the P.M. and was jailed. Mr. Nagarwala could not defend his case; and Bilimoria, too, found it impossible to get any one who would believe him. Before his death he could however confess the matter to his old friend Gustad and there was apparently no cause to disbelieve him. He described how he had been trapped by the Prime Minister and how he put aside ten lakh rupees for his friends after he found that the huge amount of money taken presumably for the freedom fighters in Bangladesh, had been rerouted by the P.M.'s office.

Major Bilimoria had no family of his own and he loved his friends as his own brothers. He had lived in Khodadad Building for almost as long as the Nobles. Gustad always pointed him out to the children as a good example, urging them to walk erect like Major Uncle. A brave soldier, Major Bilimoria had fought against the Pakistanis in 1948 and also encountered the tribesmen from the North-West frontier. Being a retired army man he was recruited by RAW and was engaged in secret service for the country. He was an out and out patriot and was ready to do anything for the sake of the country. Mistry projects him as a Parsi patriot who was devoted to India and was yet rudely betrayed by the Indian Prime Minister. He was a simple man at heart and that is why he was so easily trapped. His pathetic death puts a question mark on the integrity of the politicians who profited by the selfless work of the patriots like Major Bilimoria.

Gustad was obliged to Bilimoria for taking him to the bonesetter after the accident. He had always been more than just a neighbour. At the very least he was like a loving brother. When Gustad was carried home after the accident, it was Bilimoria who advised that the physicians would be of no help in that situation. Being a military man he knew about Madhiwalla Bonesetter and took the trouble of taking Gustad to him. Even when Gustad was hurt by his behaviour, he remembered Bilimoria's help and felt obliged to him for making him able to come back to normal life.

The only flaw in the Major's character was his decision to put aside ten lakh rupees for his friends who were needy. When Gustad asked him why he had not disclosed the fact to him, he answered that Gustad would never allow him to do such immoral work. He was right. He understood Gustad's character well. And he confessed that he had done an immoral job, as he was frustrated at the shameless show of corruption at the highest level. He also made a mistake in thinking that they would not bother about ten lakh rupees after getting fifty lakh rupees. Mistry's keen observation made him aware of the way corruption in highest places spreads like gangrene everywhere. However, this flaw of Major Bilimoria makes him a man of flesh and blood. Otherwise he would remain an instrument for expressing grudge against Indira Gandhi.

Ghulam Mohammed

Ghulam Mohamed has an important role in the narrative. As we learn later, he carried Gustad home after the accident and Gustad had searched for him to express his gratitude for the kind service, but did not see him. After a long period of time he could see Ghulam on a Lambretta only in a flash and the Lambretta collided with a car and Ghulam seemed injured. That time also Gustad did not have the opportunity to talk to him. Much to his surprise he saw Ghulam in the Chor Bazaar and learnt that he was also attached to RAW. Major Bilimoria had sent the packet through Ghulam and that day Gustad had a friendly talk with him.

Gustad's attitude to Ghulam was changed after he found that the packet contained rupees ten lakh which he was to deposit in the account of some Mira Obili. Gustad tried his best to contact Ghulam as he was afraid of the money and sought to be relieved of the huge amount. But he could not meet Ghulam, and as he was late in depositing the amount, he was repeatedly being threatened by him. Gustad could not however imagine that it was Ghulam who had flung a dead rat and a dead cat with their heads severed, in his bush in order to threaten him. Only after he received a piece of paper on which someone was threatened for stealing Bilimoria's rice, that Gustad realized that everything was the brainchild of Ghulam, and that he had no other way open but to deposit the money. When the money had to be withdrawn, the entire amount was returned to Ghulam. Gustad's cold behaviour was quite natural, for Ghulam appeared no more than a hardcore criminal. It was Ghulam, again, who appealed to Gustad to meet Bilimoria in jail. And after he heard Bilimoria's confession, Gustad came to know that Ghulam was also trapped, that he had tried desperately to save Bilimoria.

Gustad's attitude to Ghulam was totally changed when he came to know that Ghulam had arranged for the funeral of the Major. "He had seen many sides of the man: jovial, threatening, callous, cajoling, sarcastic. But never like this, never so emotional." (322) With the use of some bold strokes Mistry sketches the emotional man who was so long known as hard-hearted:

> Ghulam raised his face, up towards the hill, up where the vultures were circling. Then he dropped his head and closed his eyes. Gustad waited. When he looked a few seconds later, Ghulam was waiting. Gustad averted his gaze and stood in silence.
>
> Ghulam wiped his eyes with the back of his hand. He said, his voice steady now, "Your Parsi priests don't allow outsiders like me to go inside."
>
> Gustad nodded guiltily. (322)

Ghulam Mohammed, the only Muslim character in the Parsi novel, is thus portrayed as one, devoted to Major Bilimoria since the days of their joint fighting in the battlefield.

Dinshawji

Dinshawji as a character draws ambivalence, as the readers often get puzzled to find which face of Dinshawji was the real one. He is introduced as a jovial man who is able to bring laughter in the faces of children and grown-up men alike. At Roshan's birthday party, he amused the children with his songs and stories and in the office he would always amuse his colleagues with the use of erotic slang. Unlike Gustad who was by nature afraid of expressing his views publicly, Dinshawji was vocal about his strong liking and disliking. A strong critic of Indira Gandhi and the Congress government, Dinshawji was in the habit of using slang to express his disgust towards the corrupt politicians.

Dinshawji was a staunch Parsi and the fear of the minority community is expressed in his comments on the rise of such fanatic groups as Shiv Sena. He described with much satisfaction how the Shiv Sena supporters, who came to attack their bank, were compelled to run away. "Because of the Pathans and their guns, all those Sakarams and Dattarams and Tukarams only stood outside, screaming like fishwives. . . . 'Bhum!' That's all, and the Maratha brigade ran like cockroaches." (40) Dinshawji had the marvellous quality of managing rising conflicts that grew out of serious debate with his humorous comments. "When the bank clerks and tellers debated the reformers' proposal to introduce cremation, tempers flared and there were bitter personal attacks. But Dinshawji would manage to end matters on a light note, saying things like: "Better that my dear domestic vulture eats me up than the feathered ones. With her I have a guarantee—she at least won't scatter pieces of my meat all over Bombay." (72) For such comments Dinshawji was better known as a clown or a joker.

Dinshawji could also express serious views without being light. For example, when he expressed his dissatisfaction with the change of place names, he turned very serious at Gustad's suggestion that change of names hardly mattered. Without the slightest mark of fun on his face he said,

> Names are so important. I grow up on Lamington Road. But it has disappeared; in its place is Dadasaheb Bhadkhamkar Marg. My school was on Carnac Road. Now suddenly it's on Lokmanya Tilak Marg. I live at Sleater Road. Soon that will also disappear. My whole life I have come to work at Flora Fountain. And one fine day the name changes. So what happens to the life I have lived? Was I living the wrong life, with all the wrong names? Will I get a second chance to live it all again, with these new names? (74)

This is not merely accusation against the change of names. This suggests an identity crisis of the Parsi community. The Parsis felt comfortable with the British and could learn English language very early. They were profited thereby and acquired a central position on the national scenario. During the postcolonial days their position became marginalized again, and the change of place names, which were all British names, were sad reminders of their lost glory.

Dinshawji's moral courage and fellow feeling are explicit in his volunteering the risky job of depositing ten lakh rupees in the account of fictitious Mira Obili. He was happy that he could somehow be engaged in a great work like helping the freedom fighters in Bangladesh. He even disclosed the matter to Laurie Coutino, the P.A., while chatting with her. It was he, again, who noticed the news about Bilimoria's arrest in newspaper and gave Gustad proper advice. Just as he deposited rupees ten thousand per day, so also he withdrew rupees ten thousand every day till the entire amount was withdrawn, lest there be any doubt in someone's mind about the huge amount. "Dinshawji handled it so well, thought Gustad, filling with admiration for the cool courage and good sense. Here was no clown or buffoon, but a solid, dependable friend." (207) Gustad was shocked to learn that he was hospitalized just after the entire amount was withdrawn and he also felt guilty that Dinshawji must have been pressurized for the job and his condition decreased because of the pressure. Dinshawji's death was a real shock to Gustad.

Dinshawji's flirtation with the new P.A., Laurie, who complained against him to Gustad, seems incompatible with his real nature. When Gustad told him all about Laurie's complaint, Dinshawji became serious and it came out from his words that he posed to be a clown so that nobody would bother about his activities and he could safely withdraw the amount. Dinshawji had no issue and he was not much wrong when he referred to his wife as domestic vulture. His unhappy family life may also be a cause behind his flirtation. The details of his funeral make it clear that he was a pure soul, capable of unselfish love. The capacity to make others laugh is not an insignificant quality. Dinshawji was blessed by the Almighty for that rare quality.

Dilnavaz

Gustad Noble's wife Dilnavaz is sketched as a housewife who hardly bothers about anything except the well-being of his family. She is like the wise sparrow in the story of a foolish crow and a wise sparrow retold in Shashi Deshpande's *That Long Silence*. Deshpande wonders how such an ugly, sadistic tale was used as a bed-time story for children. In that story, the foolish crow made his house of dung and the wise sparrow made hers of wax. When rain came, the house of dung was washed away, but the house of wax stood firm. The poor crow, shivering and sodden, requested the sparrow to let him in. The sparrow delayed to open her door as she was busy with her children, and when she actually opened, the crow was all wet and she showed her the oven to sit on. The foolish crow sat on the oven and was burnt up. Deshpande comments sarcastically, "There's the foolish, improvident, irresponsible, gullible crow; and there is the cautious, self-centred, worldly-wise, dutiful, shrewd sparrow. . . I have a feeling that even if little boys can forget this story, little girls never will. They will store the story in their subconscious, their unconscious or whatever, and eventually they will become that damnably, insufferably priggish sparrow looking after their homes, their babies . . . and to hell with the rest of the world."[1] Like the sparrow in the tale, Dilnavaz was devoted to her family and was unconcerned for others.

Mindless drudgery is the destiny of Dilnavaz. As Nilufer E. Bharucha observes, "In British India, unhampered by the taboos of the Hindu caste system and the isolationism of the Muslims, the Parsis surged ahead and became the most westernized. But it was mainly confined to men. Even though some rich Parsis educated their daughters, who became doctors, lawyers and teachers, the majority of Parsi women received little education and was subjected to the taboos and repressions of a strict patriarchy."[2] Dilnavaz was one among the majority of Parsi women who got little education. Thus, Dilnavaz got angry with her husband when he purchased books from Chor Bazaar and she hardly showed any interest in outside matters. She is a female stereotype, much liked by traditional Indian writers. Her only concern was her family and she could go to any extreme for the benefit of her family. As she was superstitious, she was always in the habit of touching wood so that any undesirable incident would not happen in their family. She is a perfect foil to Gustad in every aspect. Gustad is rational and she is superstitious, conspiring with Ms. Kutpitia in creating spells for her family. Gustad loved his friends like his brothers. She did not much like outsiders. She was not happy with Dinshawji's jokes and with his attempts to make Roshan laugh. While Gustad reached the height of moral supremacy, Dilnavaz deteriorated morally. Gustad's realization of Tehmul's character—his adult's body and child-like mind and also the likeness between his blessed face and the face of any saint painted on the wall—is the result of his progress towards an ethical realization. Dilnavaz, on the other hand, joined hands with Ms. Kutpitia in using Tehmul for Sohrab's return. One, who has no faith in black magic, may argue that Dilnavaz's performance of black magic and Tehmul's death were coincidences. Be it anything, Dilnavaz could not evade her moral responsibility. That she longed for Sohrab's return even at the cost of Tehmul's life is clear and her moral degeneration is also marked. Mistry does not show Dilnavaz's reaction after Tehmul's death and intentionally leaves the character mid-way. Her reaction is left up to the readers' imagination.

Ms. Kutpitia

Ms. Kutpitia is the archetypal spinster who is much reviled by the neighbourhood. In Gujarati, the name 'Kutpitia' means quarrelsome. She is introduced as a lonely person who did not allow others to enter her flat. She had adopted her brother's son after the untimely death of the child's mother, but both her brother and the son lost their lives in accident. There was a rumour in the neighbourhood that she had embalmed and preserved the dead bodies of his relatives in her flat instead of handing them over for proper disposal at the Tower of Silence. Some persons did not believe in this rumour; they said that she only preserved the bones after the vultures had cleansed them. However, she lived like a miser, "a typical loose-screw eccentric, with dust and cobwebs everywhere."

Mistry sketches her character both from external and from internal perspectives. Externally, she was miser, superstitious and believer in black magic. In the neighbourhood, she alone had telephone in her flat and she took thirty paisa for each telephone. But she was against pretensions. That is why she gave back the rose sent to her by Gustad and took thirty paisa after Gustad telephoned from her flat. Raising her skinny, trembling finger she told Gustad, "All this pretence with a rose no one needs. Just remember one thing. Old age and sorrow comes to everyone some day." (87) Though she is rendered as silly, superstitious woman, she is internally a pathetic figure. She had decided not to marry for bringing up her nephew and that nephew along with his father died in a car accident, leaving her alone in the unsympathetic world. Her sorrow led her more and more towards a secluded existence and in her seclusion she was habituated to explain matters in her own way. Her irrational female nature has been rendered as a matter of fun and the writer informs that she was "the ubiquitous witch of fairy stories come to life" to the children. She was treated by her neighbours in a way that could drive anybody to despair. "She was a wizened woman of seventy, and seldom went out these days, she said, since her bones got stiffer day by day. But there were not many in the building she could talk to about her bones, or anything else, for that matter, because of the reputation she had acquired over the years, of being mean and cranky and abusive. . . . [The children] would flee past her door, screaming, 'Run from *daaken*!' as much from fear as to provoke her to mutter curse, and shake her fist." (2) The details of the rituals associated with her magic only make her a laughing stock. No one is expected to believe that whatever she did with a lizard caused Tehmul's death. Her imaginative nature, her capacity to persuade others towards her line of thinking and her knowledge of the surroundings could make her a wise lady only if she were provided with proper modern education. Otherwise she is strong enough to run an independent life of her own and intelligent enough to feel what others are thinking about her. She is an example of what extent one can go to if one is led by superstitious thoughts. The pathos underlying her lonely life enriches the novel.

Tehmul

Tehmul was an orphan idiot who lived with his brother in the Khodadad Building. His brother had to go out of station for his work and Tehmul remained alone most of the time. He was lame as his hip was fractured in an accident. "Tehmul-Lungra, as everyone called him, was a supreme pathetic example of hip-fracture victims who had had the misfortune to be treated by conventional methods, condemned to years on crutches and walking sticks, with nothing to look forward to but a life of pain." (30) Tehmul did not mind staying alone. In his mid-thirties, he still preferred the company of children to adults, except Gustâd. Tehmul's relationship with Gustad forms a sort of under-pattern in the narrative.

In the beginning Tehmul liked Gustad who being gentle, never used hard words against him. But Gustad did not develop any relationship with him at that time. When Gustad found that Tehmul had seen the heaps of notes in his room, he even threatened the idiot with a knife lest he would tell others of what he had seen. Gustad was surprised to see Tehmul among the prostitutes who did not entertain him but made fun of him. Thanks to Gustad's interference, Tehmul could come out without being hurt. Next time when Gustad found that Tehmul had stolen Roshan's big Italian doll and was trying to satisfy his sexual desires upon that life-size doll, he got angry for some time. Then he could understand the idiot perfectly. "Gustad's anger began to ebb slowly. Poor Tehmul. A child's mind and a man's urges. Shunned by the whores, turning to the doll in desperation. Somehow, it seemed a fitting solution. He imagined Tehmul undressing the doll each night, caressing it tenderly. Gustad remembered the day he had come home with the doll by taxi from Sister Constance, and met Tehmul in the compound. How gently he had patted the cheek, stroked the tiny fingers, gazed wonderfully into the deep blue eyes." (303) Though Gustad did not express his feelings to Tehmul, he was very sorry that Tehmul was denied the genuine rights and virtues of mortals. He wished he had the power of miracles, the power to cure Tehmul's ills, so that he would be able to enjoy life in all its aspects. Gustad realized that he could not take away the doll. "Somehow, the loss to Roshan would not be as great as it would to Tehmul." (303) This encounter is revealing as it highlights both Gustad and Tehmul. After that incident Gustad saw him in the compound one evening, groping in darkness. Gustad clicked on his pocket torch and Tehmul was enlightened by the beam. Sadness and affection filled Gustad's heart as he noted a 'blissful smile' on Tehmul's face when he found the little beaded bracelet from the doll's wrist that had been lost. "In this pose, with his blissful smile, he thought, Tehmul's picture would fit right in among the others [the portraits of gods and saints] upon the black wall." (309)

Gustad's changed feelings towards Tehmul explain his behaviour after Tehmul's death while trying to catch a flying brick at the time of the clash. Mistry highlighted Tehmul's fascination for anything flying. "Things that travelled through the air enchanted him—things that soared, swooped or dived, things flying and fluttering in freedom. Whether it be bird or butterfly, a paper dart or a falling leaf, he never tired of trying to possess it." (31) It is because he was handicapped and could not move freely he developed an attraction towards flying or moving things. This attraction was a satisfaction of his desire to move freely and this attraction also caused his death. Tehmul's character-sketch is thus an example of Rohinton Mistry's hold on psychology.

NOTES

1. Shashi Deshpande, *That Long Silence* (Penguin, 1989), p. 17.
2. "From behind a Fine Veil: A Feminist Reading of Three Parsi Novels," *The Fiction of Rohinton Mistry: Critical Studies*, ed. J. Dodiya (New Delhi: Prestige, 1998), p. 53.

Special Features of *Such a Long Journey*

The Title and the Epigraph

The title of the novel *Such a Long Journey* has a symbolic significance. It is taken from T.S. Eliot's poem "Journey of the Magi" and three lines of the poem containing the words chosen as the title are quoted as an epigraph:

> A cold coming we had of it,
> Just the worst time of the year
> For a journey, and such a long journey.

The title has a symbolic significance: it refers to the spiritual progress in the life of the protagonist, Gustad Noble. In the beginning of the novel Gustad was god-fearing, and without greed. He was then much concerned with his family, with his eldest son's enrolment in I.I.T. and with his daughter's illness. Yet he immediately agreed to Bilimoria's proposal of taking the packet sent by him from the Chor Bazaar, as he stuck to the point that a friend should not be let down. Whatever happened in his life enriched his experiences and at the end of the novel his sensibilities were broadened so much that he could trace the blissful face of a saint on the face of Tehmul, the idiot. Gustad's agony at the death of his friend and colleague Dinshawji, and after some days of Major Bilimoria, who had once been like his brother and who had confessed his sin and suffering to him in jail, changed him altogether. 'Such a long journey' refers both to his physical journey—his financial troubles after his father became bankrupt and his continuous struggle since then—and to his spiritual journey; the latter is highlighted by the title and the epigraph.

The magi or the wise men from the east came to see newborn Jesus in His birthplace. They also had both physical suffering and spiritual suffering. The lines "Just the worst time of the year/ For a journey. . . . The ways deep and the weather sharp,/The very dead of winter" refer to the physical sufferings of the magi. But the conflict in their mind when they could not get themselves adjusted to the old ways of life after gaining the new experience refers to their spiritual suffering.

> I had seen birth and death,
> But had thought they were different; this Birth was
> Hard and bitter agony for us, like Death, our death
>
> "Journey of the Magi"

This suffering is essential when one tries to attain higher and nobler values of life. The experience they gathered made them spiritual foreigners in their own land. Gustad also became a spiritual foreigner in his own surroundings: he alone came forward to carry the dead body of Tehmul. Inspector Bamji asked him not to carry Tehmul's heavy body alone, but he did not listen to him.

> Gustad ignored him and began walking down the compound, away from them all, towards the stairway to Tehmul's flat. They looked in silence now, too ashamed to follow. Sohrab gazed after his father with fear and admiration. (325)

After Tehmul's death Gustad prays not only for his children but also for others. "He kept his eyes closed and started a second cycle of prayer. Tears began to well in his closed eyes. His voice was soft and steady, and his hand steady and light upon Tehmul's head, as the tears ran down his cheeks. He started another cycle, and yet another, and he could not stop the tears." (337) Those tears were purifying his soul that was on its journey ahead. The motif of 'journey' is further exemplified through the pavement artist who is always on his way. He thought of settling near the Khodadad Building after the compound wall was fully decorated with the portraits of gods and saints, and people began to offer flowers, incense sticks and money. The pavement artist even replaced the crayon paintings with oil paintings which are permanent. After the wall was broken by the municipality, the pavement artist realized how he was mistaken with the idea of permanence. There is no place of permanence on his way which is the other name for life; there is only journey ahead. That is why he took only the materials for crayon painting and left those for oil painting when he started his journey again. When Gustad wished him good luck, he replied, "Luck is the spit of gods and goddesses." He reveals the author's message that man must carry on whatever may come in his way.

The lines from Rabindranath Tagore's *Gitanjali,* quoted as another epigraph, also suggest the motif of journey. Poet Tagore accepted life on earth as journey ahead and he also conceived of God as the fellow traveller, suffering with men and yet consoling them and encouraging them for undertaking further journey. The epigraph is as follows.

> And when old words die out on the tongue, new melodies break forth from the heart; and where the old tracks are lost, new country is revealed with its wonders.

The lines suggest that life is always changing and along with it changes man's language and also the scenario of his surroundings. Man's embarking on new land, as is suggested in the lines, does not imply his adventurous nature, but his inward journey, his urge to develop a broader consciousness.

Mistry used another quotation from Firdausi's *Shah-Nama* which runs as follows.

> He assembled the aged priests and put questions to them concerning the kings who had once possessed the world. "How did they," he inquired, "hold the world in the beginning, and why is it that it has been left to us in such a sorry state? And how was it that they were able to live free of care during the days of their heroic labours?"

The quotation from Firdausi's Iranian epic, *Shah-Nama* also suggests a journey of mankind from the ancient time to the present age. The question is about the beginning of the journey when the kings were famous for their heroism. It recalls both the glorious heritage of a mighty empire, as well as hints at the downgraded condition of present day Paris. It is a riddle that the heroes of the past had not been able to remove the sufferings of mankind. Is it man's fate then that they will have to embrace suffering as long as they continue their journey? The way Gustad suffered and the way his hopes were denied show that the epigraphs symbolize the essence of the novel. It is implied that life has to get going. The writer's message is perhaps best expressed through the activities of the pavement artist:

> Over the years, a precise cycle had entered the rhythm of his life, the cycle of arrival, creation and obliteration. Like sleeping, waking and stretching, or eating, digesting and excreting, the cycle sang in harmony with the blood in his veins and the breath in his lungs. He learned to disdain the overlong sojourn and the procrastinated departure, for they were the progenitors of complacent routine, to be shunned at all costs. The journey—chanced, unplanned, solitary—was the thing to relish. (184)

The pavement artist made a mistake when he stopped in one place, allured by the agreeable neighbourhood and the solidity of the long, black wall. When the wall was broken, he could decipher the causes of sorrow: "a yearning for permanence, for roots, for something he could call his own, something immutable." (184) 'Journey' in the title is therefore, not mere physical journey, but a journey of the spirit, one that requires non-attachment. Purvi N. Upadhyay explains the concluding lines of the novel in terms of Gustad's spiritual journey:

> At the end of the novel, Gustad tears off the black paper covering the ventilators of his flat that had for years "restricted the ingress of all forms of light, earthly and celestial," and a moth, a symbol of past, flies out, a sign of new beginning, a new birth, that emerges from death. Like the journey of the Magi, Gustad's arduous trek through pain, heart break and loss has brought him to a new awakening and the promise of the ultimate victory of human spirit. Ultimately the novel *Such a Long Journey* celebrates through the metaphor of the journey the all inclusiveness of life and the indestructibility of the human spirit.[1]

Religion

Though *Such a Long Journey* is a Parsi novel, it does not project Zoroastrianism as the best religion whatsoever. That is why Gustad went to the Church of Mount Mary to pray for Roshan and Dinshawji and this posture did not diminish his faith in Zoroastrianism. He even followed the Catholic rituals of offering wax-made parts of human bodies for curing those parts of his friends and children. "Gustad knelt, following his friend's example, then Malcolm indicated that the wax purchases should be relinquished and the candles lit. . . . Gustad joined his hands, bowed his head and thought of Roshan, wishing her healthy and well again; of Dinshawji, that his suffering may ease; and of Sohrab, that his good sense be restored to him." (228) It was not by the miraculous story of Mount Mary that Gustad was impressed, but by the serenity of the place, of the sea with its rising tides.

> The rush of the approaching tide, the blue-pink sky filled with comforting white shapes, the dancing foam and sea-glistened rocks, the touch of salty breezes on his face: all this was working to bestow gently upon Gustad a serenity he had not known for a very long time. (230)

That is why Gustad sat there even after Malcolm; who brought him there, had gone for a piano-session. Alone, he gazed at the horizon. He felt the tranquillity at the far edge, where the water met the sky. While the waves crashed against the rock on which he was sitting, he felt as if he were listening to the sonata. He saw that the sun was sinking in the ocean, "its journey done for the day." Thus he discovered a link between nature and human beings. And love of God and love of nature become synonymous for him.

Rohinton Mistry's attitude to religion is best expressed through the pavement artist. Gustad had requested him to paint portraits on the compound wall of the Khodadad Building and he started with Trimurti of Brahma, Vishnu and Shiva. Then he painted gods, goddesses and saints of different religions. He also painted sacred religious places of different religions. And the place was miraculously changed. The stink was replaced by fragrance of flowers and incense sticks. Instead of flies and mosquitoes buzzing, a thousand colours danced in sunlight. Not that all the people were happy. There were lots of sceptics and malingers. Some even meant by religion only mysteries and magic. When asked by Gustad if he really believed in miracles, the pavement artist said,

> I don't like to weaken anyone's faith. Miracle, magic, mechanical trick, coincidence—does it matter what it is, as long as it helps? Why analyze the strength of the imagination, the power of suggestion, the power of auto-suggestion, the potency of psychological pressures? Looking too closely is destructive, makes everything disintegrate. As it is life is difficult enough. Why to simply make it tougher? After all, who is to say what makes a miracle and what makes a coincidence? (289)

After the compound wall was broken and the pavement artist was on his journey again, he said to Gustad, "Luck is the spit of gods and goddesses." (338) Through the views of the artist, the author's views are highlighted. Mistry feels that fanaticism is the worst enemy in today's world. There is no use of hurting others' feelings in the name of religion. Religion is necessary for upliftment of one's ethical standard, broadening of one's consciousness and for mental peace.

Rohinton Mistry's Interest in Psychology

Such a Long Journey reveals Rohinton Mistry's interest in psychology. Sohrab's adolescent mind came into conflict with his father's as his father imposed his own will on his son. Sohrab's enrolment in I.I.T. was so much aspired by Gustad that he was engrossed with the idea and as a result Sohrab felt humiliated. Moreover, Sohrab had a genuine interest in arts and this interest was not reciprocated in the surroundings he was in. The way he protested was quite natural for a boy of his age group. Mistry sought to delve deep beneath the surface of his mind. The seed of Sohrab's troubles germinated long ago, when his parents discovered how easily things came to their first-born, at home, in school, at work or play. "There seemed to be nothing Sohrab could not do, and do well. Whether it was arithmetic, or arts or crafts, or moral science, he bagged several prizes each year on Prize Distribution day." (64) His failures were ignored by his parents. Gradually the dream of I.I.T. took shape, then took hold of their imagination. "And the Indian Institute of Technology became the Promised Land. It was El Dorado and Shangri-La, it was Atlantis and Camelot, it was Xanadu and Oz. It was the home of the Holy Grail. And all things would be given and all things would be possible and all things would come to pass for he who journeyed there and emerged with the sacred chalice." (67-68) Sohrab's mind protested against this mad rush and he wanted to satisfy his inner urge for learning more about arts and literature. His father was not in a mood to understand the mind of his son and he insisted on his getting enrolled in I.I.T. which was supposed to bring material prosperity to the family. The conflict between the father and the son was thus inevitable and the conflict reveals Rohinton Mistry's hold on adolescent psychology.

Besides adolescent psychology, the novel also reveals Rohinton Mistry's interest in the psychology of the old person, socially secluded and abused. Ms. Kutpitia is projected as a strong personality and capable of running an independent life of her own. She was alone because of the misfortune in her life that came in the form of the death of his brother and his motherless son whom Ms. Kutpitia had adopted. Her way of life was different from others as he remained in the imaginary world of the past and could not accept the hard reality. She remained alone inside her and yet people could hear her voice. It suggests that she developed the habit of remaining in the past world and would talk to her nephew imagining that he was in the room. Her flat was filled up with old papers, old books and dress which she could not remove. After performing the magic with lizard's tail that was burnt in a lamp, the room caught fire and all the old things that she could not fling were destroyed. Mistry shows that she looked happy and relaxed after the old things were destroyed. Mistry wants to say that she badly needed to be relieved of the past but she could not do so. The fire helped her to get relieved of the past that was a burden on her and she became relaxed. The sketch of Ms. Kutpitia reveals Rohinton Mistry's hold on psychology.

The character of Tehmul is another example of Rohinton Mistry's sympathetic understanding of an idiot's mind and activities. A physically handicapped male Tehmul was denied mental development. As a little boy he had fallen from a big 'neem' tree in his attempt to rescue a tangled kite, and as a result his hip was broken. Although he had not landed on his head, something went wrong inside him due to the jolt of the accident. He was never the same after the accident. He was not happy to go to the school, trudging on his little crutches. His parents also died leaving him to the custody of his brother who had to move from place to place for his work. Tehmul got used to live alone and most of the time played with the children in the compound. In his mid-thirties, he still preferred the company of children to adults. He no longer used crutches, but walked up and down indicating his rolling gait and twisted hip for their benefit. As he was handicapped, his latent desire for free movement was expressed through his fascination for flying things. "Things that travelled through the air enchanted him—things that soared, swooped or dived, things flying and fluttering in freedom." (31) This fascination for flying things brought about his tragic death. When the compound wall of the Khodadad Building was being broken and the excited mass flung bricks, Tehmul was so fascinated by the sight that he tried to catch a piece of brick and was seriously injured. That injury led to his death and Mistry made the incident plausible through exposing Tehmul's fascination for moving things which was an outward revelation of a handicapped person's desire for freedom.

The way Tehmul stole Roshan's big doll and satisfied his sexual desire with the doll, is another example of Rohinton Mistry's powerful dealings with what is commonly called perversion. The author's sympathetic understanding of Tehmul's psychology renders his activity as natural, and not as perverted. The writer's view is expressed through Gustad who became angry after he found that Tehmul had stolen Roshan's doll and satisfied his sexual urge on the naked doll. But very soon, Gustad's anger ebbed and he felt sorry for him. "A child's mind and a man's urges. Shunned by the whores, turning to the doll in desperation. Somehow, it seemed a fitting solution." (303) Without using any catchy tricks, Rohinton expresses his deep knowledge of human psychology in a traditional way. His humanist stand helped him to delve deep beneath the surface level of man's mind.

Social Reality

Rohinton Mistry comes out as a satirist so far as the treatment of social reality is concerned. Though he exposes the personal life of Gustad Noble in *Such a Long Journey* in the background of the contemporary political scenario, his awareness of the society to which he belonged is revealed in his writing. The setting of the novel being Bombay, the problems faced by the middle class and the lower-middle class people in Bombay are highlighted. The novel starts with the water-crisis: Dilnavaz had to get up early in the morning only in order to keep in store the necessary water for her family for the entire day. The familiar hissing, spitting, blustering sound in the water pipe was like a summon. Details are given of Dilnavaz's activity in the early morning: "She went to the bathroom and connected the transparent plastic hose to fill the water drums, even though today there was time enough to brush her teeth first, and make tea. It was only five o'clock—two whole hours before the taps went dry. She turned the brass handle, and the head of water surged through the hose. A long tail of air bubbles followed close behind." (7) All this is described only to point at the scarcity of water in Bombay.

The simple faith of the common Indian people who were ready to do their best when their dear motherland was attacked by China is put side by side with the corrupt practice of stealing the things contributed by the common people. The slant remark that there was competition among the persons, who donated, makes the picture more realistic.

> And the people were moved to staunch the flow of yellow invaders. They throw blankets and sweaters and scarves out of their windows into the open lorries that passed below. In some wealthy localities, the collection drive turned into a competition, with neighbours trying to outdo one another in their attempts to simultaneously seem rich, patriotic and compassionate. Women removed gold bangles and earrings and fingerings from their persons and gave them away. Money-notes and loose change was wrapped in handkerchiefs and tossed into the fund-raisers' grateful hands. Men tore shirts and jackets off their backs, yanked shoes off their feet, belts off their waists, and flung them into the lorries. What a time it was, it brought tears of pride and joy into the eyes of everyone to see such solidarity, such generosity. Afterwards, it was said that some of the donated goods had turned up for sale in Chor Bazaar, and in the stalls of roadside hawkers everywhere, though not much attention was paid to that nasty allegation; the glow of national unity was still warm and comforting. (10)

The above quotation reveals Rohinton Mistry's keen observation of the surroundings and of the attitudes of the people. Corruption is rendered as an integral part of Indian life.

As a social realist, Mistry pointed out how the poor people suffered financially at the time of the war. The refugee Relief Tax is referred to again and again as a burden on the people who had to try hard for making the two ends meet. "The Refugee Relief Tax is terrible," said Gustad. "It's killing the middle class." "He described how, working at the bank, he could see the trend: more and more people had to draw on their savings." (230) Gustad said to Dilnavaz, "This refugee relief tax is going to make all of us into refugees." (83) The humorous description of Dr. Paymaster's inability to remove the signboard with the name of one Dr. R.C. Lord—the name with which the patients were habituated and which they did not want to get changed—displays the reality that most of the Indian people are lacking in proper education and are often guided by some superstitions. That is why the patients who would come to Dr. Paymaster did not bother to see if it was the same doctor who had treated them; they interpreted that the change of signboard implied the change of doctor. "Dr. Paymaster sorrowfully realized something they never taught in medical college: like any consumer product, a doctor's name was infinitely more important than his skills." (113)

The discrimination between the rich and the poor is revealed through the crazy remarks of Cavasji, an old resident of Khodadad Building. With his white hair shining on his head, Cavasji appealed to God, "Monsoon is coming, so you be careful! Year after year, your floods are washing away poor people's huts! Enough now! Where is your fairness? Have you got any brains or not? Flood the Tatas this year! Flood the Birlas, flood the Mafatlals!" (127) The wretched condition of the whorehouse where Gustad went in search of Ghulam is revealed through Rohinton Mistry's description of the House of Cages.

> The rooms he could peek into were sordid. Bed, thin lumpy mattress, no sheet, ceiling fan, chair, table. In one corner, a basin and small mirror. Where were the scented silk sheets, the air-conditioned rooms, drinks, refreshments? The luxuries that they talked of in their stories of this place? Where were the skilled practitioners of the art said to possess secrets that could drive a man insane with pleasure? (201)

Discarding the romantic descriptions favourite with some authors, Mistry presents the harsh reality of the profession. It is not the magic world of the Arabian Nights but poverty that leads so many women towards this profession.

The description of the railway platform—of the tea-stall with its pyramid of dirty cups and saucers, the dirty water, the security man, announcement of trains and the waiting of the travellers—and the corrupt practice of the coolies are taken from real life.

> A well-dressed man in his thirties was stretched out on the overhead luggage rack. He laughed. "Coolies are controlling the whole show. Railway ministry thinks it is in charge, strikers think they are in charge. But the coolies are the real bosses. I paid twenty rupees for this deluxe sleeping-berth." (258-59)

Dr. Paymaster's accusations against the municipality are not imaginary. They are very much real pointing at the varied problems of the common people.

> For months and years now. Problems wherever you look. Leaking, broken waterpipes. Sewer overflowing. Inspectors come and inspectors go, but the gutters overflow for ever. And police corruption on top of that. They want weekly 'hafta' from people who are using pavements. Harassment from health inspectors also. They want baksheesh from House of Cages, even though it is properly licensed. (305)

The fictional world created by Rohinton Mistry is thus a replica of the real world. It is a world in which all forms of corruption, knavery, hypocrisy, tyranny, ugliness and decay have become the order of the day. Flies and mosquitoes are also included in this world. It is a world that includes both the stink and the fragrance of flowers.

Language

Rohinton Mistry's use of language in *Such a Long Journey* is a fine specimen of Indian English. Mulk Raj Anand once said that he had to bear the burden of both the Alps and the Himalayas. He meant that he had to keep in mind both the tradition of English language and the Indian sensibility. He made necessary changes in English language in order to reveal Indian sensibility through it. His language is termed as 'Mulkese' by Khushwant Singh. Mistry has proceeded almost in the line of Mulk Raj Anand, inserting maximum Hindi and Gujarati words whenever he felt that translations of those words would fail to render Indian sensibility. It is possible to make a big list of Hindi and Gujarati words used in the novel. And the list may be divided into three parts. First, there are common Hindi words; then there is slang;

and lastly, there is English translation of Hindi idiom as in the expression, 'turn tail and run.'

The novel starts with such Hindi expressions as 'Arre bhaiya,' 'Hindi-Chinee bhai bhai,' 'Humko kuch nahin maaloom' which at once reveal the Indian sensibility and at the same time blend well with the English structure. There are words such as 'chawl' and 'subjo' which are common Hindi words and Mistry rightly felt that these words are better than rice and vegetable for expressing the Indian scenario. There are typical Parsi words like 'kusti,' 'sudras' which cannot be expressed in English. And the non-Parsi readers, both Indian or non-Indian, are required to know the meaning of those words which very well express the Parsi identity. 'Goaswalla' is used instead of butcher, 'seth' instead of 'sir,' 'langra' instead of lame. For such words as 'sev-ganthia,' 'basmati,' 'sappat,' 'goteloo' there are hardly any English words. 'Ole' may not be replaced with any English word; and if it is done, the Indian fervour would be missing. 'Gilly gilly gilly,' 'Chaalo, chaalo,' 'Theek hai! Theek hai,' 'jaadu mantar' etc. are other examples of Hindi expressions which attribute an Indian fervour to the English language used by Mistry.

Rohinton Mistry's use of language adds a special charm to the novel and reveals the social reality better than any thing else. A passage that describes jokes of different provinces may be quoted in this context:

> They told the perennially popular Sikh jokes (What did the Sardarji runner say, after finishing first in the Asian Games, when asked: 'Are you relaxing now?' He said: 'No, no, I am still Arjun Singh); they told Madrasi jokes, mimicking the rolled-tongue sounds of South Indian languages (How does a Madrasi spell minimum? Yum-i-yen-i-yum-u-yum); they told Guju jokes, capitalizing on the askew English pronunciations of Gujaratis and their difficulties with vowels, 'o' in particular (Why did the Guju go to the Vatican? He wanted to hear pope music. Why did the Guju bite John Paul's big toe? He wanted to eat popcorn); they told Pathani jokes, about the Pathan's supposed penchant for rear-entry (A Pathan went to

> his doctor: 'Doctor Sahib, in my stomach is a lot of pain.' So the doctor gave him an enema. The Pathan left in ecstasy, told his friends: "Arre, how pleasureful modern science is—belly in pain, but medicine beautifully arse-way rammed." The next day his friends lined up at the doctor's clinic for enemas). (70-71)

Here is an excellent example of Indian English as used in different provinces in India.

There are frequent uses of typical words such as 'meherbani,' 'toba, toba' which are blended with the English language. 'Dubbawalla,' 'jaripuranawalla' are typical names indicating trades. Dinshawji and Inspector Bamji often use slang such as 'madder chod,' and the use of slang gives the novel a subaltern look.

Fate in *Such a Long Journey*

The novel is full of co-incidences and many things happen by chance. In an article "Thematic Concerns in *Such a Long Journey*," Anita Myles compares Rohinton Mistry's ideas about destiny to those of Thomas Hardy.[2] Hardy's poem 'To Life' is quoted by her:

> O, life with the sad sacred face
> I weary, of seeing thee,
> I know what thou wouldst tell
> Of death, Time, Destiny—
> I have known it long, and know, too well,
> What it all means for me.

In his novels Hardy projected human beings as playthings in the hands of destiny. But his characters hardly surrender meekly. They face the fate with all their might and like the old man in Hemingway's *Old Man and the Sea,* they do their best for survival. Gustad's suffering as well as his capacity to fight ill fate is compared by Anita to the struggle of Hardy's heroes. In fact, Gustad fought against his ill fate and prayed to God calmly. He was fortunate to have a good friend like Dinshawji who took the risk of depositing the huge amount and of withdrawing the entire amount on behalf of Gustad. It was mere chance that just after depositing the amount, Dinshawji was hospitalized. Again, it was a coincidence that just after the magic was performed in the presence of Tehmul, he was killed while trying to catch a flying brick, and Sohrab, for whose return the magic was performed, was united to his father over the dead body of Tehmul. Mistry arranges coincidences in such a way that one may get the impression that Tehmul's death and Sohrab's return were the effect of Ms. Kutpitia's magic. The writer's views in this respect are best expressed through the words of the pavement artist:

> Miracle, magic, mechanical trick, coincidence—does it matter what it is, as long as it helps? Why analyze the strength of the imagination, the power of suggestion, the power of auto-suggestion, the potency of psychological pressures? Looking too closely is destructive, makes everything disintegrate. As it is, life is difficult enough. Why to simply make it tougher? After all, who is to say what makes a miracle and what makes a coincidence? (289)

Mistry accepts man's helplessness at the hands of relentless destiny, and yet he feels that man may prove him to be worthy only through the calm acceptance of the burden of life.

NOTES

1. "The Journey as Motif and Metaphor in Rohinton Mistry's *Such a Long Journey*," *Parsi Fiction,* Vol. 2, ed. N. Kapadia, J. Dodiya and R.K. Dhawan (New Delhi; Prestige, 2001), pp. 175-76.
2. *The Fiction of Rohinton Mistry, Critical Studies,* ed. J. Dodiya (New Delhi: Prestige, 1998), p. 87.

Menace to the Cocoon of Petit Bourgeois Security: *Such a Long Journey* as Domestic Melodrama, Tragic Farce and Religious Parable

DAVID MYERS
University of Queensland

> He learned to disdain the overlong sojourn and the procrastinated departure, for they were the progenitors of complacent routine, to be shunned at all costs. The journey—chanced, unplanned, solitary—was the thing to relish.[1]

On occasion, when we are accustoming ourselves to Rohinton Mistry's world of infinite, realistic detail, repetition of leitmotifs and his insistence on the evocation of apparently trivial domestic routine, we may well be seized by impatience. Why doesn't he get on with the story, we mutter to ourselves, the pace is so slow. But after persisting, we realize that the details and the routine *are* the story. We are witnessing the attempt of the unlikely hero, Gustad Noble and his petit bourgeois family to construct a cocoon of security against the disruptions and turbulence of the outside world. It is an impossible attempt to create permanence, to stop all development, all change, all destructive intrusion from manifold menaces. It is an attempt which has some tragic results, but which nevertheless, in a testing pilgrimage through death, culminates in Gustad's spiritual growth and moral triumph.

Gustad has at least two or three character foils who are his opposites. Gustad's dearest friend, Major Jimmy Bilimoria, does not shrink back from war, menace and criminal activity. As a leading figure in the Indian secret service (RAW), he tries to make a heroic, glamorous game of fighting against Pakistan in their invasion of East Pakistan. He actively supports the Mukti Bahini guerillas. He relishes the danger and the clandestine manoeuvering of the secret war. But the ten lakh rupees which he entrusts to Gustad become Gustad's nightmare. They open a rift in his cocoon and menace him through his own enforced, criminal involvement and his fear of losing that mainstay of his stability, his job.

The second foil to Gustad is his next best friend, Dinshawji. Dinshawji tries to escape from his knowledge that there is no ultimate security in life by clowning and joking. Jokes, as we know from the brilliant analysis of Sigmund Freud, are the escape valve from unbearable pressure in the subconsciousness. Dinshawji finds many things unbearable: his bossy wife "the domestic vulture," the hostility between India's ethnic and religious groups, his menial position as a bank teller, his lust for Laurie Coutino the typist at the bank, his responsibility for the criminal deposit in the bank of ten lakh rupees for Gustad, and most of all his terror of the cancer that has attacked him. Therefore he clowns and makes jokes about all these things. His fellow employees and Gustad's little daughter Roshan are very grateful to him for his levity. His jokes afford them relief, too. They rely on his effervescent wit to help them get through their monotonous days. But when the pressure of possibly being reported for his indecent caperings in front of Laurie and then being found out in his illegal deposit of the ten lakh rupees becomes too much for him, he lapses, overnight, into dejection and despair. He has begun to let the truth show and his life-threatening illness grows apace because the defence of humour that is his lifeline has been lost.

The third foil to Gustad is the pavement artist who draws religious pictures on the pavement and subsequently on the long black wall outside Gustad's tenement building. Gustad tries very hard to keep everything the same, unchanging, as in daily routine. He is trying to stop time, to freeze time so that his children will not grow up, challenge him and move away. But the pavement artist shuns routine because it breeds complacency; he is devoted to the unplanned journey of each unknowable day. In his wisdom he senses that the "yearning for permanence, for roots, for something he could call his own, something immutable" is "the source of human sorrow." (184)[1] The pavement artist's drawings are derived from "assorted religions and their gods, saints and prophets: Hindu, Sikh, Judaic, Christian, Muslim, Zoroastrian, Buddhist, Jainist." He deliberately aims "to promote tolerance and understanding in the world." (182) The pavement artist bears the heavy burden of the novel's philosophical theme as moral parable.

The Cocoon of the Family

Gustad's whole life is devoted to protecting and nurturing his wife and children. This is not to say that he is a saint: he is self-righteous, self-pitying, stubborn, authoritarian and bad-tempered. He does everything he can to help the gifted Sohrab win admission to the prestigious I.I.T., but he also drives his son out of the home by bullying him into a career path that he doesn't want. He fights with his wife about whether his wife is right that Roshan has fallen dreadfully ill because Gustad has said it was not necessary to boil their drinking water. He has flaws. But unlike his father who collapsed into tears when his playboy brother brought him down to bankruptcy, Gustad has vowed never to cry, but to struggle on. The biggest threat to his cocoon of security occurs when the mentally handicapped Tehmul sees the ten lakh rupees through the window and blabbers the gossip; this threat becomes worse when a beheaded rat and a beheaded cat are ominously thrown in his tiny garden and he is warned in a mysterious anonymous note to deposit the money in the bank. So, the threats to Gustad's cocoon stem from disease, filial disloyalty, poverty, fear of unemployment, losing his nerve, and getting caught up in criminal activity out of friendship. Gustad has to learn that there is no absolutely secure cocoon and no permanence.

Repression and Safety Valves

The mounting threats to his petit bourgeois stability are ignored, downplayed or repressed by Gustad, as he struggles to cope. The most obvious symbol of repression and shutting out the outside world is Gustad's refusal to remove the black paper stuck on all the windows, originally for a blackout in the 1962 war with China. It is now 1971, but still Gustad keeps the blackout. It has become a neurosis and a metaphor for the way his mind uses repression of everything unpalatable from outside.

Gustad's momentary thought of lust for the typist Laurie or his curiosity about the prostitutes in the brothel are largely repressed. His son Sohrab's left wing accusations of the corruption of Prime Minister Indira Gandhi in favouring her son with taxpayers' money for his failed motor car enterprise are heatedly refuted by Gustad: corruption at the top would imperil the political stability of his nation, so he refuses to believe it. The notion of seven million refugees from East Pakistan pouring into an India that has no way to feed them is a lurking horror that is repressed. Every now and then it rears its menacing head and is quickly tucked away again as an insoluble problem. The sounding of the air defence siren in Bombay is trivialized with jokes. The threat by Shiv Sena to the democracy and stability of Bombay is avoided as a topic of conversation. The nefarious and illegal activities of Major Jimmy Bilimoria for RAW are hushed up and not spoken about. The beheaded rat and cat are terrifying and push Gustad into quick compliance so that the menace will go away.

The defence used by Dinshawji against these menaces is clowning. The defence used by Gustad's wife Dilnavaz is superstition, taboos and black magic to ward off the evil eye. Gustad himself retreats into doing his duty in stern silence and repression. But as the pressure builds slowly in this novel, clearly his tactics will no longer work. The novel culminates in tragedy with three bitter, untimely deaths and three funerals which Gustad must endure.

Taboos and Superstition

Dilnavaz Noble tries to guard her family against menace and disruption with taboos and superstition. She is sure that one must never speak out loud the worst disasters that one fears. If she does this inadvertently, then she invokes the ritual of *oowaaryoo*, imploring the gods to delete all record of this breaking of a taboo. The taboo is her version of repression. She invariably consults the local witch, the elderly spinster Miss Kutpitia, for remedies against misfortune, either sewing and hanging up a chain of lime and green chillies or passing a lime seven times around her son Sohrab's head to ward off the evil eye and to restore peace and domestic tranquillity. These scenes are part farce and part melodrama. The cures show no sign of working. Gustad tries to mock these superstitions, but he himself has nothing better to offer when the chips are down and everything he has built up is falling down around him.

Roshan's Doll as Lucky Talisman

Just as there are evil omens in this novel, there are also favourable omens of good luck. When Roshan wins a lifesize doll in a school raffle, the doll quickly becomes a talisman. The doll, with her immaculate, old-fashioned clothing, is also a symbol of wealth and security, or for the mentally retarded Tehmul an object of erotic perfection and sexual desire. When the doll is undressed and the naked doll and her clothes are packed away, she loses her symbolic power. But when she is re-dressed and put on display, Roshan responds with a temporary recovery from her mystery illness. When the doll is stolen, the mystery deepens and the fears of evil grow. Mistry's art is to invest these mysteries and fears with a quite extraordinary narrative intensity.

Sickness and Mortality

Awareness of mortality and decay first threaten the characters in this novel when Gustad flings himself from a bus to save his son's life and dislocates his hip. Much is made of this, especially in the image of the selfless father who sacrifices himself for his son but in the end is rewarded, as he sees it, with ingratitude and refusal to accept his fatherly authority. In truth the boy Sohrab is just going through the normal teenage phase of self-assertion and independence which is necessary for his development. But Gustad says, melodramatically, that he no longer acknowledges this son. It is a typical, blustering over-reaction, a cutting off of his nose to spite his face, and all because Gustad fears all change. The curing of the hip dislocation is used to suggest the superiority of the Indian bonesetter to western medicine and to help uphold Gustad's masculine dignity, so that he doesn't have to limp badly for the rest of his life. It is nevertheless a sign of encroaching physical frailty and mortality.

Far more threatening are both the mystery illness of daughter Roshan, where orthodox medicine doesn't seem to help much, and the stomach cancer of Dinshawji. This is where Gustad is at his most vulnerable, most panic-stricken and most guilty. This could almost degenerate into the pop culture genre of domestic soap opera and melodrama, but although Mistry gives the sicknesses plenty of focus and deliberately plucks at the readers' heartstrings, he does avoid all purple language and hyperbole. Thematically, the sicknesses underline Gustad's tragic inability to protect his family and friends from the intrusions of fate and bad luck.

Local and International Politics

Gradually, the number of references to the faraway war in East Pakistan increase, together with estimates of the number of rapes and massacres and the number of terrified refugees (up to 7 million). This combines with the eerie sounding of the air alarm siren. Evidence of the corruption and treachery of the Indira Gandhi government mounts and becomes incontrovertible. Major Bilimoria is betrayed by Mrs. Gandhi and arrested while secretly following her orders and extracting 60 lakh rupees from the Bank of India by impersonating her voice. The RAW activities of Major Bilimoria and the secret funding and fighting of the Mukti Bahini guerrillas increase Gustad's and Dinshawji's sense of unease and fear of an impending war, an invasion, war-rationing, extra refugee-taxes and so on. The structural function of international politics in this novel, such as the easy military triumph of China over Nehru's India in 1962, Pakistan's rattling of the war drum over Kashmir and East Pakistan and the covert support by the American CIA for Pakistan to keep Russia away from access to a southern port—all these factors contribute to the lower middle class's fear of destruction of their precarious standards of living. The sectarian thuggery of the ultra right wing group Shiv Sena and mob violence in protesting against municipal corruption increase this fear of lawlessness and chaos.

Sexuality

At first it seems as though sexuality is simply not a theme in *Such a Long Journey*, but this is because of the puritanical repression. The hints and signs of repression are there: the simpleton Tehmul rubbing at his genitals in public and his drooling lasciviousness for Roshan's doll when it is undressed are such signs. The son Sohrab's teenage adoration for the plump daughter of the insulted dog-wallah is a sub-theme. But the two main hints of repression are these: First, Dinshawiji's indecent clowning in front of the very feminine typist Laurie Coutino in which he goes too far and refers to his genitals. Second, Gustad's flash of sexual desire as he follows the typist up the stairs to a private booth. Third, the repeated references to the House of Cages which is the local brothel and into which Gustad has to enter in pursuit of the RAW officer Ghulam Mohammed. These hints of sexual desire all have in common that they are portrayed as potential causes of chaos and mayhem. They threaten the established order. They threaten Dinshawji's job and they constitute a secret menace to the innocence of daughter Roshan. Petit bourgeois society has to preserve its sense of order by repressing sexual desire, but this desire has scandalous and bizarre ways of escaping from its cage and rearing its menacing head.

The Fear of Unemployment and Poverty

There is constant scraping and saving with every last rupee and paise being jealously guarded. Old newspapers have to be sold as waste paper in order to meet household expenses. Gustad's salary as a bank teller is clearly very small. The family has fallen on hard times since the grandfather owned one of India's biggest bookshops and his playboy brother gambled the lot away. They have to put up with the stink of people using their front wall as a public urinal, an unreliable supply of disease-carrying water, watered-down milk and basic rations. To buy a second hand book is a luxury. Gustad's centre of refuge is his job as a bank teller and his main terror is somehow to inculpate himself and lose this job. This may sound rather pedestrian as the main issue in an imaginative work of art, but Mistry manages to make this fear, and the other security fears of his main protagonist into philosophical and even tragic problems and presents them very persuasively.

A Hero Who Grows in Courage

When you think about it, there is very little plot to *Such a Long Journey.* What there is, consists of a sequence of menaces to the domestic security of Gustad's cosseted, little domestic realm. Mistry presents these menaces with intensity and detailed verisimilitude and he has us nervously turning pages in worried concern for the Noble family.

Gustad is a stoic and obscure hero with no grand deeds but a man who accepts his impoverished lot in life, does his duty and shows resolute decency to everybody. Above all, he never gives in to self-pity, or to rages against God and fate or to tears of helplessness. Only once does he abandon his principles as a man of science and progress: downcast by the continuing serious illnesses of his beloved daughter and his friend Dinshawji and the unjust imprisonment and illness of Major Jimmy Bilimoria, he resorts to populist superstition by going with his friend Malcolm to Mount Mary shrine, buying wax effigies to represent his loved ones in need of a miracle cure and lighting candles and praying to the virgin mother of Jesus. We do not see this as a flaw in his character. On the contrary. He is motivated by protective and unselfish love. Gustad is noble by name and noble by nature.

But Gustad has the idiosyncratic weakness of needing to keep the black-out paper glued to his apartment windows. This black-out paper is the symbol of his attempt to blot out all outside menace, to ignore it, to repress it, so that he can keep his family secure. The menaces are varied and range from war with China and then with Pakistan, dire threats by the murky representatives of the Indian Secret Service, disease, unsanitary living conditions, fear of dismissal, unemployment and abject poverty, undercurrents of sexual lasciviousness and any change to the status quo. When at the end of the novel, he finally has the resoluteness to tear down the black-out paper, it is because he no longer has a need to cower within his walls or to repress his fears of the worst. He has been through the tragic loss of his two best friends, Dinshawji and Major Bilimoria. He has behaved equally with compassion and dignity in the accidental death of the retarded Tehmul. He has been steeled in combat with disease, intrigue and death, and he has grown inwardly to a deeper courage. He was loyal and humane when he visited the dying Major Bilimoria in prison in Delhi; but he was even more humane when he understood why the simpleton Tehmul needed his secret lust for Roshan's stolen doll. It was a moving gesture when he dressed the doll in her finery to be laid alongside Tehmul on his death bed.

Genre: Domestic Melodrama with Villains? Or Tragic Farce? Or Religious Parable?

Perhaps the key to understanding the genre in which Rohinton Mistry is writing is held by the words of the title. On the basic, realistic and childish level, the words "such a long journey" refer to a childhood journey made by Gustad with his parents to a hill station for a holiday. The words are the kind of thing you say when you put a child to bed (242).

Symbolically, however, the title refers to Everyman's very long journey from cradle to grave: it is the pilgrimage of Gustad from the traumatic experience of his father's bankruptcy, which in a way was worse than death (243), through the tests and trials of his manhood and his loyalty towards the winning of wisdom and serenity.

Religiously, the title's words also refer to the last long walk up the gravel path of the hill to the Tower of Silence where the corpse will be left to the vultures. Gustad holds the hand of the frightened little boy on this final walk in order to reassure him: it is the final rite of the Parsees. When Gustad bids farewell to his dead friend, Dinshawji, he derives solace from the traditional Parsee prayers, spoken in the ancient language of Zoroaster that no one understood any longer (247). He is also deeply impressed by the peace and even the apparent smile on the dead man's face. Gustad overcomes his fear of death, menace and the unknown and begins to see the peace of death (248). This is reinforced when he is the sole Parsee mourner for his old friend Major Bilimoria and he must again walk up the gravel path to the Tower of Silence. He learns much from bidding farewell to his two best friends at these two funerals. The serenity that he learns equips him spiritually to be able to show sympathy and dignity for Tehmul in his accidental death shortly afterwards. As shown in Mistry's novel, life is ideally a pilgrimage towards wisdom, courage and compassion.

This pilgrimage is accompanied in *Such a Long Journey* by "a miraculous transformation" (286), a transfiguration of the black wall outside Gustad's tenement building. It had been misused as a public urinal, attracted hordes of mosquitoes and was a "horrid shit and piss hell." The pavement artist transforms it with his religious paintings with the themes deliberately drawn from every major religion in India: Zoroastrianism, Hinduism, Islam, Judaism, Jainism, Christianity and Buddhism. The pavement artist is the prophet of a non-sectarian God for all. The religious drawings attract offerings of flowers and the stink is transformed to the scents of heaven. It is a grotesque farce when

Municipal workers arrive to tear down the sacred wall for no good reason other than bureaucracy, but that brings us to another genre in this novel of many genres.

Typical of Mistry's deliberate mixing of moods and genres is this example. Gustad's pious participation in the Parsee funeral of his joker-friend Dinshawji is undoubtedly the tragic climax of the novel and it is deeply moving. The gloom of defeat and failure are deepened with the lonely funeral of Major Jimmy Bilimoria. But no sooner is Jimmy bade a sad farewell than Mistry launches abruptly into a farce. He depicts the greedy, overstuffed vultures leaving the corpses and wearily dropping leftover titbits as they fly past high-rise residences. This is in itself gruesome and grotesque. But Mistry then transforms the scene into farcical satire when the rich tenants of the luxury apartments make formal legal protest against the vultures for bombarding their prestigious balconies with morsels of human flesh (317).

The abruptly changing tones and moods of *Such a Long Journey* make it quite difficult to classify within any one genre. Mistry was well aware of this and he gives us an ironic clue about how he sees his art when he suggests a comparison with the popular, folk-oratory of Peerbhoy Paanwalla. Panwalla transfixes the Bombay crowd during the 1971 war in East Pakistan with his propaganda parable of the Pakistani President as an impotent drunkard who overcompensates for his impotent sexual weapon with an aggressive misuse of other, larger, destructive military weapons (306-209). What is the nature of this comparison of the art of Peerbhoy and Mistry?

Mistry wants to transfix his audience, just as Peerbhoy has done, regardless of the rules of literary criticism governing such literary genres as "tragical-comical, historical-pastoral . . . epic, . . . mock-heroic . . . ballad, . . . ode, masque or anti-masque, fable or elegy, parody or threnody." (306) Mistry wants his audience to join him in thumbing his nose at literary criticism and to respond to his tale "with every fibre of their beings." He wants us to "see and smell and taste and feel the words that . . . conjured the tale" and made Peerbhoy's audience "oblivious to the gutter stink." This is Mistry's self-defence against the possibility of literary critics charging him with having written a novel that combines the minute details of kitchen-sink realism (2) with the pathos of melodrama.

Indeed *Such a Long Journey* is partly classifiable as domestic and political melodrama. The ultimate villains are the power- and intrigue-driven Indira Gandhi and her greedy, corrupt son. The shining knight is played by Gustad Noble. The novel can be seen as a peculiar mixture of tragedy, farce and the grotesque (but then so are some of Shakespeare's tragedies). Equally, the novel is an Everyman religious parable of pilgrimage. Finally, it is also a political satire against corrupt government at all levels. According to Mistry, this deliberate mixing of the genres really doesn't matter. All he wants is for us to acknowledge that he has conjured up the magic to make us turn the pages and to become absorbed in the terrors and the joys of his petit bourgeois hero and his fictional world. Mistry wants to be seen as an unconventional magician and conjurer and I for one am happy to see him in this light.

The religious and philosophical hero of *Such a Long Journey* is the homeless pavement-artist. In a true *sunnyasi* spirit he suggests that the simple religious parables of all religions inspire people and help them to grapple with their miseries and woes, so why look down on these parables from the would-be lofty, rationalist heights of science and scepticism. To do so would be smug and destructive of ordinary people's religious needs and would be without moral justification.

The pavement artist philosophically embraces transience and the inevitability of change. He packs up his drawing-crayons and prepares for the next stage in his wandering pilgrimage he knows not where and says: "In a world where roadside latrines become temples and shrines, and temples and shrines become dust and ruin, does it matter where? . . . Luck is the spit of gods and goddesses." (338)

Not all of us can hope to emulate this stalwart sunnyasi pilgrim. But we can hope to strive towards the acquired wisdom, loyalty, decency and compassion of Gustad Noble. For all its quirks and unconventionalities and mood-changes and flaws, *Such a Long Journey* is an inspiring and thought-provoking read and more than deserved its short-listing for the Booker Prize.

NOTES

1. Rohinton Mistry, *Such a Long Journey* (London: Faber and Faber, 1991).
2. The issue of whether realism is artistically respectable in today's postmodernist world is debated by Chelva Kanaganayakam in *The University of Toronto Quarterly*, Vol. 71, No. 4, Fall 2002. York University, Toronto, seems to have adopted Rohinton Mistry as a Canadian author and maintains an inventory of Mistry's works called the Clara Thomas Archives (see http://archivesfa.library.york.ca/fonds/ON00370-f0000180.htm)

Mistry's Hollow Men: language, lies and the crisis of representation in *Such a Long Journey*

PETER G. MOREY
University of Eastern London

> Truly there are two primal Spirits, twins renowned to be in conflict. In thought and word, in act they are two: the better and the bad. And those who act well have chosen rightly between these two, not so the evil-doers.
>
> (*The Gathas*, Yasna 30, v. 3)

> We are the hollow men
> We are the stuffed men
> Leaning together
> Headpiece filled with straw.
>
> (T.S. Eliot, *The Hollow Men*, lines 1-4)

Commenting on the possibilities of narrating the colourful story of India's historical experiences, Rukmini Nair writes:

> It sometimes seems apt to imagine the history of this subcontinent as a palimpsest of literary forms. First a substantial layer of myth and epic, then a burning layer of tragedy, then farce and so forth. Lately, the furious discovery of political scandals we've witnessed might suggest that it is now an action thriller, Hindi-film style, which is currently being written out in subcontinental space. (Nair 14)

Rohinton Mistry's first two novels, *Such a Long Journey* and *A Fine Balance*, appear to bear out this suggestion. Both have something of the political thriller about them, although, as always in Mistry's writing, the operations of history are linked to, and impinge on, humdrum, quotidian life. In the earlier novel, published in 1991, political events put pressure on a family already under strain. Gustad Noble becomes alienated from his disobedient elder son, his precious daughter falls mysteriously ill, and he struggles with memories of a financially secure and emotionally stable past that only serve to highlight his family's current plight at a time of shortages and rationing. Additionally, the outside world with its political intrigues and threat of war seeps into their flat in the Khodadad Building, a Parsi housing development in Bombay. As a Parsi loyal to Indira Gandhi's government, Gustad finds himself, along with his friend Major Jimmy Bilimoria, used and duped as part of an apparent plot hatched by the Prime Minister to embezzle money. The Bilimoria sub-plot is based on a true-life financial scandal that engulfed Indira Gandhi's government at the beginning of the nineteen-seventies, and offers a point of entry to one of the text's central concerns, the manipulation and misuse of language. The theme of language versus reality is played out in the doublespeak of the government: the Prime Minister's vocal denial of involvement in a conspiracy bearing the hallmark of her arbitrary power; the renaming of Bombay streets by the Shiv Sena which leads to acute existential anxieties in Gustad's dying friend, Dinshawji; the discrepancy between the propaganda offered by the newspapers at time of war—about evil, baby-bayoneting Pakistani troops confronted by their impossibly heroic and virtuous Indian counterparts—and the reality which seems to involve shady dealings at the highest level; and a 'hollowness' at the heart of language more generally in this tale of misunderstanding and the limitations of verbal communication. This, in turn, is linked to a wider Platonic investigation into the relationship between shadow and reality operating on a number of levels, and which can also be connected to the Zoroastrian struggle to reconcile the spiritual (*menog*) and material (*getig*) realms. Many situations and characters are multi-layered or enigmatic, and there always appears to be a gap between events and the power of language to describe them and encompass their various resonances: a disjuncture between appearance and actuality, intention and outcome, utterance and reception, object and surrogate. Gustad's initial desire to hold the outside world at a safe distance, symbolised by the blackout paper he keeps over his windows even in peace time, is part of the related theme of activity versus withdrawal, traceable to the Zoroastrian demand that the true devotee be actively engaged in the fight against evil. *Such a Long Journey* is in part the story of Gustad's battle to confront and overcome the urge to withdraw. After all, it is only through the activity of the righteous that evil may be defeated and good advanced. As always, in this novel about contending evils of various kinds, Mistry gives the Zoroastrian ethical imperative a political dimension. Many paths to truth are charted, some of them spiritual or supernatural, and some of them mundane and material. Yet the important thing is never to be merely passive, always to go on with the journey.

The novel is set in 1971, the turbulent year of the struggle between what were then the East and West wings of Pakistan, which eventually drew in India and culminated in a brief, two-week war and the creation of Bangladesh. It also harks back to the political history of India in the 1960s, the decade that saw the death of Jawaharlal Nehru and the accession of his daughter Indira Gandhi. Events in the Sixties—including the Indo-Chinese War, the sudden death of Nehru's successor Lal Bahadur Shastri, superpower meddling, and the rise of Indira and her tearaway son Sanjay—are all mentioned in the text and seem to be characteristic of a political landscape of decline, deceit and corruption.

However, the most important background feature of all, described in the later part of the novel, is the Indo-Pakistan War of December 1971, triggered by a divided election result in the two wings of Pakistan. The larger force in West Pakistan, led by Zulfikar Ali Bhutto and General Yahya Khan, refused to accept the election result in the East which had gone against them and in favour of Mujib-ur Rehman's Awami League. They ordered the arrest of the East's victorious candidate and embarked on the suppression of opposition in the territory in an unprecedented clampdown. Brutal repression led to an enormous refugee crisis with, eventually, approximately ten million people fleeing across the border into Indian controlled Bengal (Adams and Whitehead 230-39). Of course, such an influx was inevitably a severe strain on India's resources; one result was the Refugee Tax which pushed up prices, and which characters complain about in the novel. There was also a groundswell of popular opinion supporting the deployment of Indian troops in defence of the Bengalis. Not wanting to appear the aggressor, Indira Gandhi initially rejected such a move, preferring instead to train and equip guerrilla bands based in India but operating across the border. And this is, of course, the point of overlap with the political subplot of *Such a Long Journey*.

Major Jimmy Bilimoria, Gustad's close friend from the Khodadad Building, suddenly disappears, leaving no other explanation than that he has embarked on a covert mission in the interests of national security. Eventually we discover that he is involved in the activities of RAW—the Research and Analysis Wing of India's secret service. It seems that he is engaged in providing funds for the cross-border guerrilla groups. However, it is soon apparent that Jimmy has become deeply embroiled in an altogether more murky set of events, involving the embezzlement of large sums of money. The outline of his story is based on that of a parallel historical figure—also a Parsi and, by all accounts, an agent of RAW—Captain Sohrab Rustom Nagarwala. On 24 May 1971, the chief cashier of the State Bank of India received a telephone call, apparently from the Prime Minister, instructing him to withdraw six million rupees and hand them over to a person whom he would find waiting on a road, and who would identify himself simply as 'a man from Bangladesh'. The cashier obeyed these instructions and then went to the Prime Minister's residence to ask for a receipt. To his surprise, he was told by the Prime Minister's private secretary that she had made no such telephone call, and advised to contact the police. He did so, and Captain Nagarwala, who had taken deliverv of the money, was swiftly arrested. He seemed to have left an easy trail for the police to follow, and confessed that he had impersonated Indira Gandhi's voice to obtain money to support guerrilla activities in Bangladesh. However, what began to raise suspicions at the time, and what was never adequately explained, was the hasty and highly unorthodox manner in which Captain Nagarwala's trial was conducted. Three different judges presided over the case in just three days, at the end of which he was sentenced to four years' imprisonment. The police failed to produce in court the tape they claimed to have of Nagarwala's remarkable impersonation of Mrs Gandhi, and contradictions between his story and that of the State Cashier were never investigated. Moreover, after his arrest, Nagarwala appears to have had a change of heart. From prison he appealed for a retrial and tried unsuccessfully to gain an interview with a journalist and fellow Parsi from a Bombay weekly newspaper. A few months later, Nagarwala was removed to hospital, allegedly complaining of chest pain, where he died in March 1972 (Sahgal 83).

In Mistry's fictionalised version of these events, the Nagarwala substitute, Jimmy Bilimoria, tells Gustad that he has been made a stooge in the interests of Mrs Gandhi and her family who act extra-constitutionally and for their own ends: 'it is beyond the common man's imagination, the things being done by those in power' (280). Mistry partly undercuts these shocking allegations by having Jimmy utter them on what turns out to be his deathbed, in disjointed fashion, and in a drug-addled daze. Yet they do appear to represent more insistent, gnawing malefactions in the body politic as a whole.

Against this, the Parsi world of the Khodadad Building seems something of a haven: the novel commences with Gustad's morning orisons to Ahura Mazda, while ritually tying and untying his *kusti* cord, and later he reflects fondly on his elder son's *navjote* ceremony, initiating him into Zoroastrianism. Such moments are often retrospective, and the narrative works through a shuttling temporal schema that is the formal corollary of the thematic concern with memory and identity. Of course, the locus for the most powerful memories is to be found in the tender minutiae of family life. Gustad recalls the halcyon days when the family had servants, whereas now they cannot even afford to buy milk from the Parsi dairy. He therefore invests his hopes for the future in his elder son, Sohrab. However, rather than appreciate the sacrifices his parents have made to facilitate his education, Sohrab refuses to accept entry into the prestigious Indian Institute of Technology, preferring, much to his father's outrage, to pursue an arts degree elsewhere. The generational split that results, culminates in a series of bitter arguments, after the last of which Gustad disowns his son. In fact, by attempting to impose his personal ambitions on his son, Gustad is at once hoping to reclaim vicariously his own lost opportunities, clinging to the remnants of the old father-child relationship and attempting to perpetuate his role as protector: a role which once saw him seriously injured in a traffic accident while thrusting the young Sohrab to safety. This inability to come to terms with time, change and endings—fundamental to human life—characterises Gustad's dealings with those around him. He aims to keep everything, family, friendships, his environment, pristine and inviolate. Beyond his domestic habitat he is much less confident, and recalls Eliot's Prufrock, diffident, paralysed by doubt and confronted by seemingly hostile forces in the outside world; during one misunderstanding with his wife, Dilnavaz, he even laments, 'That is not what I meant at all' (292).

Most redolent of this mindset is the physical space of the Khodadad Building itself. It is a Parsi enclave in the heart of Bombay, almost a ghetto, with all the attendant paranoia such an environment suggests. At one point, the complex is likened to a museum, and it is no coincidence that many domestic items in Gustad's apartment seem to be in a state of atrophy and decay too. In this atmosphere, municipal proposals to demolish the wall surrounding the compound as part of a road-widening programme take on the qualities of a threatened invasion, further underlining the community's sense of being at siege. The wall keeps the hectic, disordered world out. Yet even this space cannot be maintained in its purity: it is used as a public latrine by passers-by, like dogs marking their territory, and as events unfold, Gustad's worries start 'walling him in, threatening to crush him,' (177). In *Gitanjali*, one of the intertexts that provide epigraph quotations at the start of the novel, Tagore describes a devotional crisis which, nevertheless, mirrors Gustad's own self-inflicted isolation: 'I am ever busy building this wall all around; and as this wall goes up into the sky day by day I lose sight of my true being in its dark shadow' (Tagore 17). The dark shadow cast by the wall becomes Stygian gloom within the apartment on account of the blackout paper Gustad has put up at the time of the Indo-Chinese War, and which he has refused to remove ever since. We are told that the paper restricts 'the ingress of all forms of light, earthly and celestial', and despite Gustad's regular dawn prayers, Dilnavaz remarks, 'In this house, the morning never seems to come,' (11). The blackout answers a psychological need in Gustad in that it keeps out the frightening historical events he reads about in the newspaper everyday, as the nation prepares for war and its propaganda machine grinds into action. Moreover, as he has discovered in his dealings with Sohrab—and with his neighbour Jimmy Bilimoria, whose sudden and unexplained disappearance leaves him baffled and angry—to reach out to others, even members of one's own family, is to risk betrayal.

Ironically, it is the Major himself, Gustad's best friend and, in many respects a surrogate brother for him, who is the 'agent' that brings the outside world in and destroys Gustad's insulated existence. He does so by embroiling his friend, and a work colleague, Dinshawji, in the embezzlement scam, sending bulky packages of crisp new banknotes along with a prevaricating letter requiring them to make regular bank deposits on his behalf. As an undercover operative, Jimmy has certain affinities with Verloc in Joseph Conrad's novel of intrigue and evasion, *The Secret Agent*. Both novels explore the theme of loyalty, and the respective protagonists keep secrets even from those nearest to them. Secrecy and agency are themes in a more general sense too, as characters are empowered or disempowered to varying degrees according to the amount of knowledge they possess. And, crucially, both texts are concerned with the way language can be used to obscure and disinform as much as to enlighten.

Indeed, *Such a Long Journey* demonstrates an insistent concern with the slippery, malleable nature of language, and how reality can often be very different from appearance. This is nowhere more evident than in the nature of names and naming. Characters adopt and discard names, give and take nicknames, and find that certain names stick, while others are forgotten: the bank manager, Mr Madon has a secret first name that no one knows; old Mr Cavasji did have a nickname, 'the watermelon', but shed it along with the pounds as he aged; Ghulam Mohammed knows Jimmy as 'Bili-boy', while the latter uses the anagram Mira Obili, when communicating with Gustad incognito; and Dr Paymaster, who treats Roshan's unnameable illness, is completely in thrall to nomenclature when he finds that his patients will not allow him to replace the name of the previous doctor on the sign outside his surgery with his own.

As this last example indicates, to name is to exert power. In an interesting essay on the novel, David Williams invokes Jacques Derrida on the appropriative nature of naming: '"The Battle of Proper Names" in *Of Grammatology* concludes that what's in a name is nothing less than the whole coercive network of relations bounding the subject' (Williams 59). Nowhere is this more evident than in the ailing Dinshawji's lament over the Shiv Sena's campaign of street renaming in Bombay, designed to expunge signs of the British presence and reassert majority Marathi identity:

> Names are so important. I grew up on Lamington Road. But it has disappeared, in its place is Dadasaheb Bhadkamkar Marg. My school was on Carnac Road. Now suddenly it's on Lokmanya Tilak Marg. I live at Sleator Road. Soon that will also disappear. My whole life I have come to work at Flora Fountain. And one fine day the name changes. So what happens to the life I have lived? Was I living the wrong life, with all the wrong names? Will I get a second

> chance to live it all again, with these new names? Tell me what happens to my life. Rubbed out, just like that? (74)

Unfortunately, Dinshawji fails to take on board the lesson about names and power inherent in his disorientation. His own behaviour when flirting with the alluring new secretary at the bank, Laurie Coutino, is an example of the potential sexual violence involved in language and naming. He tells Laurie that he would like to introduce her to his own 'little Lorri', neglecting to mention that *lorri* is the Parsi slang word for penis. When she finds out, Laurie feels demeaned and insulted, telling Gustad, "If someone speaks my name now . . . I feel bad. It reminds me of the dirty meaning. Mr Dinshawji has ruined my own name for me" (176). Although Dinshawji means no offence, the misalliance between intention and effect here offers a prime example of how, in Eliot's words, 'Between the idea / And the reality / Between the motion / And the act / Falls the Shadow' (80). As if to compound both the indignity and the linguistic vacillation, Laurie's complaints about the harassment take place in one of the 'private' upstairs rooms at a local restaurant, where illicit sexual encounters take place, and which contains a sign proclaiming, 'Please Ring Bell For Waiter Under The Table': '"Now why would they put a waiter under the table?" said Gustad' (174).

From Dinshawji's crude double entendres, to the damaged Tehmul with his rapid-fire speech, words have a habit of sliding around, of changing meaning between sender and recipient. Throughout the book attempts at communication tend to obscure as much as they reveal. Gustad and Dilnavaz use a special '*asmai-kasmai*' code when they want to communicate without the children understanding, and a Gujarati child's rhyme is cryptically deployed as a veiled threat to Gustad as he wavers over the bank deposits. When Jimmy realises that he has been framed he sends an apologetic letter to Gustad, imploring him to undertake a visit to the jail in which he now languishes, as, '"you will not believe words on paper, because *I sent you words on paper before and could not keep them from turning false* . . . I want you to know and understand, *hear from your own lips* that you forgive me"' (216, emphasis added). Yet, despite Jimmy's faith in the power of direct verbal communication, the deceptive characteristics of writing also turn out to hold true for the spoken word. On Gustad's arrival, Jimmy's jailor asserts that his charge is suffering from 'jungle sickness', despite the clear textual indication that paralysing drugs are being administered. The story of the set-up emerges little by little, stifled and blurred by the injections: Jimmy's words require patient listening and disentanglement, emerging slowly, 'As though each one was being sculpted painstakingly, out of stubborn granite' (272). And during his account he recalls an observation by that 'Very clever woman', Indira Gandhi, at a personal briefing: '"under the proper conditions, people will believe anything"' (277). During a lull in the interview when Jimmy lapses into catalepsy, Gustad emerges, exhausted, to seek refreshment: 'The policeman said there was tea and snacks in the canteen downstairs. He pronounced it snakes' (272).

As all this suggests, Gustad offers the main example of how misrecognition and the fundamental gap between appearance and reality are played out in *Such a Long Journey*. Initially, this relates to his bewildered and resentful dealings with Jimmy which draw him further into the world of double-dealing and intrigue he seeks to avoid. Baffled by his neighbour's unexplained disappearance, Gustad no longer knows what to believe about him. His absence allows Gustad to project all manner of sinister motivations onto him and his actions, viewing him as a traitor to the close friendship they have shared. In this respect, Jimmy is one of several characters who invite their interlocutors—and the reader—to project interpretations onto them. For instance, Dinshawji plays the role of 'the Casanova of Flora Fountain', and maintains a façade of good humour and ribaldry despite the fact that he is actually dying. As a result of this discrepancy between appearance and reality, Gustad is shocked by the speed of his decline when, in the interests of discretion, the joking is silenced:

> When Gustad came across him later in the day, he was surprised at how authentically Dinshawji projected his new image. Till he remembered that it seemed authentic because Dinshawji was no longer playing a role; reality, at last, had caught up with him; and Gustad felt awful for confiscating his mask. (181)

Another character onto whom it is even easier to project interpretation is Tehmul-Lungraa. With his swaying gait and impaired mental faculties, Tehmul lurches around chasing butterflies, running simple errands, and disconcerting residents by his tendency to follow them around; he becomes particularly attached to Gustad with a child-like loyalty and faith. In the novel as a whole, Tehmul functions as a kind of divine idiot or fool figure. Like Dostoyevsky's eponymous character, Prince Myshkin, in *The Idiot*, Tehmul appears too good, too innocent for the duplicitous society in which he is placed. Likewise, both Tehmul and the Prince have no knowledge of women, although Tehmul's beatific innocence is alloyed with a disturbingly adult sexuality: his drooling and crotch-rubbing antics alarm Dilnavaz, particularly when he appears to set his sites on the attractive pink plaster doll Roshan has won in a school raffle.

Both Gustad and Dilnavaz in their different ways take advantage of Tehmul and project their anxieties onto him: Gustad, by frightening him with the threat of violence when he finds out about the hoard of money; Dilnavaz by conspiring with Miss Kutpitia to displace onto him the 'evil spirits' afflicting little Roshan and making her ill. Indeed, the text appears to maintain the possibility that Tehmul has been gifted some extraordinary qualities and powers to compensate for his other disabilities. We are told that he has the 'ability to ferret out information ahead of others with whole minds and bodies' (112), and there is enough evidence to support a reading of his urgent desire to 'touch' Roshan's doll as more than simply an urge to sexual self-gratification. Is it some kind of proxy healing gesture, a laying on of hands, to draw the malevolent forces from her and, thus, effect a cure? Like Joseph Conrad's half-witted Stevie in *The Secret Agent*, Tehmul is an incoherent victim of the machinations and intrigues of those around him. However, unlike the hapless Stevie, Tehmul becomes a redemptive figure: he is the receptacle into which the bad spirits plaguing Roshan will be poured, and his death at the end of the novel effects a reunion between the estranged Gustad and Sohrab over his corpse. He is, on one level, a kind of sacrificial lamb—just as, one might say, Major Jimmy Bilimoria is made a sacrificial lamb on the national level (although, in the latter case any redemption is rather more ambiguous and short-lived, as Mistry will show in *A Fine Balance*).

Tehmul, like Jimmy, is one of Mistry's 'hollow men' in *Such a Long Journey*, embodying the text's insistent concern with shadows and doubles, surrogates and simulacra. For example, at one point Jimmy poses alongside a projection of the crime fighting superhero the Shadow to entertain Gustad's children, but is later described on his deathbed as 'nothing more than a shadow. The shadow of the powerfully-built army man who once lived in Khodadad Building' (267). Similarly, in a last trip to the Noble home before the hospitalisation from which he will not emerge, Dinshawji is little more than a shadow of the ebullient joker Dilnavaz remembers from a previous visit: 'The man who had laughed and sung that night, drunk beer and recited rhymes . . . was not the man who stood before her,' (187) shrunken and visibly sick. Meanwhile, Roshan's doll operates as her double—when he hears of his daughter's raffle success Gustad exclaims, 'my doll has won a doll' (84)—but it also serves as a surrogate sexual partner for Tehmul, who has been denied the physical comforts of the 'painted dolls' working in the local brothel, the 'House of Cages'. The image of synthetic supplements for organic entities, begun with the doll, reaches a semi-surrealistic pitch in the plethora of surrogate body parts—torsos, limbs, digits, heads—sold to supplicants at the Church of Mount Mary, hoping for miraculous cures to a variety of ailments; just as the statue of the Virgin, supposedly found under supernatural circumstances, like all icons acts as a receptacle for the hopes and dreams of the faithful.

The line between what one might call the deep structures of these psychic correspondences, and 'mere' simulation, is never entirely clear. Dinshawji simulates vitality and cheerfulness for as long as he can; Tehmul simulates sex with Roshan's doll; Ghulam Mohammed—the contact through whom Jimmy communicates with Gustad—alters his appearance to play the roles of taxi-driver or bookseller as the exigencies of espionage require; and the government of India simulates openness and accountability while actually being mired in corruption and ruthlessness. Ghulam Mohammad makes a comment about Jimmy's predicament that might almost stand as a refrain, or a surrogate title for the novel as a whole: 'things are not what they seem' (215).

At one point, when Gustad goes to Chor Bazaar for a rendezvous with Ghulam Mohammad he purchases a copy of Plato's *Dialogues* at a bookstall. Probably the most famous of these dialogues is *The Republic* in which Plato advances his Theory of Ideas or Forms. Here, Plato explains that most people live as if in a darkened cave. We are chained, facing a blank wall, and behind us is a fire. Between the fire and our backs, others move carrying all manner of vessels, statues and figurines of various shapes and materials. All we can see are the flickering shadows of these objects playing on the screen offered by the wall in front of us. It is only by learning to break our shackles and turn away from the wall and its shadows, that we can hope to escape into the true light of day, and view those archetypal Forms—the ideal paradigms, of which all earthly entities are merely imperfect copies (Plato 177-78). Although Plato is talking about a general philosophical conundrum, it is tempting to apply his ideas to Gustad in *Such a Long Journey*: trapped in his own dim cave, the earthly and celestial light kept out by the blackout paper and his own fear of change, chasing the shadows that have become threatening only because he cannot face them fully. Throughout the book, the lure of the illusion, of what one wishes to believe, is stronger than that of reality.

These Platonic interests and echoes work not merely to lend intellectual *kudos* to Gustad's personal tribulations, but to point up the thematic continuity between Plato and the cosmological and theological preoccupations of Zoroastrianism. Correspondences between Platonism and Zoroastrianism include the tendency both systems have to privilege the verbal over the written. In poststructuralism, Derrida's critique of logocentrism questions that elevation, traceable to Plato, of the spoken over the written in human communication. The comparatively late transcription of the Gathic texts of Zoroastrianism likewise ensured the pre-eminence of oral performance in ritual observance: 'The sound of the words themselves were thought to convey power and instil religious experience, a power and experience which could not be captured by the written word' (Clark 16). Similarly, Platonism, like the revealed religions, of which Zoroastrianism is the oldest, interprets truth as an absolute hidden from humankind, but which can yet be attained by those following the path of light.

Indeed, it is in their mutual recourse to images of light that Platonism and Zoroastrianism seem most apposite as compatible modes of approach to *Such a Long Journey*. In the parable of the cave, light becomes, for Plato, a symbol of the ultimate Good: the nearest we can approach to the Divine Form itself; 'the good may be said to be not only the author of knowledge to all things known, but of their being and essence' (Plato 174). He continues:

> my opinion is that in the world of knowledge the idea of good appears last of all, and is seen only with an effort; and, when seen, is also inferred to be the universal author of all things beautiful and right, *parent of light and lord of light* in this visible world. (Plato 179, my italics)

In Zoroastrianism, the *Yasna* ceremony, the highest of the liturgies, may only be performed at sunrise, 'since this is said to represent the fire of *asha* scattering light and heat over creation' (Clark 99). And in the ninth century *Pahlavi* text, the *Bunda-*

hishen, *Ohrmazd*, otherwise known as *Ahura Mazda*, dwells outside time, 'in a realm of pure light', while the evil spirit, *Ahriman*, exists, 'in a realm of utter darkness' (Clark 51). *Asha*, associated with truth, is represented in Zoroastrian ceremonial by fire. It is the opposite of evil or the lie, *drug*, and represents that ideal form by which the cosmos should be regulated. Considering the battle between truth and lies that is conducted on all levels in *Such a Long Journey*, Mistry's novel appears to raise once again one of the central questions from the *Yasna* hymns: 'This I ask you, O Ahura, tell me truly: How can I deliver deceit into the hands of truth'? (Clark 31-32)

It has also been suggested that the two planes of existence recognised in Zoroastrianism—the *menog*, or spiritual, and the *getig*, material—correspond to Plato's notions of physical and Ideal realms. The *getig* plane serves as the battlefield between the forces of good and evil, while the *menog* has been read as a prototypical stratum, inhabited by the spirits. According to Clark:

> Both Plato and Zarathushtra advocated a dualistic view of the universe, though their respective forms of dualism are only superficially related. . . . In Zoroastrianism, unlike Platonism, there is an ethical struggle to make the *menog* accessible through the *getig* on the basis that the more good there is in a spatially and temporally finite world the less evil can reside there, whereas the Platonic view tends towards the eventual rejection of the *entirety* of the mundane, allowing the 'ideal' world of forms to be realised and experienced in its totality (Clark 78-79).

In view of this, Zoroastrianism requires of its devotee a conscious choice to participate in the battle against evil. As a result, asceticism is discouraged as it constitutes a retreat from that worldly engagement on behalf of truth. (This desire to engage is what Gustad lacks at the beginning of the novel, and needs to develop. His horror of contamination and urge to withdraw can be seen as an indulging of an ascetic instinct.) Whether or not final victory is achievable in this world is a moot point. What is important is to be always endeavouring to move, to journey, towards perfection.

Thus, Gustad's long journey is to a kind of enlightenment on two levels: that of political reality, and that of personal affections and mortality. The central image of the journey recalls that paradigmatic journey of the Parsis in their flight from Iran to India in the eighth century, alluded to in the novel and recorded in the talismanic seventeenth century chronicle known as the *Kisseh-i Sanjan* (Eduljee). Yet it also encompasses a range of experience, resonating outwards to affect all the characters and situations in the novel. As Anjana Desai says, 'The journey is the journey of a nation, of a city, of an ethnic minority, and of an individual man of this community—and the question it raises is the same one that baffles Eliot's magi—was it for a birth or a death that they travelled?' (Desai 134) Meditations on this theme are memorably focalised through the figure of the pavement artist, who is persuaded to turn the stinking compound wall into a canvas on which are depicted the sacred personalities and sites of a variety of religions. The peripatetic pavement artist lives and deals in the mutable and transient. In art as in life, permanence is an illusion, a false consolation: the pavement artist works in coloured chalks and crayon that can be rubbed out or washed away. For him existence, the stuff of art, is 'a cycle of arrival, creation and obliteration. . . . The journey—chanced, unplanned, solitary—was the thing to relish,' (184). By contrast Gustad's own fear is of the end of journeys: a paralysing horror of change, termination and death, which does not allow him to yield to the pavement artist's maxim and start enjoying the journey for its own sake. The acts of betrayal and deception of which he feels himself a victim are experienced as mini-deaths, confirming him in his isolationist outlook. It is only with the actual deaths of his friends Dinshawji and Jimmy—and his decision to undertake the long journey to the latter's bedside—that, through the soothing balm of the funeral rites he participates in, Gustad is able to come to terms with those losses which constitute human experience through time.

Despite the conceptual common ground of Zoroastrianism and Platonism, *Such a Long Journey* is not simply an illustrative Platonic tract. Instead, Mistry appears to be offering what one might describe as a Zoroastrian revision of Plato. To begin with, Gustad is not one of the initiates, the philosopher-kings or guardians of his society. Indeed, the novel as a whole shows a nation state whose governance appears predicated on mendacity, and teeters on the brink of a tyranny that will become overt in the 1975 State of Emergency. Likewise, the proliferation of storytelling, and the power of art more generally, are celebrated in *Such a Long Journey*, making a final, decisive distinction from Plato who famously wished to banish artists and storytellers from his republic. Thus, the novel is replete with storytellers. Jimmy is a great storyteller, regaling the children with heroic tales of India's previous post-partition clashes with Pakistan: Dinshawji is an accomplished story and joke teller; and Dr. Paymaster metaphorises the political situation between Pakistan and Bangladesh as a 'diarrhoea of death', municipal corruption as gangrene, and, along with his faithful compounder, is likened to Don Quixote with Sancho Panza as he joins the *morcha* to tilt at the local government's incompetence and sloth. The doctor's surgery is near both the cinema, where the unending appetite for stories is temporarily sated, and the House of Cages, where the gaudily arrayed prostitutes, like fantastically plumed birds, draw punters into a fantasy environment. The latter is presided over by the local *paan* salesman and raconteur, Peerbhoy Paanwalla, whose racy stories inspire and elevate the sordid and carnal, encouraging clients to think of their sexual powers and encounters as something grander than they really are. His repertoire also includes an erotic satire, attributing the Pakistani leader's fascination with military hardware to the recent failure to function of his own sexual hardware.

Yet the stories in *Such a Long Journey* syncretise experience in non-linguistic forms too. For instance, the pavement artist's polytheistic mural turns the Khodadad building's perimeter wall from a latrine into a sacred site, enshrining India's portable notions of the sacred in a synthesis, albeit temporary, of religious iconography. It reconciles the different religious stories so fundamental to the nation's sense of itself. In figuring the saints and sages, mosques, churches and temples, on the blank canvas offered by the wall, the artist's work foregrounds the role of representation in the perception of 'truths', whether interpersonal, national or metaphysical. On inspecting the rapidly expanding mural, Gustad notices on one of the panels 'a painting of the wall featuring a painting of the wall, featuring a . . .' (288). The pavement artist explains this *mise en abime* by pointing out that the wall itself is now a sacred place, drawing its own share of pilgrims and worshippers. This draws attention once more to the inherently reproductive nature of attempts to give access to 'the real', especially in art and literature, in terms that recall the various other simulations which, as we have seen, epitomise this novel. This, in turn, might act as a metaphor for the issue, amplified throughout, of how versions of reality are created through, and dependent on the vagaries of representation. As Michael Ryan has written:

> what we take to be real does not exist prior to simulation; rather it is simulated into being and lent ontological reality by virtue of acts of *representation*, *masquerade*, and *posturing* that are themselves more prior, fundamental, generative (of the real). Reality is the successful repression of these processes. (Ryan 69, my italics)

In a sense, Rohinton Mistry's first two novels can be read as a diptych, diagnosing the ills of a nation in the early 1970s. The powerful blend of political chicanery and casual brutality which descends on the fiercely guarded private world of sensitive individuals, intrinsic to *Such a Long Journey*, also provides the lineaments of Mistry's novelistic analysis of an even greater constitutional outrage, the 1975 State of Emergency, in his next novel, *A Fine Balance*. Throughout his work attention is given to deception, miscommunication and misrecognition: interests which, when traced to the level of narrative technique too, offer ample evidence for a reading of Mistry's writing as something more than simply realist.

Works Cited

Adams, J. and Whitehead, P. (1997) *The Dynasty: The Nehru-Gandhi Story*, Penguin, Harmondsworth.

Clark, P. (1998) *Zoroastrianism: An Introduction to an Ancient Faith*, Sussex Academic Press, Brighton.

Conrad, J. (1997) *The Secret Agent*, J.M. Dent, London.

Desai, A. (1994) '"Was I There?" Rohinton Mistry's *Such a Long Journey*', in *Indian-English Fiction 1980-1990: An Assessment*, ed. Nilufer E. Bharucha and Vilas Sarang, BR, Delhi.

Dostoyevsky, F. (1955) *The Idiot*, trans. D. Magarshack, Penguin, Harmondsworth.

Eduljee, H.E. (1991) *Kisseh-I Sanjan*, K.R. Cama Oriental Institute, Bombay.

Eliot, T.S. (1961) *Selected Poems*, Faber and Faber, London.

Mistry, R. (1991) *Such a Long Journey*, Faber and Faber, London.

Nair, R.B. (1996) 'Bombay's Balzac: *A Fine Balance* by Rohinton Mistry', *Biblio: A Review of Books*, vol. 10, no. 2, pp. 14-15.

Plato (2000) *The Republic*, Dover Publications, New York.

Ryan, M. (1999) *Literary Theory: A Practical Introduction*, Blackwell, London.

Sahgal, N. (1983) *Indira Gandhi: Her Road to Power*, Macdonald, London.

Tagore, R. (1976) *Gitanjali*, Macmillan India, New Delhi.

Williams, D. (1996) 'Cyberwriting and the Borders of Identity: "What's in a Name" in Kroetsch's *The Puppeteer* and Mistry's *Such a Long Journey*', *Canadian Literature*, no. 149, pp. 55-71.

Such a Long Journey: Interrogating Multiculturalism

SANJAY KUMAR
B.H.U., Varanasi

While reading Rohinton Mistry's *Such a Long Journey*[1] a reader is inevitably faced with the question—can this novel be classified as a work of Canadian literature. There is hardly anything in the novel which connects it even remotely with Canada, neither the setting, nor the characters, nor the events—except for the two references in the acknowledgement where the novelist thanks the Ontario Arts Council and the Canada Council for their assistance. And yet this novel has gone on to win the Governor General's award and Smith's First Novel award in Canada besides having been shortlisted for the Booker Prize in 1991. This has also been made into a much-acclaimed movie of the same name by Sarah Gurnarsson with assistance from Canada Film Council. The only criterion by which this novel would then apparently qualify as a work of Canadian literature is the fact that Mistry is a Canadian citizen and he lives in Toronto. What confounds this vexed question further is the puzzling remark in the blurb of the novel that "*Such a Long Journey* is a brilliant first novel by one of the most remarkable writers to have emerged from the *Indian literary tradition* in many years" (emphasis added). So, does it belong to the Canadian literary tradition or to the Indian one, or can it belong to both the traditions at the same time. Such a question has become increasingly urgent and persistent in the face of the fact that "national literature is not only increasingly seen as a product of the nation coming into being, but it is also seen as playing a decisive role in the formation of the nation."[2] Underlying this notion of national literature being a product of nation are the specific issues of identity construction in the larger discourse of nation formation and the space assigned to racial/ethnic minorities in it. In asking such a question one presumes that there are a host of factors which coalesce to give rise to a Canadian (national) identity and a work is to be classified as such to the extent it conforms or does not conform to this identity.

But this notion of single homogeneous Canadian (national) identity has always been problematic. The discourse of nation formation always tends to be monologic, appropriated by the dominant group which always declares itself to be the mainstream and thus the norm and excludes others from this construct because of race/ethnicity. In fact, race and ethnicity have been used as floating terms to demarcate some people as totally inassimilable to the mainstream culture (the racial other) and others as partially assimilable (the ethnic other), while the mainstream is held as norm, having neither race nor ethnicity. But, of late, the project of nation has come under severe strain and what seemed to be a seamless unity has come to be frayed at edges. In fact, it has become a heavily contested site in modern/ postmodern discourse, marked by contemporary struggles between what has been constructed as the national cultural mainstream and those who belong to groups that have been traditionally excluded from this construct because of race/ethnicity. Describing the ambivalence of nation Homi Bhabha says that "the locality of national culture is neither unified nor unitary in relation to itself, nor must it be seen simply as 'other' in relation to what is outside or beyond it. The boundary is Janus-faced and the problem of outside/inside must always itself be a process of hybridity, incorporating new 'people' in relation to the body politic, generating other sites of meaning and, inevitably, in the political process, producing unmanned sites of political antagonism and unpredictable forces for political representation."[3]

Canada has always been multicultural, at least, a bicultural society because of the presence of both the English and the

French settlers. Even in the eighteenth and nineteenth centuries, the Anglo-Celtics who dominated both economically and politically had to contend with the French-speaking people in Quebec. It is a matter of historical record that in the nineteenth century Canada, the mainstream Anglo-Celtic Canadians tried to suppress the French-speaking Quebeckers by denigrating them and describing them as the racial other, but met with stiff resistance they had to settle for a bicultural and bilingual society. So Canada has always been characterized by what Sutherland calls "two nations in one state"[4] or what MacLennan calls "Two Solitudes."[5]

The twentieth century witnessed new waves of immigrants from almost every part of the world including India. Stranded between the French and the English mainstreams of Canada, the Indian immigrant writers have experienced difficulties in making their voices heard. While the mainstream continues to pay lip service to the notion of multiculturalism, in actual practice it continues to ignore the immigrant voices. On the one hand, it is claimed that Canada is a multicultural mosaic and that immigrant literature has come of age, on the other writers of outstanding merit such as M.G. Vassanji, Rohinton Mistry, Uma Parameswaran, Arnold Harrichand Itwaru, Arun Prabha Mukherjee, John Ramsaran, Neil Bisoodhnath, Naznin Sidique etc. are not considered worthy to be included in the celebrated White anthologies or even to be mentioned in any history of Canadian literature written or compiled by the White authors.

This refusal to give recognition to the voice/s of the 'other' is to be seen as an endeavour to contain the threat, on the part of the dominant mainstream White Anglo-Saxon culture, of defilement and disruption of the monolithic national culture by the racial other. But this act of guarding jealously the national culture, or the very fact that such a need has been perceived, ironically and paradoxically enough reveals the deep fissures in the façade of the nation—that it is not given, natural and primordial, but it is made and constructed. This made-up-ness reveals the element of coercion in forging this nation-ness, an identity which is only provisional and whose stability is constantly threatened by the rhetoric of the other lurking on the margins. The margin thus becomes the space from where to mount the challenge to the dominant cultural discourse of the nation.

The marginalization of the immigrant writers fails to deter them from writing their versions of Canada. From their position on the margin they create narratives which challenge the static borders of national and cultural identities by disrupting the dominant discourse of the nation. These narratives seek to extend the boundaries of the nation, neither by assimilation into the dominant narrative nor by its simple subversion, but by hybridizing the discourse through a process of creative dialectic tension.

Living in a multicultural society and being characterized by an ethnic identity, the Indian community in Canada has been invariably required to negotiate the problem of ethnicity. They have been engaged in active economic and cultural competitions. They have experienced ethnic discrimination, either explicit or covert. Having a unique socio-cultural history, the Indian community in Canada has evolved as a distinct diasporic entity. 'Home' for them becomes a mental construct symbolizing their distinct socio-cultural identity in an unsullied and distilled form. Safran has observed that it is a general characteristic of diaspora that "they continue to relate, personally or vicariously, to the homeland in one way or another, and their ethno-communal consciousness and solidarity are importantly defined by the existence of such a relationship."[6] Thus the diasporic Indians do not sever their relationship with their ancestral land. And, naturally the writer in his role as a preserver of the collective tradition, a folk historian and mythmaker, recreates this sense of community in his writings by invoking the past and history.

Mistry is one such writer who invariably goes back to India in his writings, to the Parsi community to which he belongs, to be precise. But this going back to his past is characterized by neither nostalgia nor bitterness as it happens in the case of most of the writers of the Indian diaspora. He seems to have a matter-of-fact attitude in his portrayal of the Parsi community in India. He does it with compassion and warmth but there is also a sense of gentle irony. If there is a sense of frustration at the social injustice, ineptitude, corruption and numerous problems that India faces, then there is also a sense of celebration and joy for the essential nobility and virtues of human life. In fact, invoking the past becomes a positive attribute with him as it becomes a strategy to cope with the present by resisting assimilation into the mainstream Anglo-Saxon culture. By asserting and maintaining a distinct cultural identity he presents a better vision of the future by strengthening the multicultural fabric. From his position on the margin, Mistry presents an alternative worldview which not only interrogates and challenges the hegemony of the Eurocentric discourse and worldview but also leads to a better appreciation and understanding of Canada's multicultural fabric. Sutherland points out that "ethnic writers . . . distil their experiences of Canada through a variety of rich cultural heritages. Perhaps it is this very process of diverse cultural distillation that will become the distinct characteristics of Canadian Literature."[7]

Canada is paradoxically present by its absence in Mistry's *Such a Long Journey*. One cannot help but read this novel as an allegory of multiculturalism. It presents Mistry's vision of a multicultural society and the place of minorities in it. Set in Bombay in 1971 against the backdrop of the Indo-Pakistan war and the birth of Bangladesh as a nation, *Such a Long Journey* deals with the life of the Parsi community in India. On the one hand, this novel opens up a new world for the readers in Canada—the life and ways of the Parsi community—and thus helps them in developing a better understanding and appreciation of their culture. On the other, it also presents to us a model of multiculturalism in its delineation of this minority community in India and how well they have integrated into the Indian society without losing their cultural and religious identity. This can, Mistry proposes, act as a model for the Canadian society and will go a long way in strengthening the fabric of multiculturalism in Canada.

The novel focuses on the lives of Gustad Noble and his family, residing in Khodadad building together with other Parsi families in Colaba and how the Indo-Pak war impinges on their lives. Parsis as we know are a closed and insular community, strictly regulating and preserving their cultural and religious identity by not allowing any intermingling with other communities at the familial, kinship and religious levels. Having been driven away from Persia around eighth century AD, they have lived in India for 1300 years. Though now declining in numbers, this minority community has maintained and preserved their separate identity and they have also contributed significantly to the public life as architects, industrialists, merchants, bankers, statesmen etc.

In its loving evocation of the details of the cultural milieu the novel manifests a specificity and rootedness which are rare to be found in immigrant writings. It beautifully and faithfully renders the life of the minority Parsi community—its religious beliefs, rituals, mores, social norms, modes of dress, food habits, linguistic habits and idioms etc. But amidst all these particularities which show their distinctiveness from other people, there is also emphasis on the universals of human experience. There is a tension between the particular and the universal. Even readers in Canada can easily identify themselves with these characters in spite of the different socio-cultural space that they inhabit; they can find in them many similarities to their own situation. If these characters appear different outwardly in their religious beliefs, social norms and mores, and linguistic habits, inwardly there beats the same heart in all of them, betraying the same range of emotions and feelings—love, joy, happiness, anger, frustration, helplessness, anxieties and fears which ordinary human beings do. In fact, showing universal in particular becomes Mistry's way of showing unity in diversity and thus presenting a paradigm of a stable multicultural society.

The Khodadad building with its Parsi residents comes to stand for the Parsi community. And the six feet high compound wall running around it becomes the symbol of its insularity, protecting and sheltering it from the eyes of the majority community, and thus rendering that space sacred where they can practise their faith unhindered. If this wall becomes the symbol of their insularity, it also becomes the target of attack of the majority community which shows its contempt by pissing against the wall. Safe within this sacred space, they occasionally betray their anxieties and fears and insecurities as members of a minority community, although they have done better than other communities including the majority Hindu community:

> What kind of life was Sohrab going to look forward to? No future for minorities, with all these fascist Shiv Sena politics and Marathi language nonsense. *It was going to be like the black people in America twice as good as the white man to get half as much.* How could he make Sohrab understand this? (55, emphasis added)

> He turned and slipped into my seat! Insult to injury! What to do with such low class people? No manners, no sense, nothing. And you know who is responsible for this attitude—that bastard Shiv Sena leader who worships *Hitler and Mussolini*. He and his "Maharashtra for Maharashtrians nonsense." They won't stop till they have complete Maratha Raj. (23, emphasis added)

These references to the plight of the Blacks in America and to Hitler and Mussolini internationalize the dimension of racism and thus alert us to the Canadian situation. This also simultaneously points to the phenomenon of racism/ethnicity/ communalism as the darker side of the discourse of the nation which India has inherited as a legacy from the West. This cannot be dismissed as an example of deviant or distorted nationalism. In fact, the racial/ethnic/communal other is the necessary condition for the discourse of nation which achieves its identity in difference not only from outside but from inside as well.

The compound wall of the Khodadad building, a symbol of the insularity of the Parsi community, is soon transformed into a multi-religious shrine, a mosaic of different religions and cultures, as a pavement artist draws pictures of deities of different religions and renders stories from epics of different religions on this wall. People of all faiths and religions come to worship and pay their obeisance. This wall symbolically becomes a multicultural and multi-religious space where different cultures and religions exist in harmony. In the end the wall is brought down by the municipal corporation in the name of widening the road but this does not happen without stiff resistance of the people who spontaneously rise up to save the wall. What the novelist seems to be suggesting here, in my opinion, is that the multicultural fabric of the society can be preserved, sustained and strengthened only with the will and commitment of people, not just through some official policy.

If the novel portrays the Parsi community in India on the large canvas with broad brush-strokes, then it also draws the miniature paintings of individuals with fine brush strokes. At the individual level, the novel tells the story of Gustad Noble, a bank clerk and the peculiar way in which the Indo-Pak war of 1971 makes an impact on his life as well as that of his family. It becomes the story of a common man living and surviving in hard times. Having seen better days during the time of his grandfather and father, Gustad now lives in straitened circumstances in the Khodadad building with his wife Dilnavaz, two sons Sohrab and Darius, and a daughter Roshan. Gustad has dreams and aspirations which, though quite modest and ordinary, prove difficult to fulfill. He finds it quite baffling that things do not happen the way he wants them to. His dreams slowly crumble and his hopes die a slow death as he has one frustrating experience after the other.

Life for him seems to be an endless series of trials and tribulations. First, he feels betrayed by his long time friend, Major Jimmy Bilimoria who suddenly decides to leave the Khodadad building without even bothering to inform him. Then, his eldest son, Sohrab, after having qualified for the I.I.T., refuses to join it and all his efforts to persuade him fail and it leads to quarrels and fights at home, and finally Sohrab leaves the home in a huff. "How to make him realize what he was doing to his father, who had made the success of his son's life the purpose of his own? Sohrab had snatched away that purpose, like a crutch from a cripple." (55) Then, he is worried no end over the illness of his daughter Roshan whose condition continues to deteriorate even after medication. On top of that, for the sake of friendship he gets drawn into a cloak and dagger operation of helping the Mukti Bahini on the request of Major Bilimoria. And then comes the illness and death of his friend Dinshawji. His problems seem to be endless.

> He returned to his desk, kneading his forehead. It was becoming too much to bear, Roshan's sickness, Dilnavaz blaming him for potassium permanganate, Jimmy's treachery, Dinshawji's stupidity, Laurie's complaint, Sohrab's betrayal, nothing but worry and sorrow and disappointment piling up around him, walling him in, threatening to crush him. He moved his massaging hand from the forehead to his nape and closed his eyes. (177)

What redeems his character in our eyes is his manner of facing his problems. These experiences fail to break him. Though angry and frustrated at times, he does not give in to any prolonged bout of despair or cynicism. As his name suggests, he maintains the essential nobility of his character all through. He endures his trials with dignity, courage and equanimity without losing faith in humanity. The novel is, in fact, the story of his education that man does not always control his destiny, that there are forces beyond his control and larger than he is and of his learning to come to terms with it.

The ordinariness of his life makes Gustad the symbol of every man just as the Khodadad building is the symbol of the Parsi community. If on the one hand, Gustad as an individual becomes every man in his aspirations and anguish, on the other he as a member of his community shows his independent cultural and religious identity. Through the character of Gustad, Mistry shows that in spite of the cultural and religious differences, there is a lot which people have in common with each other as human beings and it is this commonness which unites people despite the differences. And this is Mistry's way of offering a paradigm of multiculturalism for Canada, though Canada does not figure in the novel.

NOTES

1. Rohinton Mistry, *Such a Long Journey* (Delhi: Rupa, 1991).
2. Anthony D. Smith, *National Identity* (Nevada: University of Nevada Press, 1991), p. 20.
3. Homi K. Bhabha, "Of Mimicry and Man: The Ambivalence of Colonial Discourse," *October*, 28 (Spring 1984), p. 127.
4. Ronald Sutherland, "The Mainstream of Canadian Literature" in M.G. Vassanji, ed., *A Meeting of Two Streams: South Asian Canadian Literature* (Toronto: TSAR, 1985), p. 76.
5. Hugh MacLennan, *Two Solitudes* (Toronto: General Paperbacks, 1991), p. 26.
6. William Safran, *Nationalism and Ethnoregional Identities in China* (*Nationalism and Ethnicity*, 1), (New York: Frank Cass, 1998), p. 18.
7. Ronald Sutherland, "The Mainstream of Canadian Literature," p. 74.

Realism in *Such a Long Journey*

CELESTE FERNANDES
Smt. Parvatibai Chowgule College , Margao Goa

Realism is used to denote a literary movement of the nineteenth century, in prose fiction, beginning with Balzac in France, George Eliot in England and William Dean Howells in America to designate a recurrent way of representing life in literature which was typified by the writers of this historical movement.[1]

The realist is deliberately selective in his material and prefers the average, the commonplace and the everyday over the rarer aspects of the contemporary scene. His characters are usually of the middle class or the working class-people without highly exceptional endowments, who live through ordinary experiences of childhood, adolescence, love, marriage, parenthood, infidelity, and death, who find life rather dull and often unhappy, though it may be brightened by touches of beauty and joy; but who may, under special circumstance, display something akin to heroism. There is a link between literature and life in the work of the realist writer—in this case Rohinton Mistry. It is the main focus of attention in his writings and his novels are closely linked with social realism.

Rohinton Mistry is a writer who makes up a part of the Indian diaspora in Canada. He is also a Zoroastrian whose ancestors were exiled by the Islamic conquest of Iran, making him and his kind in diaspora in the Indian subcontinent. Mistry's work is guided by this experience of double displacement, like other diasporic writers. He explores the relationships at the heart of the Parsi community, their cultural identity and the uniqueness of their community living in the city of Bombay. He has written

Tales from Firozsha Baag (1987), *Such a Long Journey* (1991), *A Fine Balance* (1995).

Such a Long Journey is a fascinating book with the ability to hold the reader spellbound. It has won several prizes; the Governor General's Award, the Commonwealth Writers' Prize for Best Book, and the Smith Book/Books in Canada First Novel award. The book is in line with the realist tradition, when we can firmly believe that, "Before a work of literature can be a work of realism, it must be a work of art and conform to the canon of art, and in art the artist is an indispensable medium through which we see things."[2] And that is what happens in this first novel by Rohinton Mistry. We are made to 'see' and to 'live' the story of Gustad Noble, a simple ordinary man, trying to cope with life and its difficulties.

The novel is set in Bombay in 1971. Gustad Noble lives in a typical building at that time in Bombay called Khodadad Building. He is a family man, devout, hard-working with aspirations for his children, in particular his older son, Sohrab, who he hopes will join I.I.T. one day. "Sohrab will make a name for himself, you see if he doesn't Gustad had said with a father's first pride. At last our sacrifices will prove worthwhile." (3)

But this is not to be as several things change in Gustad's life—certain events take place in the building, in the office, in his home and in the country, that leave an indelible mark upon him and eventually turn the tide for him. The novel then dwells upon these events in Gustad's life and the action takes place at the moment when the war breaks out between India and Pakistan over what later becomes Bangladesh. So this gives the novel a political background, contributing to its realism. Gustad Noble's family is a microcosm of a society that is fast changing. It is becoming corrupt and greedy and insensitive to the needs of the mentally challenged or the marginalized.

So in the novel, we have the protagonist, Gustad Noble, quite content with his situation, with his little flat, with the blackout paper taped over the glass panes of the windows and ventilators. Gustad had put it up nine years ago, the year of the war with China. His wife Dilnavaz is quite happy with life too but not with the darkness caused by the blackout paper. "In this house, the morning never seems to come," Dilnavaz continued to complain. (11) In the midst of his everyday routine, his daily prayers, his reading on the political developments of *The Times of India* and making his usual observation, Gustad thinks about his childhood friend Major Jimmy Bilimoria, who vanished suddenly from the building the previous year. He had been very close to Gustad who used to point him out to the children as a good example, urging them to walk erect, with chest out and stomach in. The Major used to regale the children in the building with stories of army and battle. His sudden departure from the building disturbed Gustad, more than he allowed anyone to see. Only Dilnavaz could sense the depth of his pain. "To leave like this, after being neighbours for so many years, is a shameful way of behaving. Bloody bad manners." (14)

Dilnavaz, ever optimistic and trusting, believes firmly that Bilimoria would never have left without a reason whatever that might be. Events in the novel are built around Major Bilimoria and the letter he sends to Gustad, asking him to receive a package for him. And so Gustad unwittingly gets involved in a clandestine operation involving the RAW (Research and Analysis Wing) of which Bilimoria is a member. The contents of Bilimoria's next letter would have compromised Gustad's position at the bank if it were not for his good friend Dinshawji's cooperation. Further developments lead Gustad to Delhi to meet with an emaciated and disillusioned Jimmy Bilimoria, making him realize how life changes its course. Gustad Noble gets involved in so many situations—he confronts problems but manages to do so honourably. A few incidents reveal his character and his resilience making him emerge stronger and better as a person.

Gustad is planning to have a family dinner for his daughter Roshan's birthday in the same way, as there were celebrations in his childhood. Chicken becomes the central motif at this point of the novel and the quest for the perfect chicken begins. This quest takes him to Bombay's famous Crawford Market but "unlike his father who enjoyed this game, Gustad felt intimidated by Crawford Market." (20) He is also conscious of several things—and these are all recalled by him at this point especially how, on his way back from the market, after buying the meat.

> Throughout the trip, he felt anxious and guilty—felt that in his basket, was something deadlier than a bomb. For was he not carrying the potential source of Hindu-Muslim riots? Riots which often started due to offences of the flesh, usually of porcine or bovine origins? (21)

He eventually buys a live chicken, much to his wife's chagrin and Roshan's initial consternation. The arrival of the chicken means some amount of change in the family's routine—there is feeding and cleaning and definitely some chasing to be done, which is when we are introduced to Tehmul-Lungraa, Miss Kutpitia and several others in the locality. Tehmul is roped in to catch the errant chicken and does so successfully. The creation of certain characters like Tehmul, the mentally and physically challenged individual, by Mistry arrest our attention. It is in the creation of such characters among others that we see his realism and his prowess as a writer.

> For Tehmul-Lungra, as everyone called him, was a supremely pathetic example of hip-fracture victims who had had the misfortune to be treated by conventional methods, condemned to years on crutches and walking-sticks, with nothing to look forward to but a life of pain, their bodies swaying frighteningly from side to side while they strained and panted and heaved in their pitiful pursuit of ambulation. (30)

He also had an abbreviated vocabulary, speaking the words at breakneck speed and incomprehensibly. At this moment when the chicken is chased and eventually caught, he says: "GustadGustadchickenrace. GustadGustadchickenranfast. Icaughtcaught Gustad." (32) The chicken is readied for cooking by a butcher and provokes much sobbing from Roshan and discontent from his sons. The party, at which the chicken is to play an important part, brings to the fore, Dinshawji, Gustad's best friend who refers to his wife as "domestic vulture." He regales everyone with his ribald humour. Sohrab explodes at the dinner when everyone toasts to his future in I.I.T. He responds to his father's toast by saying, "I'm sick and tired of I.I.T., I.I.T., I.I.T. all the time. I'm not interested in it. I'm not a jolly good fellow about it, and I'm not going there." (48)

Later on, there is an argument between Gustad and Sohrab, and the latter leaves home in a huff. Yet Gustad lives his life, follows his daily routine at work and at home, interspersed with Dinshawji's lewd jokes at the expense of Laurie Coutinho the typist. Gustad takes his son's departure later on from home in his stride although he does grieve within himself. When informed by Dilnavaz that Sohrab has left home, "He hid his surprise and hurt and blandly repeated his harsh words from two nights ago: 'What is it to me?'" (124)

The illness of his daughter Roshan also leaves Gustad confused and worried. She has a stomach infection that does not respond immediately to the treatment of the trusted Dr. Paymaster, who not only has his own views on what is ailing Roshan but also on what is ailing Pakistan. When Gustad asks him if Roshan has diarrhoea he replies:

> "Not diarrhoea. But no need to worry." He began writing a prescription. "Sometimes, of course, even a case of diarrhoea can be worrying. Look at East Pakistan—a patient with a simple sickness, but very difficult to cure. A patient in critical condition, needing the intensive care unit. But, no one in the world cares." Dr. Paymaster believed that politics, economics, religious problem, domestic strife, all could be dealt with methodically; observe the symptoms, make the diagnosis, prescribe medicine, offer the prognosis. But he also believed that just as some diseases of the human body were incurable, there were diseases of countries, of families, of theological dogma, that had fatal outcomes. "East Pakistan is suffering from a diarrhoea of death," he continued. Death is flowing there unchecked, and the patient will soon be dehydrated." (164)

So Mistry manages here to brilliantly provide a political backdrop to this story of family life. He expertly connects, through the rantings of the doctor, the situation at the present moment in time between India and East Pakistan. References are made to the Mukti Bahini guerillas who the doctor feels are incapable of dealing with the situation. "Not strong enough medicine. Only the complete, intravenous injection of the Indian Army will defeat this virus." (165)

The medical analogy brings out the intensity of the situation very vividly and explicitly. And Gustad patiently bides his time when Roshan's illness will be completely controlled and when he manages to finish the task that Bilimoria has entrusted to him revolving around the ten lakh rupees which he has received. His friend Dinshawji has been taken into confidence but one day in a conversation with Laurie Coutino, he realizes that Dinshawji has betrayed his trust even while he has been flirting with Laurie. She tells Gustad:

> You know, I don't mind his jokes and all his acting. I used to think it was so sweet. A cute old man, trying to impress me. The things he says. He was telling me he works for the secret service, that he is in charge of ten lakh rupees, to fully equip the Mukti Bahini guerrillas. Can you imagine that? Mr. Dinshawji in the secret service? (176)

It was all too much for Gustad who was naturally very angry at the revelation and the breach of confidence by Dinshawji. But in a truly honourable way Gustad does not let his friend down. He placates Laurie and manages to restrain her from complaining to the boss, Mr. Madan, about Dinshawji's lewd jokes. He also tells her that his friend is a very sick man. At this stage in the story Gustad does feel that life is becoming too much for him to handle.

> It was becoming too much to bear, Roshan's sickness, Dilnavaz blaming him for potassium permanganate, Jimmy's treachery, Dinshawji's stupidity, Laurie's complaint, Sohrab's betrayal, nothing but worry and sorrow and disappointment piling up around him, walking him in, threatening to crush him. (177)

The one bright spark in Gustad's life is his engaging of a pavement artist to paint the compound wall of the building with pictures of deities, transforming it to a holy place in order to keep passersby from using it as a public latrine and causing the unbearable stench and mosquitoes breeding all around. The artist he appoints for the purpose for no monetary consideration (except for what devout people might place near the wall later) confidently tells Gustad that he could cover three hundred miles of wall if necessary, with pictures of gods.

> Using assorted religions and their gods, saints and prophets: Hindu, Sikh, Judaic, Christian, Muslim, Zoroastrian, Buddhist, Jainist. Actually Hinduism alone can provide enough. But I always like to mix them up, include a variety in my drawings. Makes me feel I am doing something to promote tolerance and understanding in the world. (182)

Gustad is told that the artist has a BA in world religions and a specialty in Comparative Studies before he went to the School of Arts. Soon the wall is transformed and is no longer an eyesore.

> Over the next few days, the wall filled up with gods, prophets and saints. When Gustad checked the air each morning and evening, he found it free of malodour. Mosquitoes and flies were no longer quite the nuisance they used to be; with their breeding grounds drying up, the numbers diminished dramatically. (183)

Gustad is pleased at the result of the artist's efforts because his handiwork elevated the wall to a place of sanctity with flowers placed near some picture of a deity and money being placed which was of great help to the artist. However this redeeming feature—the wall—was torn down later and the small attempt at maintaining the beauty of the neighbourhood came to naught.

Gustad's trust in his friend Bilimoria is sorely tested when he sees a newspaper report on him being arrested on charges of fraud and extortion. Mention of ten lakh rupees is also made. He does not know what to believe and Bilimoria's friend, Ghulam Mohammad, tries to convince him that Bilimoria is being framed and that several people higher up are involved, including the then Prime Minister, Indira Gandhi. His doubts are sought to be allayed by Ghulam Mohammad who insists that he should go to Delhi to visit Jimmy and see the truth for himself. The truth is not easy for Gustad to stomach. He visits Jimmy Bilimoria in the hospital:

> What he saw made him want to weep. On the bed lay nothing more than a shadow. The shadow of the powerfully-built army man who once lived in Khodadad building. His hairline had receded and sunken cheeks made his bones jut sharp and grotesque. The regal handlebar moustache was no more. His eyes had disappeared within their sockets. The neck, what he could see of it, was as scrawny as poor, befhesti Dinshawji's while under the sheet their seemed barely a trace of those strong shoulders and deep chest which Gustad and Dilnavaz used to point out as a good example to their sons, reminding them always to walk erect, with chest out and stomach in, like Major Uncle. (267)

Worse than what Gustad beholds at the hospital is what he hears from Jimmy—a horrific account of intrigue, crime and corruption in the highest of places and a massive cover-up operation. Ten lakh rupees that Jimmy has siphoned off the total sum of sixty lakh rupees that was appropriated ostensibly for the guerillas in Bangladesh is still unaccounted for and Jimmy has been targeted in an attempt to retrieve the amount. All this intrigue and the inevitable interrogation has taken its toll on Jimmy who is now lying in hospital and looking forward to completing a four year sentence in prison. He tells Gustad that there is nothing he can do, as the Prime Minister is involved and the courts and lawyers are in the control of the people in power. Gustad is sceptical of the whole scenario and says as such:

> "Everyone knows there's corruption," said Gustad. "But to this level? Hard to believe." "Gustad, it is beyond the common mans imagination, the things being done by those in power. But I did not call you here to make you worry . . . feel sorry for me. What has happened has happened. I just wanted to talk to you, to make sure you don't think I tried to trick you. You were so angry. Ghulam told me . . . in your place. I would also have been. But I was hoping

> . . . you forgive me? There was only one answer to give: "Rubbish! Nothing to forgive, Jimmy." (280)

At this moment, Gustad feels better for having met Jimmy and cleared his doubts. After all, Jimmy was his dear friend. The redemptive quality of this episode is matched by another in the novel—the episode of the morcha, during which Tehmul is fatally hit by a stone. On his return to Bombay from Delhi, Gustad learns that India is now at war with Pakistan. But he has his own problems still, on the homefront, among them being the inspection of the blackout paper on the windows and preparing for air raids. He is still besieged with thoughts about Sohrab and how things would have been different if he was still around. Mistry very realistically portrays life during a war—how the family responds to the air-raid siren in Bombay and dutifully switches off the main switch and hide under the bed. Gustad's concerns are the concerns of the ordinary man as usual: "What if some idiot in the building gets nervous because of the guns and decided to put on the light? Or opened a window to see what was going on?" (300) He is further troubled by Tehmul when he accidentally stumbles upon his guilty secret and missing doll, now in the possession of Tehmul used by him to satisfy his sexual urges. The doll was Roshan's most treasured possession, won by her at a school lottery. And all Gustad can do is feel a great sympathy for Tehmul.

> Poor Tehmul. What was to become of him? . . . Gustad wished he had the power of miracles, the power to cure Tehmul's ill, restore to him all the rights and virtues of mortals. And as Tehmul stood there, shamefaced, tears running down his cheeks, Gustad realized he could not take away the doll. Somehow, the loss to Roshan would not be as great as it would to Tehmul. One day, when she was old enough, perhaps he would tell her what had happened. (303)

The war comes to an end and the blackout paper is removed, having served its purpose. Gustad reads in the newspaper about the death of Jimmy Bilimoria of a heart attack while serving his sentence in prison. He attends his funeral and wonders all the while who could have paid for it and arranged for the expenses until he realizes that it is Ghulam Mohammed. He is grateful to him for this gesture and says as much to him. Sohrab who visits his mother often is apprised of the death of Jimmy but does not want to meet his father. He tells her,

> "It's no use. I spoilt all his dreams, he is not interested in me any more." "Don't talk like that!" she said sharply, and then softened again. "He is your father. He will always love you and want the best for you." (321)

His refusal to commiserate only reminds her now that he is proud and strong-willed like Gustad.

But there is great love and compassion in Gustad too, who shows this at different other parts in the novel. There is a great morcha underway and Dr. Paymaster is at the helm of affairs. He crows with delight: "What a powerful morcha we have produced! Seeing is believing. The greatest morcha in the history of our city!" (329) It appears that his emotions, which had been bottled up for so long, were suddenly coming to the fore. There is a clash between the municipality workers who have congregated to demolish the beautified wall and the construction workers. Gustad arrives at the truth about his friend Malcolm Saldanha, now in charge of the mindless project and unable to question it or to delay it. He is simply a stooge in the hands of the government, with no powers at all. Gustad realizes:

> So this was Malcolm's fate. My college friend, who used to summon the notes like magic, from the realm between wakefulness and sleep. For Chopin's nocturnes. Those evenings, so long, long ago. Now supervising pickaxes and churning concrete. (331)

Tehmul refuses to keep away from the confusion of the morcha and all the excitement. He wanted to be a part of the action. So when a brick sailed towards him, he moved to catch it, enchanted as he was by all such things: "The impact of the brick was so great that he dropped to the ground; his figure folding gracefully. The dance was over." (333) There is much confusion now as everyone rallies around to attend to Tehmul who is bleeding profusely. The realization that Tehmul is no more causes still more confusion and the insensitivity of people in the neighbourhood only serves to annoy Gustad. Finally, Gustad bodily lifts Tehmul and walks toward the building.

> They looked in silence now, too ashamed to follow. Sohrab gazed after his father with fear and admiration. People watched from their windows as Gustad strode under their eyes without faltering, as though he and Tehmul were all alone, as if the dead weight of the grown man in his arms was naught but a child's. (335)

And when he was in Tehmul's room, he prayed softly, crying all the time. Then, in the stillness of the moment, he notices his son Sohrab who has returned to his father, drawn by the compassionate action of carrying Tehmul's dead body and attending to the final prayers.

> Gustad turned around. He saw his son, standing in the doorway, and each held the other's eyes. Still he sat, gazing upon his son, and Sohrab waited motionless in the doorway, till at last Gustad got to his feet slowly, then he went up and put his arms around him: "Yes" said Gustad, running his bloodstained fingers once through Sohrab's hair. "Yes," he said, "Yes," and hugged him tightly once more. (337)

The "Yes" that he utters is an affirmation of all that his son means to him, of all his emotions and feelings for his son. He had made mistakes but is now prepared to start anew—he is prepared to affirm that life must go on. And that's what Gustad decides later on, after the pavement artist leaves and goes on his way, his work having been rudely intercepted by the demolition squad. Yet he refuses to leave with any of his things—his box of oil paints and brushes. He merely tells Gustad, "I have taken everything I need for my journey. . . . My box of crayons is in here." (339) The artist does not want to compromise himself and his art any more for monetary pursuit or any other motives. Gustad returns to his flat and then: "He stood upon the chair and pulled at the paper covering the ventilators. As the first sheet tore away, a frightened moth flew out and circled the room." (339)

So, at the end of the novel, we have Gustad, a man with principles and dreams and aspirations, realizing that some compromise has to be reached in life. He emerges out of his problems, a survivour with tremendous resilience. As a realist novel, Mistry brings out the reality of life—the novel becomes a telling commentary on social life, political life and morality. His focus is the Parsi community in Bombay with all the problems they face, their reaction to political change and corruption. His focus is also on life in Bombay in the early 1970s—a city in transition with the backdrop of the war. He captures the essence of Bombay—the good, the bad and the ugly, dwelling upon the cosmopolitanness, certain landmarks whether of universal interest or religious interest—Crawford Market, the Irani restaurants, the dudhwalla 'bhaiya,' the water problems of people in the city, the red-light areas etc. He uses typical terms—native of the language adopted by the Parsis—which is Gujarati and refers to the Parsi customs, food, religious ceremonies all of which contribute to Mistry's realism. In conclusion I would like to point out that Rohinton Mistry has presented a novel with truly exemplary characters who provoke our laughter and sympathy but who like the protagonist will remain in the minds and hearts of readers for a long time to come because the writer succeeds in making us "see" and having done so, makes us respond accordingly.

NOTES

M.H. Abrams, *A Glossary of Literary Terms* (New Delhi: Macmillan, 2001), p. 141

Daymond Douglas, Leslie Monkman, *Canadian Novelists and the Novel* (Ottawa: Borealis Press, 1981), p. 138

Rohinton Mistry, *Such a Long Journey* (New Delhi: Rupa, 1991).

Such a Long Journey: A Sociological Study

JAGDISH BATRA
Hindu College, Sonepat

The pioneers of the Indian novel written in English imbued their works with social realism. Stalwarts like Mulk Raj Anand, Raja Rao, R.K. Narayan and Bhabani Bhattacharya analyzed the social scenario and suggested remedies before the focus shifted to the individual psyche in due course of time. Anand, for one, used Auguste Comte's sociology, illustrating how such social phenomena as untouchability or poverty in *Untouchable* and *Coolie* could be read in terms of the three stages of development—theological, metaphysical and positivistic. These three stages can be traced in history but they also co-exist, as for example, on a single day in the life of Bakha. In the long journey of the Indian novel written in English, sociological reading of Indian milieu lost its hold, giving place to newer readings. However, the old emphasis on sociology has returned, as for example, in Rohinton Mistry's *Such a Long Journey* which presents sociological perception of human nature. Before we take up this novel in detail, it would be fruitful to ascertain how the sociologists themselves view life.

Sociologists like Max Weber claim: "modern industrial society is characterized by 'rationalization and intellectualisation.' The world is no longer charged with mystery and magic; the supernatural has been banished from society."[1] On the other hand, we have scholars like Vilfredo Pareto who have shown the weak foundations of a rationalistic approach to society. He believes that human actions, for the most part, are guided not by logic or reason but by sentiments. Pareto represents one of the most distinguished intellectual currents in the European tradition. "That broad school of thought includes such diverse figures as Burke, Taine, Dostoevsky, Burckhardt, Nietzsche and Spengler and stands in opposition to rationalism, liberalism, egalitarianism, Marxism, and all of the other offspring of Enlightenment doctrinaires."[2] And it is this school of thought that seems to inspire Rohinton Mistry's work under study here.

In the first epigraph of the novel *Such a Long Journey*, quoted from Firdausi's *Shahnama*, Mistry has sought to underline the fact that the early rulers held populace subjugated precisely because the masses lived by beliefs, at times, transcending their minds such as the theory of the divine right of kings. That is why these early rulers exploited people's beliefs to the hilt, and as Firdausi learnt they left nothing worthwhile for the newer generations to fall upon.

As we open the reading of the novel, we find that it is not only the people in the past who have been gullibled at the hands of the Machiavellian rulers, our own lives are none too logically and scientifically lived. This novel is a story of a Parsee family. The head of the family Gustad, his wife Dilnavaz and their three children—Sohrab and Darius, both boys, and Roshan, a girl, live in Khodadad Building in Bombay. Their very ordinary middle class existence receives a jolt as they find themselves involved in a political scandal of international stature. This sensational event known as the Nagarwala scam is the one that rocked the Indira Gandhi government in the wake of the Bangladesh liberation struggle. The novel lays equal stress on the communal as well as the individual lives.

The novel has drawn heavily on that side of human life and activity which can be described as non-rational in the philosophical sense. Religious activity, for example, is one such facet which finds wide mention in the novel. The novel begins with the central character Gustad offering prayers to 'Ahura Mazda.' After finishing the prayer, as is the custom, Gustad cracks the *kusti* which action is symbolic of driving away the devil. But he does not resort to it merely as a religious gesture. In his mind are stored images of his childhood days when, with this action, he imagined driving away all sorts of ghosts and murderers. He continues to enjoy it with the same abandon even as a middle-age man.

The reader is now treated to the happy news of Gustad's eldest son Sohrab's admission to the I.I.T. That is a dream-come-true for any middle-class youngster and his proud parents. As such, Gustad plans to celebrate it on the ninth birthday of his daughter Roshan but surprisingly Sohrab is not amused. Things go haywire on the party day with an unbridgeable gulf developing between the father and the son. Sohrab would just not listen to the suggestion of entering the portals of the hallowed precincts of I.I.T. as he does not like the idea of getting separated from his friends, who ostensibly have taken up arts. All this appears so illogical and unreasonable to Gustad who blurts: "Throwing away his [Sohrab's] fortune without reason. What have I not done for him, tell me? I even threw myself in front of a car. Kicked him aside, saved his life, and got this to suffer all my life (slapping his hip). But that's what a father is for."[3]

His tiff with his son reminds us of the intransigence of his own father. 'One proud man's stubbornness' (101) is how Gustad referred to his father's soft corner for his dissolute uncle at the expense of Gustad's college fees. He never forgave his weak father for his 'effeminacy' and decided to grow strong as a rock. Now, that rock-like strength was being put to test by his own son who found him stubborn in wishing him to join I.I.T. Anyone would dub Sohrab's action as non-rational because it means honouring his emotional links with his buddies but Gustad also cannot be called a rationalist because it is his son who has to study and ultimately shape his life according to his own interests. The point Mistry makes is that our wishes, propped by beliefs and sentiments, are not necessarily realized because there is no logical connection between what we wish and what happens.

Mistry, through this fiasco of the central wish, underlines his views about human nature which for all its evolution is still steeped in non-logical ways of thinking and acting. Mistry was not the first to present this sociological perception of human nature. I.A. Richards, in his essay 'Pseudo-statements' said that most of our attitudes are determined by emotive responses rather than by scientific views. Poets are known for making pseudo statements such as the existence of God, of immortality, of freedom but such beliefs do serve some social purpose, when it comes to organizing society around rituals and ceremonies, around common beliefs and shared sentiments. Still, on the whole, these non-logical actions have also been exploited by those who are able to free themselves from these sentiments.

In the midst of the father-son stand-off, it is Dilnavaz, Sohrab's mother, who suffers. The special chicken dish is hardly partaken of, its six out of nine pieces remaining in the pot. Sohrab's uttering a volley of audacious words right in the face of his father appears like so much blasphemy to his mother. This gulf, most unfortunately, goes on widening and at one point of time, Sohrab walks out on his father and his family. This is indeed shocking. As a mother, Dilnavaz's utmost concern is to see her son reconciled to his father and the family re-united. She cannot think of any reasoned solution to this malady and falls for the utterly irrational and superstitious counsel of her neighbour Miss Kutpitia (which in Gujarati means 'the quarrelsome one'), an elderly and freakish spinster who acts as the community advisor of queer medicines prescribing lemons and chillies to win over the estranged son of Dilnavaz, subjo leaves for Cavasji's hypertension and nails and lizard for Roshan's illness. Dilnavaz is also in the reflex habit of saying 'touchwood' and touching anything nearby—a table or a chair—whenever she hears about some accident or to avoid anything untoward happening to her family.

In his first book, The *Treatise on General Sociology*, Vilfredo Pareto has raised the issue in much the same vein as Mistry that actions resting on exact knowledge—purely logical or means-ends estimations and judgements—are very rare in human affairs. Only a very limited section of actions in society approximates to logic. The rest is relegated to specific kinds of human propensities, instincts and interests through which mankind seeks material gratification. They are the actions, as for example, the first action of Gustad, praying, is attached to sentiments or subjective desire, often without a definite orientation to ends, which are, in any case, vague, diffused and unattainable. In short, we aspire for such things which have no logic of causality. All this does some good at least psychologically; they have their utility but not their truth. Pareto calls these actions emanating as they do from primordial human nature residues.

Pareto examines multitudes of human actions that constitute the outward expressions of sentiments and classifies these residues into six major classes. Class I is the manifestation of sentiments in individuals and in society that tend toward inventiveness, and the desire for adventure. Class II residues encompass the more conservative side of human nature, including loyalty to society's enduring institutions such as family, church, community, and nation. In a society, both have their respective roles and functions and complement each other but what concerns us here is the fact that both these concepts are built around sentiments and not reason.

Another Italian thinker Machiavelli divided humans into two classes, foxes and lions. The qualities he ascribes to these two classes of men resemble quite closely Pareto's Class I and Class II residue types. Men with strong Class I residues are the "foxes," tending to be manipulative, innovative, calculating, and imaginative. Class II men are "lions" who place much more value on traits such as good character and devotion to duty than on sheer wits. They are the defenders of tradition, the guardians of religious dogma, and the protectors of national honour. Indeed, Major Bilimoria, who symbolizes 'Nagarwala' of the historical political scandal, appears to be a fox to start with but Gustad remains a lion throughout. Both are sentimental fools however. After the former withdraws himself from Khodadad Building surreptitiously, Gustad learns a bitter lesson—never to trust friends. And yet Gustad is noble enough to prove himself a true friend not only to Bilimoria and Dinshawji but also to halfwit Tehmul.

At times, Gustad resembles Roderigo of Shakespeare's *Othello,* who was advised to "put money enough in your purse" by Iago. This is the same line that occurs repeatedly towards the end of Act I and Gustad is asked by Bilimoria to mark it so that the former may be marked by his man, Gulam Mohammad. Roderigo is a poor gentleman—for he is a gentleman, though a "gulled gentleman—he has a sad life in the play, bled white by Iago, disappointed of his hopes . . . a pathetic figure . . . trying to swim in a sea much too rough for him."[4] Doesn't Bilimoria make Gustad a Roderigo? Tested on the touchstone of rationalism, Gustad's agreeing to see a languishing Bilimoria in Delhi does not appear any whit logical. However, as things unfold themselves later, Bilimoria himself is taken in by bigger foxes.

The Parsee community has been in India for quite a few centuries now and still their total population stands at a few thousands only. Seen from this angle, they can be categorized as an ethnic minority, but the sense of their great heritage, their rich contribution to the country of their adoption, i.e., India, their forward-looking attitude—all these have denied to them a minority syndrome that is normally characterized by low achievements, high crime rate and worry about amalgamation through inter-race marriages etc.[5] Parsees are also alleged to have gained a lot through collusion with the Britishers before independence in India. This is not to discount the valuable contribution made to the independence struggle by stalwarts like Dadabhai Naoroji and Sir Pherozeshah Mehta. Yet it is a fact that the bulk of the Parsees kept aloof from common Indians on account of their better economic and educational status. In the post-Independence India, their somewhat westernized life-style has ensured the continuation of the wedge between the two communities. Allowance must be made here for the very ordinary, economically speaking, Parsee characters portrayed by Mistry in the present novel. They retain residues of ordinary prejudices of their group. Durkheim believed that "the fundamental categories of thought have a social origin, and that they owe their necessity and their *a priori* character to the fact that they are the basis of all intercourse between individuals."[6] The members of the Parsee community have their thoughts fashioned by inadequate knowledge of the majority community. Dilnavaz is enchanted by the milkman's *choti* but does not know its name. She has a faint idea that some caste sports it. Born of this ignorance is the suspicion of the slum-dwellers whose eyes seem to be threatening to throw the Parsees out.

Sociologists are of the view that "every in-group constructs out-group stereotypes."[7] Therefore, all Maharashtrians could be lumped together as 'Maratha buggers' (330). Prejudices take the form of derogatory references like "The Maratha brigade ran like cockroaches" (40). The numerous jokes regarding various communities (70-71), though in good faith, do point to underestimating the value of the out-groups. Beef is humorously considered healthier "because it is holier." (23) The Parsees themselves are at the receiving end when they are referred to as 'crow eaters.' (39)

A common subject of societal conversation in India is politics. Now, the popular understanding of politics is simplistic rather than rationalistic. A fine specimen of this, couched in figurative language is provided by Gustad-Dinshawji tête-à-tête: "Where is *madar chod* America now? Not saying one word. Otherwise, if Russia even belches, America protests at the UN. Let Kosygin fart, and America moves a motion in the Security Council." (76) It is not that persons like Gustad are not aware of what goes under the title 'news.' Cautioning his son, he waxes, "Whatever you read in the paper, first divide by two—for the salt and pepper. From what's left, take off ten percent. Ginger and garlic. And sometimes, depending on the journalist, another five percent for chilli powder. Then, and only then, will you get to the truth free of *masala* and propaganda." (68) But when the son grows wiser about the activities of RAW, the self-same Gustad has a different approach, "I read the papers and I know what goes on. Rumours and allegations all the time, and no proof!" (93) Later, Gustad himself is at the receiving end of the RAW personnel's macabre modus operandi. It is Ghulam Mohammad's turn to remind Gustad of the doubtful nature of news, "You know everything that appears in newspapers is not the truth." (202) In the kind of society to which Gustad belongs, Peerbhoy *Paanwala* analyses news in his inimitable style for the benefit of his customer-audience.

In such a society, myths are born easily. Thus, Medhiwala Bonesetter, the one who set right Gustad's aching hip, is famed to have 'piercing eyes' because of which the X-ray laboratories suffer in getting business (130). Peerbhoy Paanwala makes umpteen varieties of the betel leaf to cure all sorts of ailments and weaknesses. The enthusiasm for deification is quite common. Mr. Rabadi, the 'dogwala idiot,' would like Dustoorji Baria's picture drawn on the municipal wall for he can prescribe remedies for all the ills of life related to health, job, business, social status and even pet animals (288). It is a world in which "roadside latrines become temples and shrines, and temples and shrines become dust and ruin." (338) In this world, where Tatas and Birlas are favoured as against the poor people (127), Cavasji finds God highly irrational.

However, when a catastrophe like the Chinese aggression of India takes place, a rare emotional camaraderie is seen. The aggressor is transmuted to the category of a bugbear. "The wicked Chino will carry you off if you don't finish your food," Dilnavaz would tell her son Darius (9). Even a much lesser problem like the demolition of the boundary wall of Khodadad Building brings about a feeling of camaraderie among people living within and without, regardless of their religious or regional affiliation. All this is achieved on impulsive rather than any rational consideration. One is reminded of the famous simile of freezing porcupines given by Schopenhauer, which "crowd together to save themselves from being frozen to death, but separate again as soon as they feel one another's quills until at length they discover a mean distance at which they can tolerably exist."[8]

Even though scientists and philosophers have failed to find final answers to the myriad questions of philosophy, a kind of obsession with rationalism, that El Dorado of epistemology has marked the thinking of man much against human experience in certain weak moments as is provided by the following peep into the life of the great apostle of rationalism. Descartes took it upon himself to find a body of self-evident truths which could appeal to common sense and the faculty of reasoning. He desired to see the kind of accuracy in philosophy as characterized Mathematics, "prayed for divine illumination, vowing a pilgrimage to the shrine of Loretto in case his prayer should be answered."[9]

There are perhaps limits to practical transformation of all human ideas. G.B. Shaw's 'The Revolutionary's Handbook' in his magnum opus *Man and Superman* begins with the promise to unravel the 'golden rule' but deconstructs stating simply, "The golden rule is that there is no golden rule." Major Bilimoria has learnt while working in RAW that one must not trust anyone howsoever near and dear. Unfortunately, if the worldly-wise Major had stuck to this golden principle, it would have been a rational approach and he would have saved his skin, but acting on impulse and taken in by the majestic charm of the Prime Minister, he signs his confession. (277) While the Major meets his doom at the end of the novel, Sohrab's estrangement and Roshan's illness also end. However, this latter happy development coincides with the last magic rites conducted by Miss Kutpitia before the laboratory of magic goes up in flames. The writer seems to be trying to achieve some kind of suspension of disbelief with regard to the miraculous impact of the magic.

Why does man leave the straight path of reason and get fascinated by the labyrinthine maze of sentimentality instead? The answer, if it can be called an answer, is provided by the footpath artist, "You see, I don't like to weaken anyone's faith. Miracle, magic, mechanical trick, coincidence—does it matter what it is, as long as it helps? Why analyze the strength of the imagination, the power of suggestion, the power of auto-suggestion, the potency of psychological pressures?" (289)

NOTES

1. Michael Haralambos, *Sociology: Themes and Perspectives* (Delhi: Oxford University Press, 1980), p. 484.
2. Fr. James Thornton, *Vilfredo Pareto: A Concise Overview of His Life, Works, and Philosophy* <http://www.google.com>
3. Rohinton Mistry, *Such a Long Journey* (London: Faber and Faber, 1991), p. 52.
4. M.R. Ridley, *Othello.* (London: Methuen, 1969), p. lxvi.
5. David C. King and Marvin R. Koller, *Foundations of Sociology* (San Francisco: Rinehart Press, 1957).
6. Morris Ginsberg, *Sociology* (Delhi: Surjeet, 1979).
7. Robert Bierstedt, *The Social Order* (New Delhi: Tata McGraw Hill, 1970).
8. Ginsberg, p. 103.
9. Frank Thilly, *A History of Philosophy* (New Delhi: SBW, 2005).

Presented at the UGC sponsored National Seminar on "Divergent trends in Indian Fiction in English," held on Oct. 1-2, 2005 at D.A.V. College (Lahore), Ambala City.

Distorted Angularities of Socio-Political Reality A Study of *Such a Long Journey*

B. GOPAL RAO
Osmania University

Perhaps one of the most compelling types of fiction being written today by the writers of the Indian diaspora is the political novel. According to H.A.L Fisher, the political novel "concerns itself with man and woman engaged in contemporary political life and discussing contemporary political ideas." (4) For Joseph L. Blotner, "a political novel is . . . a book which directly describes, interprets or analyses political phenomena" (19) while Irving Howe declares that "by a political novel I mean a novel in which political ideas play a dominant role in which the political milieu is the dominant setting." (19)

As several definitions indicate, the term "political novel" may denote either a piece of fiction devoted mainly to a presentation of political ideas, or a type of fiction in which action, characters and setting are all firmly grounded in politics without any distortions.

One of the essential criteria of a novel is its apparent adherence to truth, or at least its probability. It signifies its truthfulness by its wealth of corroborative detail. A fundamental building material out of which novels are made is a narrative that claims to be factual and which contains internal evidence of an appropriate kind to convince readers of its truth. One of the basic tests of the novel is probability; another is consistency in representation of socio-political aspects in a given contextual reference to time and place of its occurrence. Novels, if they are to be effective, must be coherent and the novelist should be a synthesizer, an unbiased thinker who formulates socio-political values in his fictional representations. Historical events most of the time become texts which interpret timeless human dramas that transcend their immediate circumstances.

In this respect Rohinton Mistry's *Such a Long Journey* is an attempt to draw the attention of Western readers by misrepresenting Indian socio-political and cultural ethos in a negative tone. When a writer portrays a picture of his homeland he often tends to be anachronistic, outdated in terms of over-idealization or condemnation without substantiating any concrete evidence to misrepresent factual reality. Such a long journey through an alien land and culture is bound to defeat the expatriate writer's efforts to represent a true picture of what he abandoned on the native shores and what it has evolved into the present in a relatively changed context of time-frame.

A work of literature cannot afford to peevishly shy away from social reality. As a social discourse, it is written by a sensitive being for some other members of the society to read and comprehend what is written and conveyed. A serious work of literature, created as it is within the framework of existing social relations, is not only a living document of the contemporary happenings but also of the historical processes underlying them. This is particularly true of the diasporic writers. Immigrant novelists have on several occasions revealed more biased and lopsided political and socio-cultural truths than all the professional politicians put together.

The relationship between art and society therefore cannot be ignored. A novel contributes to the reaffirmation or devaluation of people's ideas, goals and values. It cannot escape from the class power structures that shape our everyday life. Here the novelist has no choice. Whether or not he is aware of it, his work reflects one or more aspects of the intense economic, political, cultural and ideological struggles in a society. What he can choose is one or the other side in confronting sensitive socio-political contradictions. What he or she cannot do is to remain neutral. Every writer is a gifted artist and a commentator of socio-political issues of his times. Any attempt to misrepresent depending on his whims and fancies would mean debasing or devaluing a work of art. It would be interesting to evaluate the Parsis' response to great national events and political movements and their attitude to some well-known politicians, on the basis of a close study of the Parsi fiction. The present paper aims at highlighting Rohinton Mistry's dilemma and ambivalence as reflected in *Such a Long Journey*.

The brief and sketchy account of the Parsis' role in Indian politics is sufficient to make us inquisitive about the Parsis' views on Indian politics and politicians as found in their novels. The Parsis generally looked at politics with disfavour and misgivings. The Parsis's decisive influence through their chosen leaders was confined to the period 1885-1915. Later, the community strangely developed apprehensions and distrust towards the Congress politics. The Parsis were particularly disturbed by increasing radicalism of the national movement strongly influenced by the neo-Hindi renaissance. They felt that they had very limited access to the socio-religious nationalism of the Congress movement under Tilak and Gandhi. These fears encouraged the Parsis to oppose even the concept of the Home Rule in India.

The Parsis' attitude to momentous movements and events affecting the entire subcontinent such as the Quit India Movement, the Naval Ratings Mutiny, the Partition, the Independence, Pakistani wars and the creation of the Bangladesh, appears to be ambivalent. Some insiders have testified to this dilemma of their community members. "This ambivalence and alienation," writes Nilufer Bharucha, "became exacerbated during the colonial period. . . . Most Parsis . . . felt bereft at the end of Empire and the resultant loss of the special elite status they had enjoyed during the colonial period." (xiii) Kapadia also talks about what he calls the 'Parsi paradox' projected in Nergis Dalal's novels *The Sisters* and *Minari*. According to him, "Most of them are cultural hybrids, living and sharing intimately in the cultural life, traditions, languages, moral codes and value systems of two distinct peoples, which never completely penetrate or get fused." (79)

Bapsi Sidhwa's *Ice-Candy-Man* is a fine illustration of this ambivalence. The novel is at once "about the need to transcend that ambivalence." (85)

In delineating the political and social scenario in Bombay, Mistry in his fear and insecurity about his community, reveals almost a distorted and angular vision of India and its polity. The writer's sensitivity of impending dangers to his community is expressed by his character's consciousness of these changes. The Parsis being on the periphery even in India show their reluctance to mingle with the down to earth Indian masses. They suffer from insecurity especially in the postcolonial era and the same sentiment is reflected in the statements like, "And today we have that bloody Shiv Sena wanting to make us second-class citizens" (39), "Parsi crow-eaters, we'll show you who is the boss" (30), "Wait till the Marathas take over then we will have real Gandoo raj." (73)

To most of the Parsis, the departure of the British would bring untold miseries of many kinds. "Parsis were the kings of banking in those days" (38) and earned a lot of respect, but now they would be reduced to "second-class citizens." To some others, "Johnie Walker scotch [was] rare." This comment clearly indicates their self-imposed alienation and fear psychosis on the basis of their exaggerated notions of marginality.

Against the backdrop of the case of a real life State Bank cashier Sohrab Nagarwalla who was involved in a 60 lakhs scam that had rocked the Indira Gandhi government in 1971 was arrested for his dubious role in the bank scam. Later he died a mysterious death even before he could be brought to trial. Through this real life etching, Mistry tried to show by deliberate design the erosion of the Nehruvian idealism and the beginning of corruption at the highest level, nepotism, power-politics, the Hindu-Muslim riots and other vices in the postcolonial India. He blamed Indira Gandhi for all these: "How much bloodshed, how much rioting she caused. And today we have that bloody Shiv Sena, wanting to make the rest of us into second-class citizens. Don't forget, she started it all by supporting the racist buggers."

(39) Mistry follows the rhythm of postcolonial discourse and celebrates the Parsi idiom in an uncharacteristic manner and even his intemperate language shows his disgruntled vision of modern India.

The derogatory comments of the characters often reveal the Parsi background and the sense of alienation of Mistry himself. For instance Gustad thinks about the position of the Parsis in Bombay and comments: "No future for minorities, with all these fascist Shiv Sena politics and Marathi language nonsense. It was going to be like the black people in America—twice as good as the white man to get half as much." (55) Regarding the change of the street names in Bombay, Dinshwaji comments on the notion of displacement: "Names are so important. I grew up on Lamington Road. But it has disappeared, in its place is Dadasaheb Bhadkhamkar Marg. My school was on Carnac Road. Now suddenly it's on Lokmanya Tilak Marg. . . . So what happens to the life I have lived? Was I living the wrong life, with all the wrong names? . . . Tell me what happens to my life. Rubbed out, just like that?" (74) This describes the Parsi sense of comfort in the colonial era and unwarranted sense of displacement in the postcolonial age. On the basis of theme and content, some of the novels written by expatriates, especially writers like Mistry, may be regarded as political novels written with a bias. In a political novel, as Irving Howe points out, "political ideas play a dominant role." There may not be much ideological interplay in some of these novels but most of them have an ambivalent political setting. They represent the contemporary scenario seen through the eyes of the narrator or the character concerned in a narrow and subverted perspective.

Yet, the significance of the impact of recent political events on contemporary Indian novel cannot be wholly dismissed. If nothing else, such events have re-established politics as legitimate, perhaps even desirable, subject matter for fiction. Indeed, the plethora of writings from Indian diasporic writers etc., which have been produced during and in the wake of the Bangladesh and Pakistan wars is tantamount to a renaissance in political writing.

Whatever the future of Indian literature, particularly the novel as the vehicle of artistic expression among contemporary writers, "political" novels, either as novels of political ideology or works in which political events and issues serve as a backdrop for the depiction of India and its socio-political scenario, will continue to be written. Whether it will eclipse the other genre will be determined only by the talent, inspiration and commitment of the individual writer. But the contentious issue still remains unresolved with few writers, like Rohinton Mistry, who project a distorted and ambivalent picture of socio-political scenario in order to make their works saleable commodities for western reading public. This pattern of interpreting Indian political reality in the novels to suit one's convenience spells doom for aesthetic mode of creative writing. The scope and the form of the political novel, therefore, remain open to question and needless controversy.

Works Cited

Blotner, Joseph L, 1995. *The Political Novel.* New York: Doubleday.

Fisher, H.A.L. 1966. "The Political Novel". Rpt. Gorden Milne, ed. *The American Political Novel.* Norman: University of Oklahoma Press.

Howe, Irving. 1987. *Politics and the Novel.* New York: Horizon Press.

Kanaganayakam, Chelva. 1995. *Configurations of Exile:* South Asian Writers and Their World. Toronto: TSAR.

Kapadia, Novy. 1995. "The Dilemma of Marriage in Nergis Dalal's *The Sisters*," R.K. Dhawan, ed., *Indian Women Novelists*. New Delhi: Prestige.

Mistry, Rohinton, 1991. *Such a Long Journey.* Calcutta: Rupa.

Elements of Modernity in Rohinton Mistry's *Such a Long Journey*, *A Fine Balance* and *Family Matters*

C. BHARATHI
Navarasam Arts & Science College for Women, Erode

The term "modernism" is widely used to identify new and distinctive features in the subjects, forms, concepts and styles of literature and the other arts in the early decades of the present century, but especially after World War II. The specific features signified by "modernism" vary with the user, but many critics agree that it involves a deliberate and radical break with some of the traditional bases, not only of Western art; but of Western culture in general. Important intellectual precursors of modernism, in this sense, are thinkers who had questioned the certainties that had supported traditional modes of social organization, religion and morality and also traditional modes of conceiving the human self-thinkers such as Friedrich Nietzsche, Karl Marx, Sigmund Freud and James G. Frazer.

In modern Indian English novels, writers like Anita Desai, Shashi Deshpande, Upamanyu Chatterjee, Amitav Ghosh, Arundhati Roy, Manju Kapoor and Rohinton Mistry have tried to underline modernity, or significant changes, by creating illustrative situations and characters in different circumstances or an event. The additional charm of their novels also residents in the graph that they have tried to chart out in the advancement of women from tradition to modernity in family situations.

Rohinton Mistry is a product of the postcolonial Indian diaspora. In his novels, one finds a poignant picture of the Parsi diaspora, as members of this miniscule community struggle to come to terms with the baffling and complex phenomenon of Indian modernity. If modernity, as defined by Stuart Hall, can be considered "as the experience of living with rapid, extensive and continuous change" (qtd. Wadia 216) then that is amply illustrated in *Such a Long Journey*, *A Fine Balance* and *Family Matters*.

Mistry's novels have as their milieu the "City by the Sea"—Mumbai or Bombay, a city marked by constant and permanent changes in its landscape, skyscape and in the people who inhabit it. Here more than anywhere else in India, one witnesses the lives of the people being governed and even enmeshed by globalization, by networks of new and foreign media images on the one hand, and by poverty, illiteracy, unemployment, exploitation and homelessness, on the other. This gives the impression of identities getting detached and disembodied from specific places and times and becoming free-floating. Mistry's *Such a Long Journey* marks the beginning of this detachment and dismemberment, while *A Fine Balance* deals with characters who are displaced, isolated and estranged, framed against the background of the anonymous, impersonal and terrifying metropolis. *Family Matters* places the microcosm of individual's lives within macrocosmic events.

Man-woman relationship in modern Indian English novels has acquired varied dimensions. The hidden meanings and the sexual innuendoes in the dialogues point to a rapidly changing society in which conventional values are crumbling. Social norms and conventions have now been thrown to the winds. The modern Indian man and the modern woman have now become acquisitive—the age of "go-getters" has now set in. The novels reveal the flux in the world around them and there is an ease about the mixing of the real and the fantastical. The novels focus on issues like marriage, love, commercialism, destitution, communalism, crisis of the individual, conflict between father and son, education and a general dilution of values. Western influence in India and the Westernization of Indian society, especially in the upper classes stand in sharp contrast to the traditionalism of the middle and lower classes.

From time immemorial, throughout the world, there has been a fixed image of man and woman. Traditionally, the image of woman has been what men have thought it should be. A "good" woman is one who is meek, docile, passive, obedient, virtuous, humble, kind and self-sacrificing. A "bad" woman was one who was bold, adventurous, active, articulate, intelligent and questioning—conduct of such a woman was not appreciated by society—a society which was shaped by men who laid down the norms of behaviour. This image of woman is found in the cultural attitudes of the world, and departure from this has come to stand for the dividing line between tradition and modernity.

In *Such a Long Journey*, Gustad's wife Dilnavaz is passive, docile and patient. She accepts the sufferings of the family. She has to fetch water in the early morning and fill up all the vessels in the house while the man at home sits and reads the newspaper. She does not know about, or does not care about, the Indo-Pakistan war. This shows the traditional women's daily routine and poor knowledge. In *Family Matters* Roxana and Coomy prefer to spend much of their time for the family. Even though Roxana is educated, she does not know anything about Yezad's life outside the house.

Traditionally, men control and inhabit the power structures and they understand the dynamics of economics. Men make and take decisions on property and lay down the rules of morality. They have categorized women into good and bad and have indoctrinated both women and men to such an extent that, by and large, they have come to accept these categories. The modern Indian woman finds herself in a peculiar situation—her freedom to interact with men is hampered by traditions and conventions. Dilnavaz is superstitious and she is afraid to let her husband know that she has resorted to charms and spells in order to cure her daughter of her illness. This is because Gustad does not believe in such conventional cures and he does not want Dilnavaz to have anything to do with Kutpitia.

Dina's attempts to liberate herself from her brother Nusswan, first by refusing to marry after the death of her husband, only make her pass through a fiery ordeal to earn her livelihood by taking tailors and keeping paying guests to supplement her income. Along with the tailors—Ishvar and Omprakash and Maneck, she becomes the head of the family and proves that "independence came at a high price: a debt with a payment schedule of hurt and regret" (473). Dina is just an example of how society is unable to tolerate a woman who wishes to lead an independent life.

In a conventional family, the father is the authoritarian head. Gustad assumes that role. But Sohrab belongs to the new generation which cherishes independence of choice. He rejects the coveted I.I.T. admission in favour of an ordinary B.A. Gustad, for whom higher education, academic excellence and financial/social superiority are the only possible ways of clinging to an elite status and distinct religious identity, is horrified. Sohrab is compelled to leave home as a prelude to redefining his relationship with his father. While for Gustad, a coherent self is only possible through tradition, for his son a unified identity from birth to death is no longer possible. Sohrab, unlike Gustad, has accepted the fact that identity continues to be reformed and transformed as one comes in touch with hybrid cultural, political and social systems.

The rupture in the relationship between father and son could be read as one of the many casualties of modernity, where tradition and individualism are in perpetual conflict. In the eyes of Gustad,

> This was the bloody problem with modern education. In the name of progress they discarded seemingly unimportant things without knowing that what they were chucking out the window of modernity was tradition. And if tradition was lost, then the loss of respect for those who respected and loved tradition always followed. (61)

While for Gustad, a coherent self is only possible through tradition, for his son a unified identity from birth to death is no longer possible. Sohrab, unlike Gustad, has accepted the fact that identity continues to be reformed and transformed as one comes in touch with hybrid cultural, political and social systems.

Maneck Kohlah in *A Fine Balance*, too, quickly recognizes this fact of modernity. The father-son conflict is characterized by the unwillingness of the father to read the writing on the wall, as it were. Rustom Kohlah runs a small family business in the idyllic hills of North India. His specialty is the Kaycee, which he makes according to a secret formula handed down to him over the generations. When the multinationals invade the hills, with their new-fangled technology and hard-hitting advertising campaigns Kaycee is on its way to a slow but sure death. Maneck exhorts the father to advertise, to adopt new technologies, but to no avail. Modernization, like death, is a great leveller. Here it is survival of the fittest.

> But the giant corporations had targeted the hills; they had Kaycee in their sights. They infiltrated Mr. Kohlah's territory with their boardroom arrogance and advertising campaigns and cut-throat techniques. Representatives approached him with a proposition: "Pack up your machines, sign over all rights to Kohlah's Cola, and be an agent for our brand. Come grow with us, and prosper." (220)

Industrialization and capitalism are responsible for progress, prosperity and rising living standards. But they also contribute in a large measure to the angst of displacement and, in extreme cases, even for aggression against self. These constitute the worst of modernism and find a poignant reflection in *A Fine Balance*. The novel opens with Om, Ishvar and Maneck meeting for the first time on a local train. All three, unknown to each other, are bound for a common destination—to find employment. They believe that the metropolitan city Bombay will help them to earn more money. The rest of the novel deals with their attempts at securing their jobs, the traumas that accompany, and the final return to their natural families, physically handicapped and mentally frustrated.

In *Family Matters*, Yezad works in a Bombay Sports Goods Emporium. He had the dream of emigrating to Canada and takes job over there. He thinks that he would have earned more money in Canada rather than make a living in India. In the memory of that incident he keeps the certificates and the cover in his drawer and remembers them often. According to Yezad, service to other country for a higher price is better than an ordinary middle class life in India. Thus expatriation becomes a causal factor in the dislocation of family members. In *A Fine Balance*, Maneck goes abroad after finishing his diploma course in Bombay city. He thinks that he could earn more money in U.S.A. and get his three sisters married and also develop the family business which had met with a loss. Though the youth of modern India wish to be rid of conventional fetters, men like Yezad in *Family Matters* still feel so high to contribute something to their family.

If the multinationals are directly responsible for Maneck's diaspora, Om and Ishvar are propelled from the "Village by the River" to the "City by the Sea" to escape the atrocities of caste-based politics and the virtual collapse of retail family run enterprises in the face of growing industrialization. The displacement of Om and Ishvar epitomizes the widespread phenomenon of casteist politics and communal riots uprooting whole populations of poor, ragged, unsuspecting and politically unawakened masses and casting them into new identities. This is further compounded by economic and financial losses in the wake of modernization and capitalist enterprise.

Dina Dalal has no choice but to open her doors to the low caste tailors. Both are mutually dependent on each other for survival. When the small shack of the tailors in a shanty town in the slums of Bombay falls a casualty to the city beautification programme, Dina is compelled by circumstances and Maneck's insistence to let the tailors live on her verandah in defiance of the tenancy laws. Earlier, when the tailors came to work for her on a day-to-day basis, she had been very careful to keep their glasses and cups separate from those which she and Maneck used. But now she no longer sees the need to do so. Sharing a home also implies sharing of meals, and the sharing of common cutlery becomes a very significant act, one which foreshadows the breaking down of the caste barriers, a trend that was gradually gaining ground in modern India, paving the way for a mixed community family.

The new mode of eating, unknown to her brother and sister-in-law, has already heralded an era of enhanced secularization and hints at the breaking down of class barriers. Beggars eating off the same plates as the members of the sophisticated upper-class is a very revolutionary and defiant act.

In modern Indian society, the youngsters are constrained by their jobs and individual preferences, which come in the way of taking care of the elder people of the family. They consider the elders as burden to them. Due to the generation gap, the youngsters wish to be away from them and they try to spend some time with them. Coomy, defeated by the physical labour of taking care of Nariman and even bereft of her domestic help, who is driven away by the foul odours in the flat, convinces her brother to hire an ambulance and, without any prior warning, takes Nariman to Roxana's flat and leaves him till the plaster is removed and he is mobile enough again to return to their flat. She creates a situation in which it would be impossible for Roxana and Yezad to insist that she keep her side of the bargain and take her stepfather back after the stipulated three weeks.

Yezad is happy to spend some time for the old man once in a while. When the family gets together to celebrate Nariman's seventy-ninth birthday, he tells jokes and talks about the Shiv Sena. And also he invites Nariman to his house. But when Nariman comes to his house as a bedridden patient, he becomes very harsh and turns his back on his needs. After their return to Chateau Felicity, the Chenoys employed professional help to look after Nariman. Instead of taking care of Nariman, Roxana sends necessary things through the wardboy. This shows the younger generation's lack of interest towards the elders in modern society.

In modern times, people expect more money without hard work and refuse to utilise the opportunities in the right way. The youngsters refuse to listen to their parents and bring sufferings to their parents. In the case of Nariman in *Family Matters* and Darius in *Such a Long Journey*, they choose non-Parsi girls as partners. Even though Nariman's love was mature, in order to obey the customs of the Parsi community, he leaves Lucy, a Christian woman. Darius, on the other hand, is severely admonished by his father and has to relinquish his love. This shows the youngsters' behaviour in the name of modernity. Thus Mistry has portrayed the personal lives of the three families who are torn apart by the conflict between "modernistic ideas" and "orthodox confusions."

Indian society is rapidly changing and this is affecting people's personal lives and life styles. Moreover, in India, the family continues to be the foundation of society and the novels have the family as their subject. The family as a social unit is dying in the West. But both in India and in the West, relationships matter a great deal in people's lives. Cracks often appear in relationships because of some upheaval or the other. Rohinton Mistry has delineated these cataclysmic changes that are occurring in interpersonal relationships. He also explores the impact of 'modernity' on the family set up. This has directly or indirectly influenced family relationships and the psychology behind them.

Works Cited

Bharucha, Nilufer. *Ethnic Enclosures and Transcultural Spaces*. Jaipur and New Delhi: Rawat, 2003.

Chakravarty, Joya. *Indian Writing in English: Perspectives*. New Delhi: Atlantic, 2003.

Choudhury, Indra Nath. *Indian Literature after Modernism*. New Delhi: 1994.

Dodiya, Jaydipsingh, ed. *The Fiction of Rohinton Mistry: Critical Studies*. New Delhi: Prestige, 1998.

Jha, Parmanand. "Ties and Trials in Rohinton Mistry's *Family Matters*." New Delhi: Atlantic, 2003.

Kumar, Narendra. *Parsee Novel*. New Delhi: Prestige, 2002.

Kapadia, Novy, et al. *Parsi Fiction*. 2 Vols. New Delhi: Prestige, 2001.

Mathur, O.P. "The Emergency in Rohinton Mistry's *A Fine Balance*." *Littcrit*, 27, 1-2 (2001), pp. 66-74.

Mishra, Charu Chandra. "Modes of Resistance in Rohinton Mistry's *Such a Long Journey*," in Dodiya.

Mistry, Rohinton. *Such a Long Journey*. New York: Vintage, 1991.

_____. *A Fine Balance*. New Delhi: Rupa, 1996.

_____. *Family Matters*. London: Faber and Faber, 2002.

Singh, Avadhesh Kumar. "The Sense of Community in the Parsi Novels," *The Literary Criterion*, 32.3 (1996), pp. 28-38.

Wadia, Hutoxi. *Shades of Indian Modernity in the Novels of Rohinton Mistry*. Delhi: Pencraft International, 2000.